£4.50

Protecting the Co...

AN ECONOMIC AND LEGAL...

Protecting the Consumer

AN ECONOMIC AND LEGAL ANALYSIS

Peter Smith
Lecturer in Law, Nottingham University

Dennis Swann
Professor of Economics, Loughborough University of Technology

MARTIN ROBERTSON

© Peter Smith and Dennis Swann 1979

All rights reserved. No part of this publication may be reproduced, stored in a retrieval system, or transmitted in any form or by any means, electronic, mechanical, photocopying, recording or otherwise, without the prior written permission of the copyright holders.

First published in 1979 by Martin Robertson & Company Ltd.
108 Cowley Road, Oxford OX4 1JF

ISBN 0 85520 258 0 (paperback edition)
ISBN 0 85520 259 9 (case edition)

Typeset by Pintail Studios Ltd., Ringwood, Hampshire
Printed and bound by Richard Clay Ltd., at The Chaucer Press, Bungay, Suffolk.

Contents

	Preface	vii
	Table of Statutes	ix
	Table of Cases and Decisions	xii
CHAPTER 1	Introduction – The Subject Matter	1
CHAPTER 2	Institutional Background	19
CHAPTER 3	Competition Policy – Creating a European Market	40
CHAPTER 4	Competition Policy – The Domestic Market	71
CHAPTER 5	Market Interventions	97
CHAPTER 6	Preparing to Buy – Acquiring Information	132
CHAPTER 7	Preparing to Buy – Preventing Deception	149
CHAPTER 8	Preparing to Buy – Acquiring Finance	168
CHAPTER 9	Protection at the Point of Sale	195
CHAPTER 10	Redress and the Enforcement of Rights	217
CHAPTER 11	Conclusion – The Way Forward	235
	Addendum	252
	Notes	255
	Select Bibliography	275
	Index	279

Preface

Even the most cursory glance at the legislative activity of recent years in this country, as indeed in North America and Europe, indicates that the protection of the consumer has been high on the list of governmental priorities. There now exists a substantial corpus of law concerned with the subject. In North America this has been accompanied by a veritable spate of texts and articles dealing with the problems faced by the consumer and the ways in which, through both public and private initiative, he may be better protected. By contrast in the UK the academic publishing response has been very muted. Fortunately the situation has begun to improve and recently two books, one by Ross Cranston and one by Brian Harvey, have appeared. Their appearance has confirmed the view that we formed, namely that general texts on consumer protection are well overdue. Mention of Cranston and Harvey also enables us to acknowledge the benefit that we have derived from their works. However, we have approached the subject in a somewhat different way from them. Their books are the products of legal scholars; our book represents an attempt to incorporate the expertise of an economist and a lawyer. Consumer protection is after all a subject that lies on the borderline between economics and the law. Because of this we have, for example, given more attention to the role of competition. Also, reflecting the European interests of one of the authors, we have felt it important to consider the competitive process in a European context. Our concern with the economic as well as the legal dimension is also reflected in the emphasis that we have given to anti-inflation policy as it affects both incomes and prices. We have been encouraged in taking this broad view by recent publications of the National Consumer Council, which have emphasized the wide range of policies that have an impact on consumers. For example, the consumer interest is vitally at stake when economists debate the pros and cons of import controls.

We hope this book will have a broad appeal, and to that end we have sought to minimize economic and legal technicalities. In writing it we have had students on courses in business and management studies very much in mind as well as those studying law. The time is now ripe for the development of courses specifically dealing with consumer protection and we are encouraged by signs that this is beginning to happen. Although the existence of courses stimulates the writing of books, we hope that the availability of books will stimulate academics in universities, polytechnics and further education generally to start to experiment with courses on consumer protection, perhaps as the focus of interdisciplinary studies.

Whilst the manuscript was being prepared for the press, a General Election was announced and shortly before we received proofs a new Government took office. We are grateful to our publishers for allowing us to consider briefly the new direction which consumer policy may take under the Conservative Government and our first thoughts are to be found in an Addendum. The accommodation of new text at a very late stage has exemplified the speed and efficiency which our publishers have shown at all times and for which we are very grateful.

In writing this book we have benefited greatly from advice and comments from our colleagues who have read the work in whole or part. We are grateful to Peter Maunder and Michael Fleming at Loughborough University of Technology, Sally Jones at Nottingham University and Stewart Howe at Dundee College of Technology. The book was also commented on by Jim Humble and his colleagues at the Office of Fair Trading and we are greatly indebted to them for most valuable advice. Mr R.M. Rock, who is the Chief Environmental Officer for Charnwood Borough Council, also gave us the benefit of his exerience as it relates to material contained in Chapter 5 and we found this exceedingly helpful. No book can be produced without the devoted help of secretaries and we would like to express our great appreciation of the assistance rendered by Brenda Moore, Madge Lowe, Ruth Quarton and the secretaries of the Department of Law at Nottingham University. The authors are of course solely responsible for all errors and omissions.

P.F. Smith
D. Swann

18 July 1979
Ringwood

Table of Statutes

Administration of Justice Act 1969, pp. 273 n5
Adulteration of Food and Drink Act 1860, p. 118
Adulteration of Food, Drink and Drugs Act 1872, p. 118
Advertising (Hire-Purchase) Act 1967, pp. 146, 269 n29
Air Travel Reserve Fund Act 1975, p. 124
Architects Registration Act 1931, p. 121
Architects Registration Act 1938, p. 121

Banking Act 1979, p. 123
Betting, Gaming and Lotteries Act 1963, p. 264 n53

Civil Evidence Act 1968, p. 266 n7
Companies Act 1967, p. 122.
Consumer Credit Act 1974, pp. 4, 21, 137, 170–73, 176–94, 200, 246–7
Consumer Protection Act 1961, p. 127
Consumer Protection Act 1971, p. 127
Consumer Safety Act 1978, pp. 127–8
Counter-Inflation Act 1973, p. 110
County Courts Act 1846, pp. 219–21

Dentists Act 1957, p. 121

Estate Agents Act 1979, p. 123
Explosives (Age of Purchase, etc) Act 1976, p. 129

Fabrics (Misdescription) Act 1913, p. 128
Fair Trading Act 1973, pp. 21, 23–5, 26, 27, 31, 39, 85–6, 89, 90, 91, 94, 146, 167, 179, 215–16
Food and Drugs Act 1955, pp. 30, 39, 101, 119–20, 124–6, 134–5,136, 161, 249
Food and Drugs (Control of Food Premises) Act 1976, p. 125
Food and Drugs (Scotland) Act 1956, pp. 40, 119
Food and Drugs (Northern Ireland) Act 1958, pp. 40, 119

Gun Barrel Proof Act 1868, p. 128
Gun Barrel Proof Act 1950, p. 128

Hallmarking Act 1973, p. 141
Hire-Purchase Act 1938, p. 169
Hire-Purchase Act 1964. pp. 64, 268 n3

TABLE OF STATUTES

Hire-Purchase Act 1965, pp. 173, 178, 269 n21
Housing, Rents and Subsidies Act 1975, p. 263 n42

Increase of Rent and Mortgage Interest (War Restrictions) Act 1915, p. 118
Indecent Advertisements Act 1889, p. 268 n57
Independent Broadcasting Authority Act 1973, p. 38
Insurance Brokers (Registration) Act 1977, p. 121
Insurance Companies Act 1974, pp. 30, 122

Licensing Act 1964, p. 264 n53

Margarine Act 1887, p. 263 n45
Medical Act 1956, p. 121
Medical Act 1969, p. 121
Medicines Act 1968, pp. 29, 39, 119, 121, 126–7, 129, 136
Merchandise Marks Act 1887, p. 154
    Merchandise Marks Act 1953, p. 154
    Misrepresentation Act 1967, pp. 4, 146, 164
    Misuse of Drugs Act 1971, p. 128
Monopolies and Restrictive Practices (Inquiry and Control) Act 1948, pp. 26, 71, 73–6, 85, 89, 92
Monopolies and Mergers Act 1965, pp. 85, 89, 94, 240

National Health Service Act 1946, p. 270 n20

Opticians Act 1958, p. 121

Pharmacy and Poisons Act 1933, p. 129
Poisons Act 1972, p. 129
Policyholders Protection Act 1975, p. 123
Powers of Criminal Courts Act 1973, p. 152
Prevention of Fraud (Investments) Act 1958, p. 122
Price Commission Act 1977, pp. 39, 88, 114, 244
Price Commission Amendment Act 1979, p. 263 n34
Prices Act 1974, pp. 113–14, 136
Prices and Incomes Act 1966, p. 108
Prices and Incomes Act 1968, p. 108
Professions Supplementary to Medicine Act 1960, p. 121
Protection of Depositors Act 1963, p. 123
Public Health Act 1936, p. 121

Race Relations Act 1976, p. 268 n57
Rag, Flock and Other Filling Materials Act 1951, p. 121
Rent Act 1964, p. 263 n42
Rent Act 1968, p. 263 n42
Rent Act 1977, p. 263 n42
Resale Prices Act 1964, pp. 27, 87–8

Resale Prices Act 1976, pp. 21, 27
Restrictive Practices Court Act 1976, p. 27
Restrictive Trade Practices Act 1956, pp. 10, 27, 76–84, 85, 86, 88, 89
Restrictive Trade Practices Act 1968, pp. 27, 84–5, 239–40
Restrictive Trade Practices Act 1976, pp. 21, 39, 76–84, 239
Road Traffic Act 1960, p. 128
Road Traffic Act 1972, p. 128

Sale of Food and Drugs Act 1875, p. 119
Sale of Food and Drugs Act Amendment Act 1879, p. 263 n45
Sale of Goods Act 1893, pp. 71, 196–7, 201, 210–11, 213
Seeds Act 1920, p. 121
Sex Discrimination Act 1975, p. 268 n57
Slaughterhouses Act 1974, p. 125
Solicitors Act 1974, p. 121
Solicitors (Scotland) Act 1933, p. 121
Solicitors (Scotland) Act 1949, p. 121
Solicitors (Scotland) Act 1958, p. 121
Supply of Goods (Implied Terms) Act 1973, pp. 4, 173, 198–202, 268 n3, 270 n6

Theft Act 1968, pp. 146, 153
Theft Act 1978, p. 153
Trade Descriptions Act 1968, pp. 21, 23, 30, 32, 39, 146, 153–60, 165–6, 240
Trade Descriptions Act 1972, pp. 4, 153–60

Weights and Measures Act 1878, p. 71
Weights and Measures Act 1963, pp. 21, 23, 30, 135, 161
Weights and Measures Act 1976, p. 135
Weights and Measures Act 1979, p. 161

Unfair Advertising Act 1970–72 (S. Australia), p. 256 n38
Unfair Contract Terms Act 1977, pp. 4, 164, 210–14, 246
Unsolicited Goods Act 1971, p. 215

Table of Cases and Decisions

ACEC — Berliet, Re, JO 1968 L 201/7; [1968] CMLR D. 35, p. 51
Allen v. *Flood*, [1898] A.C. 1, p. 72
American Cyanamid Co. v. *Ethicon Ltd*, [1975] A.C. 396; [1975] 1 All E.R. 504, p. 232
Aniline Dye case; see *Cartel in Aniline Dyes*
Ashington Piggeries Ltd. v. *Christopher Hill Ltd*, [1972] A.C. 441; [1971] 1 All E.R. 847, p. 199.
Associated Transformer Manufacturers' Agreement, In re L.R. 2 R.P. 339, p. 82
Att. Gen. of the Commonwealth of Australia v. *Adelaide S.S. Company* [1913] A.C. 781, p. 72

BRT v. *Sabam and Fonier*, [1974] E.C.R. 51, 313; [1974] 2 C.M.L.R. 238, p. 63
Barnett v. *Chelsea and Kensington Hospital Management Committee*, [1969] 1 Q.B. 428; [1968] 1 All E.R. 1068, p. 229
Beale v. *Taylor*, [1967] 1 W.L.R. 1193; [1967] 3 All E.R. 253, pp. 163, 199
Beswick v. *Beswick*, [1968] A.C. 58; [1967] 2 All E.R. 1197, p. 231
Black Bolt and Nut Association's Agreement, In re L.R.2 R.P. 50, p. 83
Brasserie de Haecht v. *Wilkin-Janssen* (No. 2), [1973] E.C.R. 77; [1973] C.M.L.R. 287, p. 52
British Airways Board v. *Taylor*, [1976] 1 W.L.R. 13; [1976] 1 All E.R. 65, p. 159
British Bottle Association's Agreement, In re L.R. 2 R.P. 345, p. 82
Brown v. *Cotterill*, (1934) 51 T.L.R. 21, p. 205

CFA, JO 1968 L276/29; [1968] C.M.L.R. D57, p. 55
Cadbury Ltd. v. *Halliday*, [1975] 1 W.L.R. 649; [1975] 2 All E.R. 226, p. 156
Carlill v. *Carbolic Smoke Ball Co.*, [1893] 1 Q.B. 256, p. 166
Cartel in Aniline Dyes, Re, JO 1969 L195/11; [1969] C.M.L.R. D 23, pp. 48, 49, 54
Cartel in Quinine, Re, JO 1969 L192/5; [1969] C.M.L.R. D 41, pp. 47, 52, 54, 56
Cement Makers' Federation Agreement, In re L.R. 2 R.P. 241, p. 84
Chaplin v. *Hicks*, [1911] 2 K.B. 786, p. 218
Chemists' Federation Agreement, In re L.R. 1 R.P. 43, p. 81
Chiquita, see *United Brands*

TABLE OF CASES AND DECISIONS xiii

Chocolate and Sugar Confectionery Reference, In re L.R. 6 R.P. 382, p. 87
Christiani and Nielsen, JO 1969 L165/12; [1969] C.M.L.R. D36, p. 52
Cimbel, Re JO 1972 L303/24; [1973] C.M.L.R. D167, p. 50
Clifford Davis Management Ltd. v. *W.E.A. Records Ltd.*, [1975] 1 W.L.R.
  61; [1975] 1 All E.R. 237, pp. 197, 246
Clima/Chappée, Re JO 1969 L195/1; [1970] C.M.L.R. D7, pp. 51, 61
Cobelaz (No. 1) (Usines de Synthèse), JO 1968 L276/13; [1968] C.M.L.R.
  D45, p. 55
Commercial Solvents, see *Instituto Chemioterapico* etc.
Community v. *Members of the Genuine Vegetable Parchment Association*
  [1977] C.M.L.R. 534, p. 50
Concentrated Foods Ltd. v. *Champ*, [1944] K.B. 342, p. 162
Continental Can Co. Inc., JO 1972 L7/25; [1972] C.M.L.R. D11 (see also
  Europemballage Corp. etc.), pp. 63, 64, 66
Cottee v. *Douglas Seaton (Used Cars) Ltd.* [1972] 1 W.L.R. 1408; [1972] 3
  All E.R. 750, p. 156

Derry v. *Peek*, (1889) 14 App. Cas. 337, p. 165
Dick Bentley Productions Ltd v. *Harold Smith (Motors) Ltd.*, [1965] 1
  W.L.R. 623; [1965] 2 All E.R. 65, p. 163
Doble v. *David Greig Ltd.*, [1972] 1 W.L.R. 703; [1972] 2 All E.R. 195,
  p. 158
Donoghue v. *Stevenson*, [1932] A.C. 562, pp. 203, 204, 206
Duke v. *Jackson*, [1921] S.C. 362, p. 201

European Sugar Cartel, Re OJ 1973 L140/17; [1973] C.M.L.R. D65,
  pp. 54, 63, 64, 65
Eurofirma, [1973] C.M.L.R. D217, p. 66
Europemballage Corporation and Continental Can Co. Inc. v. *Commission*
  [1973] E.C.R. 215; [1975] E.C.R. 495; [1972] C.M.L.R. 690; [1976] 1
  C.M.L.R. 587. (on appeal from *Continental Can Co. Inc.*), pp. 63, 64, 66

Fabrique Nationale d'armes de guerre and cartoucherie française, JO 1971
  L134/6, p. 51
Federation of British Carpet Manufacturers' Agreement, In re L.R. 1 R.P.
  473, p. 82
Fletcher v. *Budgen*, [1974] 1 W.L.R. 1056; [1974] 2 All E.R. 1243, p. 155
Franco-Japanese Ballbearings Agreement, Re OJ 1974 L343/19; [1975] 1
  C.M.L.R. D8, p. 47

GEMA v. *Commission*, [1971] E.C.R. 791; [1972] C.M.L.R. 694, pp. 63, 64,
  65, 66
Galvanised Tank Manufacturers' Association's Agreement, In re L.R. 5 R.P.
  315, p. 84
Geddling v. *Marsh*, [1920] 1 K.B. 668, p. 201
German ceramic tiles discount agreement, JO 1971 L10/15; [1971]
  C.M.L.R. D6, p. 57

Glass Containers, Re Manufacturers of, OJ 1974 L160/1; [1974] 2 C.M.L.R. D50, pp. 54, 55, 57
Glazed and Floor Tile Home Trade Association's Agreement, In re L.R. 4 R.P. 239, pp. 83, 84
Grant v. *Australian Knitting Mills Ltd.*, [1936] A.C. 85, pp. 199, 202
Grosfillex, JO 1964 915; [1964] C.M.L.R. 237, p. 51
Grundig and Consten v. *Commission*, [1966] E.C.R. 299; [1966] C.M.L.R. 418, pp. 59, 60, 61

Hadley v. *Baxendale*, (1854) 9 Exch. 341, p. 229
Havering London Borough Council v. *Stevenson*, [1970] 1 W.L.R. 1375, p. 155
Hedley Byrne and Co. v. *Heller and Partners*, [1964] A.C. 465; [1963] 2 All E.R. 575, pp. 164, 165, 205
Helby v. *Matthews*, [1895] A.C. 471, p. 172
Hollier v. *Rambler Motors (A.M.C.) Ltd.*, [1972] 2 Q.B. 71; [1972] 1 All E.R. 399, p. 210.
Hong Kong Fir Shipping Co. Ltd. v. *Kawasaki Kisen Kaisha Ltd.*, [1962] 2 Q.B. 26; [1962] 1 All E.R. 474, p. 196
House of Holland Ltd. v. *London Borough of Brent*, [1971] 2 Q.B. 304; [1971] 2 All E.R. 296, p. 157

Instituto Chemioterapico Italiano Sp A and Commercial Solvents Corporation v. *Commission*, [1974] E.C.R. 223; [1974] 1 C.M.L.R. 309, p. 65

Jallate-Vos and Jallate-Vandeputte, JO 1965 37; [1966] C.M.L.R. D1, p. 51
Jarvis v. *Swan's Tours*, [1973] 1 Q.B. 233; [1973] 1 All E.R. 71, p. 230
Jaz/Peter, JO 1969 L195/5; [1970] C.M.L.R. 129, p. 61
John v. *Matthews*, [1970] 2 Q. B. 443; [1970] 2 All E.R. 623, p. 157

Karsales (Harrow) Ltd. v. *Wallis*, [1956] 1 W.L.R. 936; [1956] 2 All E.R. 866, p. 210
Koufos v. *Czarnikow Ltd.* ('The Heron II'), [1969] 1 A.C. 350; [1967] 2 All E.R. 686, pp. 229, 230

Linoleum Manufacturers' Association's Agreement, In re L.R. 2 R.P. 395, p. 82
Lipton's Cash Registers and Business Equipment v. *Hugin Kassa–Register AB and Hugin Cash Registers*, [1978] 1 C.M.L.R. D19, pp. 63, 64
Lloyd's Bank Ltd. v. *Bundy*, [1975] Q.B. 326; [1974] 3 All E.R. 757, pp. 197, 246

MFI Warehouses v. *Nattrass*, [1973] 1 W.L.R. 307; [1973] 1 All E.R. 762, p. 160
Metro-SB-Grossmarke v. *Commission*, [1976] E.C.R. 1353, p. 54
Mileage Conference Group of the Tyre Manufacturers' Conference Ltd.'s Agreement, In re L.R. 6 R.P. 49, p. 84
Mogul SS Co. v. *McGregor, Gow and Co.*, [1892] A.C. 25, p. 72

National Sulphuric Acid Association's Agreement, In re L.R. 4 R.P. 169, p. 80
Nordenfelt v. *Maxim Nordenfelt Guns and Ammunition Co.* [1894] A.C. 535, p. 72
Norman v. *Bennett*, [1974] 1 W.L.R. 1229; [1974] 3 All E.R. 351, p. 157

Oscar Chess v. *Williams*, [1957] 1 W.L.R. 370; [1957] 1 All E.R. 325, p. 163

Parker v. *S.E. Railway*, (1877) 2 C.P.D. 416, p. 210
Permanent Magnet Association's Agreement, In re L.R. L R.P. 119, p. 83
Phenol Producer's Agreement, In re L.R. 2 R.P. 1, p. 82
Pittsburgh Corning Europe, Re [1973] C.M.L.R. D2, p. 53
Portelange SA v. *Smith Corona Merchant International SA*, [1974] 1 C.M.L.R. 397, p. 52

Quinine case; see *Cartel in Quinine, Re*
Quinn v. *Leathem*, [1901] A.C. 495, p. 72

R. v. *Daly*, [1974] 1 W.L.R. 133; [1974] 1 All E.R. 290, p. 233
R. v. *Kneeshaw*, [1975] Q.B. 57; [1974] 1 All E.R. 896, p. 233
R. v. *Sunair Holidays Ltd.*, [1973] 1 W.L.R. 1105; [1973] 2 All E.R. 1233, p. 159
R. v. *Thomson Holidays Ltd.*, [1974] Q.B. 592; [1974] 1 All E.R. 823, pp. 159, 233
Registrar of Restrictive Trading Agreements v. *W.H. Smith and Son Ltd.*, L.R. 6 R.P. 532; [1969] 3 All E.R. 1065, p. 239
Richards v. *Westminster Motors Ltd.*, [1976] R.T.R. 88, p. 158
Rondel v. *Worsley*, [1969] 1 A.C. 191; [1967] 3 All E.R. 993, p. 203

SAFCO, JO 1972 L13/44; [1972] C.M.L.R. D83, p. 55
Saif Ali v. *Sydney Mitchell and Co. (a firm)* [1978] 3 All E.R. 1033, p. 203
Schuler A.G. v. *Wickman Machine Tool Sales Ltd.*, [1974] A.C. 235, p. 196
Shanklin Pier v. *Detel Products Ltd.*, [1951] 2 K.B. 854; [1951] 2 All E.R. 471, p. 214
Sirena v. *Eda and others*, [1971] E.C.R. 69; [1971] C.M.L.R. 260, p. 61
Sorrel v. *Smith*, [1925] A.C. 700, p. 72
Spartan Steel and Alloys Ltd. v. *Martin (Contractors) Ltd.*, [1973] 1 Q.B. 27; [1972] 3 All E.R. 557, p. 230

Thornton v. *Shoe Lane Parking Ltd.*, [1971] 1 Q.B. 163; [1971] 1 All E.R. 686, p. 210
Tyre Trade Register Agreement, In re L.R. 3 R.P. 404, p. 81

U.D.T. v. *Kirkwood*, [1966] 2 Q.B. 431; [1966] 1 All E.R. 968, p. 170
United Brands Co. and United Brands Continental B.V. v. *Commission*, [1978] 1 C.M.L.R. 429, pp. 64, 66

VCH (Veereniging van Cement handelaren), JO 1972 L 13/34; [1973] C.M.L.R. D16, pp. 47, 50, 56
Vacwell Engineering Co. Ltd. v. *B.D.H. Chemicals Ltd.*, [1971] 1 Q.B. 88, p. 205
Victoria Laundry (Windsor) Ltd. v. *Newman Industries Ltd.*, [1949] 2 K.B. 528; [1949] 1 All E.R. 997, p. 229

The Wagon Mound, [1961] A.C. 388, pp. 205, 230
Wallis, Son and Wells v. *Pratt and Haynes,* [1910] 2 K.B. 1003, pp. 196, 210
Water-Tube Boilermakers' Agreement, In re L.R. 1 R.P. 285, p. 80
Wholesale and Retail Bakers of Scotland Association's Agreements, In re L.R. 1 R.P. 377, p. 82
Wilson v. *Rickett Cockerell and Co. Ltd.*, [1954] 1 Q.B. 598; [1954] 1 All E.R. 868, p. 201

Yarn Spinners' Agreement, In re L.R. 1 R.P. 118, pp. 79, 81

1 Introduction – The Subject Matter

PLAN OF STUDY

In the light of the title of this book it will come as no surprise to the reader that a good deal of what he will find herein is concerned with consumer protection as conventionally defined. In short, we shall be dealing with topics such as controls over the composition of goods, the provision of accurate price and other information to potential consumers, the provision of redress in cases of product-related injury and so forth. But the title *Protecting the Consumer: An Economic and Legal Analysis* was deliberately designed to indicate that, while our treatment takes in the conventional area of consumer protection, *it also encompasses other activities that have a protective intent or effect*. These other activities that protect the consumer interest of our citizenry are policies designed (a) to create competition between rival suppliers and (b) to control prices.[1] The former is often referred to as competition policy and is concerned with restrictive business practices, monopolies and mergers – the Americans refer to this as antitrust policy. (The latter is a useful shorthand term and we shall use it throughout this book.) The control of prices is an aspect of the central control of both incomes and prices. It is true that policies to control wages, salaries, etc., have an indirect effect on the prices charged to consumers, and we shall take account of that fact.

Our treatment of consumer protection as conventionally conceived and of antitrust and price control policies will focus purely on the United Kingdom. We shall endeavour to provide specific examples of the problems to which policy is addressed. A prime aim of the book is to explain the content of the laws that deal with particular problems, and we shall discuss specific cases and reports that indicate how the law has been interpreted. An important element in this area of law is the question of enforcement and redress. In other words, is the individual required to right the wrong, or do central and local government agencies act on his behalf? Also, what kind of penalties does the law inflict? It is of course always possible that private and official redress may exist side by side. Incidentally, we should not place too much emphasis on the idea that it is always the law that protects the citizen. Such an assumption would ignore the existence of what we may term private enterprise initiatives such as the Consumers' Association and local consumer groups. It would also ignore two other quite crucial points. First, the force of competition and the need to secure repeat business is a potent influence that induces enterprises, private and public, to produce goods and services that satisfy the consumer. Second, enterprises (under informed public pressure) have in some cases been in the vanguard in introducing specific consumer protection devices. For example, the introduction of open dating in the UK was a private enterprise initiative which the state took up and intends to make more general. Then again there have been occasions when the withdrawal of certain commodities, on the grounds that they contained allegedly dangerous additives, was first undertaken by distributors. The state acted only after the event. Nor should we ignore the point that, although the modern state paternally interferes in the operation of the market, inevitably considerable reliance must be placed on the ability of the individual to use his intelligence in protecting himself. There is in any case a limit to the quantity of law that business and the enforcement authorities can absorb.

The sequence in which topics are dealt with below has been devised in order to parallel the process of protection in the real world. After the introductory matter of Chapters 1 and 2, Chapter 3 deals with the creation of competition between rival suppliers at the international level. The protection of the consumer is obviously served by opening the UK market up to outside suppliers. The lower the level of the tariff barriers around the UK market, the wider and more effective the choice for the UK consumer. In this sense the reductions of tariffs and quotas achieved in the postwar period, most notably in the Dillon, Kennedy (and prospectively in the Nixon (Tokyo)) Rounds, have been potent instruments of consumer protection. We have only to think of the enhanced choice and intensified competition that has emanated from the penetration of the UK market by Continental and Japanese producers of cars, televisions, cameras etc. to recognize the force of this point. The 1978 advertising slogan of Datsun dealers to the effect that 'Britain's Datsun dealers would like you to feel free to buy the car of your choice – British, French, German, Italian or Japanese' rubbed this point in rather cleverly and was bound to make the UK consumer think twice about import controls.

If we are thinking about tariff-free access to the UK market, then obviously it is UK membership of the European Economic Community (EEC) and European Coal and Steel Community (ECSC) that is of prime relevance. It should however be noted that British membership of the European Communities was accompanied by special arrangements for European Free Trade Association (EFTA) members and associates. These arrangements have created free trade in respect of industrial goods. In Chapter 3 however our focus will be on the free-trade arrangement that exists as a result of our membership of the EEC and ECSC, and we shall look at the antitrust provisions of the Rome and Paris Treaties. These deal with various restrictive business practices (here we give the term its widest possible antitrust interpretation) that have the effect of inhibiting the free flow of Community goods and services into the UK marketplace. We are in effect dealing with a form of non-tariff barrier, and it should be noted that there are non-tariff barriers other than restrictive business practices that also restrict competition (e.g. controls on the composition and design of goods, etc.), and these fall due for consideration in Chapter 5. Having discussed the provisions of Community antitrust law, in Chapter 4 we see how UK antitrust law seeks to create and maintain competition between domestic suppliers of goods and services. (Such laws relate not only to the actual production of goods but also to their distribution.) Still thinking of the factors that govern the production and supply of goods and services, we recognize a series of other market interventions that influence the price, quality and design of goods. Here we are thinking not only of direct controls on prices but also of indirect control via incomes policy. We also examine the various controls that are devised to guarantee minimum quality standards in the supply of goods and services and to obviate product-related injury. These and other factors are discussed in Chapter 5. In Chapter 6 we ask the reader to imagine that there is now an array of goods available that the consumer can purchase: this chapter deals with the provision of information in order that the consumer may decide which goods and services to buy. Here we deal with the requirements of the law in terms of the information that suppliers are obliged to give (statement of quantity, sale in prescribed amounts, unit-pricing, etc.) and the further advice that the consumer can avail himself of as to likely performance (e.g. as a result of the activities of the Consumers' Association). In Chapter 7 we deal with the possibility that in attempting to induce consumers to buy deception may arise. We discuss deceptive statements and deceptive practices, and this involves a consideration of statutes such as the Trade Descriptions Act 1968 and the Misrepresentation Act 1967. In some cases the acquisition of goods requires the extension of credit. In Chapter 8 we review the alternative ways of financing contractual transactions and this in turn leads on to a consideration of the Consumer Credit Act 1974. In Chapter 9 we invite the reader to assume that the consumer has now acquired goods or has benefited from a service: what are his rights in terms of the performance of the goods, etc? Let us suppose that the goods or services fail to live up to expectations or give rise to injury: what are the consumers' rights of redress? Can sellers insert exclusion clauses? Here the Supply of Goods (Implied Terms) Act 1973 and the Unfair Contract Terms Act 1977, etc., and the cases that have arisen out of them, fall due for consideration. In Chapter 10 we conclude our discussion of the mechanisms of protection by considering remedies and redress of grievances. Here the focus is upon the courts and court procedures. In Chapter 11 we round off our discussion by assessing progress in protecting the consumer and by asking what more, if anything, needs to be done.

THE RATIONALE OF PROTECTING THE CONSUMER IN A MIXED ECONOMY

Let us begin by asking what are the key questions that must be answered by any economic system. They are as follows. First, what goods and services are to be produced and in what quantity and variety? The basic resources of the economic system are not necessarily specific in terms of the use to which they can be put. The basic materials necessary to produce steel for a motorcar can also produce steel for a refrigerator. Diamonds may be a girl's best friend but they also have severely practical uses in industry. These basic resources do not present themselves with labels attached indicating how they should be used: it is up to the economic system to answer that question. Second, there is the question of how the goods are to be produced. Are they going to be produced by a command economy in which the means of production are owned by the state and in which a central planning system attempts to produce an integrated plan for the allocation of resources as between competing ends? Or are the resources going to be privately owned with the direction of production, the level of price, etc., being centrally influenced or controlled?

Or are the resources to be privately owned, the productive decisions being determined in a decentralized way through a price mechanism in which the pursuit of profit is tempered by the force of competition? Third, for whom are the goods and services produced? Here we come face to face with the question of the distribution of the national product.

Economic systems differ not in respect of the basic questions that they seek to answer but in the way in which they seek to answer them. If we consider a free enterprise system – and clearly the present UK system emerged from such an arrangement and still has a substantial free-market element – then the method of answering the three basic questions is as follows.

The framework is a capitalistic one in which factors of production (i.e. labour, capital and land) are privately owned. The owners of these factors hire them in the market for the highest price they can command. The key factor is enterprise. The entrepreneur is the organizing factor. He bears risks in the sense that he tries to estimate what goods and services, at what prices, in what quantities, in what varieties, at what particular times and locations, consumers are going to demand. He bears risks in that, in undertaking this entrepreneurial activity, he is guided by the prospect of profit. Profit is the reward for making the correct entrepreneurial decisions and losses are the penalty for making mistakes.

The answer to the first question – what goods and services etc. – is given by the decentralized market system. In effect, in their spending activity consumers are casting money votes and the system is supposed to respond thereto. More money voted for good X is supposed to induce entrepreneurs to produce more X. Less voted for Y is supposed to produce a contrary effect. This is actually achieved through the agency of the price mechanism in which prices act as signals to entrepreneurs. For example, in a two-good model if consumers spend more on X its price will rise. Price will have risen relative to cost. X now being relatively more profitable to produce, entrepreneurs will produce more of it. Let us assume that the more spent on X is compensated for by less being spent on Y. The price of the latter may fall, although in a modern ratchet economy, where trade unions resist wage cuts, it is more likely that the price of Y will merely mark time. Nevertheless the *relative* profitability of Y will have fallen and we may expect entrepreneurs to switch away from producing it.

We must also recognize that the changes in relative profitability and the consequent decisions to produce respectively more of X and less of Y in turn lead to a reallocation in the use of society's basic productive resources. The producers of X will be bidding for more labour, etc., in the factor (as opposed to product) market, while the producers of Y will be releasing labour, etc., on to the factor market.

It is important to note that in a pure free enterprise system what is produced and what is not produced is determined by the market test. In other words the key question is, are consumers prepared to pay a price that covers the full cost of production including an allowance for a normal return on the entrepreneur's capital (the latter is called normal profit, i.e. that profit that is just sufficient to retain capital in a particular use)? There is no question of the production of goods being subsidized, i.e. of part of the cost of production being borne by the state.

In respect of the second question – how? – it is assumed that goods and services will be produced under conditions of competition. There will be a number of rival producers in each relevant market who will be striving to increase their market shares at each other's expense. Such striving will induce them to keep price as low as possible and to produce a quality and variety of goods that will attract the patronage of consumers. Potential competition also plays an important role. Any tendency for established producers to enjoy a level of profitability above normal will induce new firms to enter the market and, by adding to supply, to force price and profitability down to the normal or competitive level.

On the question of for whom the goods and services are produced, the answer is all too obvious. Citizens do not consume because they are good or deserving. Their command over goods and services depends on their ownership of factors of production that are in demand. The scarcer the factors, the higher the price they command.

It is clear that the above system does not describe the UK economy of the 1970s. Indeed, the contemporary economy is best described as a mixed one. There is a substantial private sector, where the kind of forces described above do operate; but in addition the government, central and local, intervenes in the workings of the system. These interventions are of two kinds. First, the government undertakes certain productive activities itself or creates bodies such as nationalized industries for that purpose. Here we have the public sector. Second, the government influences the working of the private sector. These two kinds of intervention have arisen either because the

INTRODUCTION – THE SUBJECT MATTER

private enterprise system quite literally breaks down or because, although it works, it produces results that are socially unacceptable. We do not propose to review all the reasons that have led to these two forms of intervention. Rather we shall cite just a few instances to illustrate our thesis. The nationalized industries are examples of public sector productive activity. The reasons for nationalization have indeed been diverse but one important reason has been the fact of natural monopoly. It is simply uneconomic to envisage competition in the supply of water, gas, etc. Full-blown competition would involve duplication of expensive distributional pipelines with a consequent loss of economies of large-scale operation. Not only that, but major upheavals would occur whenever consumers switched from one supplier to another. One possible solution to this problem is to provide for private ownership and operation but to apply public control over prices, profits etc. – this is called regulation and is the approach adopted in the US. Alternatively, the state can go the whole hog and take such utilities into public ownership – this has been the British solution. Monetary and fiscal policy, regional policy, the activities of the Price Commission, etc., are examples of the state seeking to influence the workings of the free enterprise system in order to prevent it from breaking down. The Keynesian remedy for macroeconomic instability in the downwards direction – i.e. unemployment – is for the state deliberately to influence the supply of money and interest rates (monetary policy), tax rates and government spending (budgetary policy) in order to generate an adequate level of effective demand for goods and services and thus for labour. Regional policy addresses itself to the fact that industries tend to concentrate in certain areas and when they decline severe pockets of unemployment, low incomes and low employment participation rates emerge. The free enterprise solution would be to let the forces of the market operate. Labour would migrate to the more prosperous regions. Capital might move to the places where there was a surplus of labour – all the more so if localized unemployment meant that the relative price of labour in the problem regions fell. Experience seems to suggest that such corrective influences work only slowly, hence the battery of regional incentives and controls aimed at preventing the development of industries and services in prosperous regions and subsidizing new activity in the disadvantaged areas.

So far we have been instancing reasons, and there are many more that we could cite, why the free enterprise system has given place to the mixed economy. We have yet to identify those specific deficiencies in the free enterprise system that give rise to the interventions with which this book is really concerned. To these we now turn.

The first relates to the question of how the free enterprise system solves the question of what to produce. Such a system is based on the principle of consumer sovereignty. The consumer is king – he commands by virtue of the way in which he votes his money. (Of course, not everyone has the same number of votes.) The deployment of resources reflects his preferences. Underlying this is another principle – that of *caveat emptor*. Let the buyer beware. This doctrine, upon which early English law concerning the sale of goods was based, assumed that the consumer was responsible for protecting himself and would do so by applying his intelligence and experience in negotiating the terms of any purchase. In early times the consumer may have been able to protect himself. Products were less sophisticated. They could be inspected before purchase. The retailer would quite probably be known to the purchaser and would be readily accessible in case of fault or deception. Today, although there are some who believe that consumer protection is unnecessary, it is fairly generally accepted that conditions have changed. The consumer is in need of at least some protection if, amid a welter of advertising, he is to make intelligent choices so that society's scarce resources may produce the maximum consumer satisfaction.

If the consumer is to make intelligent choices he needs accurate information. He must know the price. This latter may sound surprising but it is all too apparent that in the past consumers obtaining credit have not had a clear idea as to the rate of interest they were being charged. Goods must be dispensed in stated quantities if value-for-money judgments are to be made – ideally the consumer needs to know not only the price and quantity but the price per unit, i.e. unit pricing. Fraud in terms of short weight or measure must be penalized and thus deterred.

A prime element in making rational choices is information about likely performance. This may require a listing of ingredients – as in the case of foods. Some have indeed argued that in respect of foods there is a case for an indication of the calorific value per quantity, serving or container. Many modern goods are essentially technological mysteries. In cases where the expenditure is large the relatively low cost 'use it and see' learning process is distinctly unhelpful. For many highly technological goods the learning process is in any case largely irrelevant since, by the time the consumer comes to re-purchase, technological progress faces him with a new set of products about which he knows little or nothing. There is therefore a need for comparative test data and for performance and care labelling. There is also a good case for protecting the consumer against deceptive claims.

The principle of *caveat emptor* falls flat on its face when we consider the questions of hygiene in production and distribution, shelf life and so forth. In the great majority of cases the consumer has no means of knowing whether goods were produced under hygienic conditions. He has no precise means of evaluating how long goods can be safely stocked. Equally, *caveat emptor* is largely irrelevant when we consider the questions of the safety of drugs and food additives. There is also much to be said for the laying down of safety standards in the design of, e.g., mechanical and electrical equipment used by consumers.

It also seems reasonable that the consumer should have some means of redress when goods fail to live up to their promise or indeed cause injury. Consumer protection has also been in part founded on the idea that, although a consumer must ultimately make his own mind up as to what he buys and from whom he borrows, he ought not to be subjected to undue pressure when doing so.

If consumer protection is one manifestation of government intervention that helps to explain the emergence of the modern mixed economy, antitrust policy is another. In respect of our second question – how? – it was assumed that in a free enterprise system goods and services would be produced under conditions of competition. But it would be false to assume that a competitive economy is a natural state of affairs. All the evidence suggests that, if we adopt a policy of *laissez-faire*, competition would not long continue intact. It would in significant measure disappear out of the window. For the plain truth is, and all experience points in this direction, that businessmen do not like to compete. It would however be wrong to conclude that, in so far as businessmen chose to collude rather than compete, or to acquire by amalgamation or whatever a control over specific markets, they would without exception do so with one aim in mind, namely to fleece the consumer. Although some might have the latter aim in mind, the possibility needs to be recognized that collusion etc. might in some instances be motivated by a desire to impose a degree of order and stability upon the hurly-burly of the business world. Modest but stable profits rather than the maximum that the market would bear might, in some cases, be the objective.

At this point the reader may begin to wonder what is the evidence that enables us to assert that competition would be significantly attenuated in conditions of *laissez-faire?* Here the answer must be based on the experience of countries such as the UK and US prior to the introduction of significant antitrust laws. In the UK, for example, towards the end of its term of office the first postwar Labour administration began to dismantle the economic controls that had been introduced during the Second World War. The process of decontrol was completed by the Conservative administration that came to power in 1951. But it would be a mistake to assume that this bonfire of controls marked the onset of a competitive economy. The early reports of the Monopolies and Restrictive Practices Commission indicated that devices for fixing prices and excluding competitors were deeply entrenched in the British industrial system. Further evidence of the widespread nature of the problem was produced as a result of the introduction of the Restrictive Trade Practices Act in 1956. This required parties to register their agreements, and as a result an impressive array of restrictions was brought into the open. Support for the notion that competition is not popular with businessmen can also be derived from a consideration of the various substitute devices for avoiding competition that were introduced in the UK when the 1956 Act began to undermine the position of overt collusion. In the US the pattern was not dissimilar.

It is, of course, important to keep things in perspective. The reader may notice that we have chosen our language carefully. We have said that the absence of antitrust policy would lead to an attenuation of the process of competition – we have not said that it would lead to its total disappearance. For example, even if through patents a company can totally control a market, the monopoly profits so enjoyed provide a powerful temptation to an outsider to get round the patent. As long as independent centres of initiative survive, the profit motive is likely to guarantee that on occasions competition will break through.

From what has gone before we conclude that it would be erroneous to see antitrust policy as being merely an aspect of a free enterprise system. Rather it is yet another example of the interventionism that helps to explain why our contemporary economy is indeed a mixed one.

In viewing antitrust policy as a device for protecting the consumer we need briefly to consider the nature of that protection. First, competition is seen as benefiting the consumer by virtue of its contribution to allocative efficiency. It (the argument is usually conducted in terms of perfect competition) leads to an allocation of resources as between the production of various goods which maximizes the economic welfare of the community. The monopolist by contrast is assumed to maximize profits by restricting output below the competitive level and raising price above the competitive level. It is then argued that the fact that some consumers are willing to pay a high price (a measure of their welfare) for the monopolized product (price being in excess of marginal cost, i.e., the cost of the resources needed to produce one more unit of output) indicates that they would benefit if more of the monopolized good was produced. At the same time, the resources not used in the monopolized industry, if redirected into the competitive industries, will add to supply and drive down price. In the latter case the lowness of price is an indicator of the low welfare derived from the resources so employed. A better allocation of resources would accrue if fewer goods were produced in the competitive industries. Under conditions of universal perfect competition price in all industries is equal to marginal cost – there is no distortion in the allocation of resources between different products. Monopoly thus leads to allocative inefficiency while competition by contrast leads to allocative efficiency.

Second, monopoly also leads to productive inefficiency – this is sometimes referred to as X-inefficiency. The argument here is simple. Competition forces firms – management and labour – to be as efficient as possible. Waste of time and materials will be minimized since if the resulting costs and prices are too high the force of competition may lead to the bankruptcy of the enterprise. Equally, management will be driven to seek out and introduce the best technology available. Competition therefore generates productive efficiency. But if a firm were to enjoy a monopoly then it would be in a position to manipulate output and prices so as to generate monopoly profits. The monopoly profits would provide a cushion which might encourage slackness within the organization. Costs might then begin to creep up above the competitive level. Monopoly may breed productive inefficiency, not to mention a general lack of concern for the particular needs of the consumer.

If we were to try to discover why governments have introduced antitrust laws it is unlikely that we would find references to allocative efficiency considerations in their legislative proceedings. Quite simply, this kind of theoretical thinking is outside the normal experience of politicians. References, perhaps crude in character, to the issue of productive efficiency might be more frequently encountered, but undoubtedly the main practical consideration in attacking monopoly has been the propensity of the monopolist to corner the market and to line his pockets at the expense of the public. In other words, the monopolist can restrict output, raise price and engineer a rate of profitability above the normal competitive level. In effect, a redistribution of income is achieved at the expense of the consumer.

It should be added that a further factor that seems to have inspired the introduction of antitrust laws has been the complaint of some businessmen that other businessmen have excluded them from particular markets or have sought to limit their freedom of manoeuvre. In such cases the antitrust laws have not sought directly to protect the consumer against the restrictive activities of producers, but have been concerned to protect some businessmen from other businessmen. The consumer may however have been an indirect beneficiary of laws designed to guarantee a right to compete.

In the light of our indictments of monopoly (and what we have said applies with varying force to all the main antitrust phenomena) it would appear that the legal form of antitrust intervention ought to be simple and unqualified. Collusion in all its forms, monopoly in all its guises, etc., should be proscribed. But in practice this is certainly not the case – particularly not in the UK. Why, we may ask, is this? The answer is that, however much the uninitiated (which phrase clearly excludes the readers and writers of this book) may prefer simple, clear-cut policy prescriptions, the theory of competition policy does not inevitably provide them. Although competition may be beneficial there may be circumstances where some trade-off advantage arises from some restriction of competition or from some industrial structure that is far from being obviously competitive. For example, because of this possibility antitrust laws do not proscribe monopoly as such (*per se*). The reason for this is that monopoly may be inevitable. If one firm is sheerly more efficient or inventive than its rivals then it may well emerge as a victorious monopolist. Having done so it can hardly be beaten about the ears for being successful. Then again the economies of large-scale production may mean that in extreme cases the market can accommodate only one fully efficient firm. Also, an effective research and development performance may require a high degree of industrial concentration. Considerations of this kind, as well as other objectives which the state feels must be given their due, mean that the maintenance of competition is an important, but not necessarily the supreme, object of policy.

This is as good a point as any at which to note that the emergence of consumer protection and antitrust policies is not purely a response to the existence of private economic activity. In UK law, as we shall see, nationalized industries are subject to investigation by the Consumer Protection Advisory Committee, and in respect of their business practices, but not their monopolies, are capable of being investigated by the Monopolies and Mergers Commission. The fact that they are enjoined to act in the public interest does not apparently free them from the need for supervision.[2]

Before leaving the subject of antitrust policy it is worthy of note that at least one economist – J.K. Galbraith – has in effect questioned whether there is a need for antitrust policy. He has based his query on the concept of countervailing power. In his view, when market power appears on one side of the market it spontaneously generates a countervailing power on the other side. Thus the emergence of monopoly or market power among sellers will automatically lead to the emergence of monopsony or buying power in the hands of purchasers. If this were inevitably true it would suggest that economists since at least the time of Adam Smith have been busily barking up the wrong tree. However we need not be unduly alarmed. The consensus of opinion among economists is that the Galbraith thesis is not proven. Countervailing power may exist, and where it does it may assist the consumer. For example, any market power among British food manufacturers is almost certainly substantially countervailed by the buying power of the supermarket chains. The latter are in vigorous competition and thus are likely to be forced to pass much of the benefit of their buying power on to the consumer. But countervailing power is not the automatic protective mechanism that Galbraith seemed to think it was.[3]

Next we turn to our third manifestation of government intervention, which relates directly to the problem of protecting the consumer. Previously we noted that one reason why the mixed economy had emerged was because the system left to itself would break down – it would be subject to bouts of macro-instability in the downwards direction, i.e. unemployment. But it is equally true to say that the system if left to itself is prone to upwards instability, i.e. inflation, and this leads to important economic interventions.

Our discussion of such interventions must however be preceded by at least an elementary appreciation of possible causes of inflation. Figure 1 attempts to provide a simple schematic presentation. Obviously, inflation may arise as a result of an excessive demand for

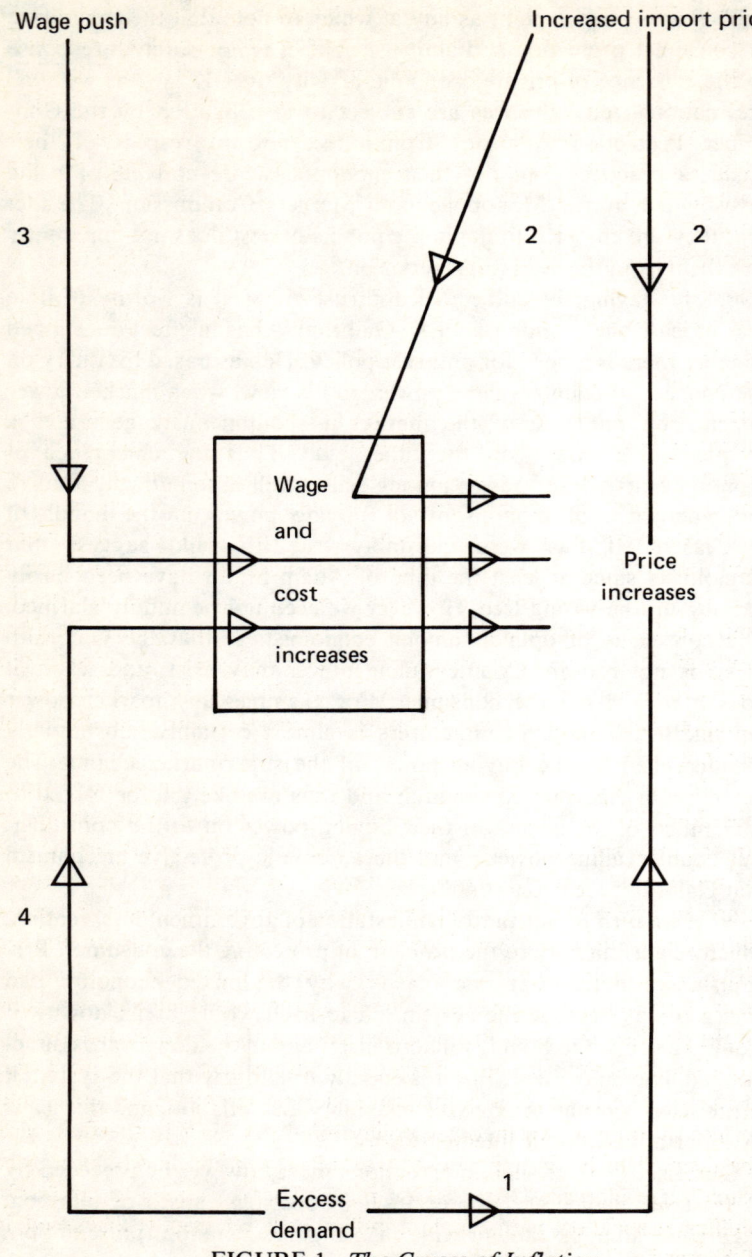

FIGURE 1 *The Causes of Inflation*

goods and services which simply and directly pulls prices up. This line of causation is labelled 1 in the diagram. Such a demand-pull causation suggests that a conventional macroeconomic policy of deflating demand by appropriate monetary and budgetary means should be adopted. The money supply should be reduced, thus raising interest rates and cutting down investment and consumption spending. Taxation (particularly direct) should be raised, thus depressing the community's consuming power, and the government's own spending should be reduced, thus directly reducing demand. (Monetarists would of course place all the emphasis on the role of the money supply and the need to control it.) Having said that we shall not venture any further into this area of policy but shall merely remind the reader that most introductory economics textbooks dwell on the theory and mechanics of such policy approaches at length. The government may however wish to hold prices down directly, and the activities of the Price Commission and the operation of the Price Codes will form an important part of our discussion in Chapter 5.

Inflation may have its origins abroad in the form of rising world and thus import prices, which increase the cost of living either directly (i.e. through dearer food) or indirectly (by inflating costs, i.e. dearer imported raw materials and fuel) – see routes 2 in the figure. There is not a great deal the government can do about this. Price control is out of the question, as we shall see when we discuss the price codes in Chapter 5. One approach is to apply to subsidies – we note this point in Chapter 5.

Inflation may however be linked to increases in wages. One obvious possibility is that, particularly at and close to full employment, trade unions may press for higher wages and salaries which outstrip the rise of productivity and thus increase costs and prompt businessmen to increase prices. This pushfulness, backed up by the strike threat, is shown as route 3. Here an incomes policy seems appropriate and we discuss the point in Chapter 5. However, an increase in wages may also be a reflection of an excess demand situation which has its origins in the product markets. Businessmen faced with an excess demand for goods may attempt to attract the extra labour necessary to meet that demand. The result is a competitive bidding up of wages, costs and prices – route 4. An incomes policy might, at least in the first case, be deemed to be an appropriate way of preventing, in whole or part, such wage increases from taking place. The objections to, and difficulties associated with, such a policy will be briefly discussed in Chapter 5.

Our diagram is deficient in that it ignores expectational factors. For example, expectations about future price rises may induce individuals to get out of money and into goods – the prophesy is then fulfilled (see route 1). There are also expectational aspects on the wages side, and we shall discuss them, and the way in which they may justify wage and price control policies, in Chapter 5.

At this point all we need to note is that in recent years incomes policies have begun to take on the appearance of a permanent feature of economic management. But during the sixties, when sustained experimentation with incomes policies really began, it became increasingly clear that trade unions would not accept control over incomes unless the policy also encompassed prices. In other words, social justice required that incomes derived from profits should also be controlled and that the purchasing power of wages should be guaranteed. Nevertheless, the main stress in preventing inflation continued to be laid upon controlling wages and salaries and thus costs and prices. The deference to control over prices was to a degree a gesture designed to secure trade union compliance with the control of wages and salaries. In more recent years the desire to prevent inflation has led governments to lay more stress on controlling prices directly and this has been done by establishing price codes that have been general rather than selective in their impact. Yet more recently price control policy and competition policy have come closer together. It has been recognized that price control is most relevant in those markets where the force of competition, which normally tends to arrest inflation, has been attenuated by virtue of the existence of anti-competitive industrial structures.

We must now say a few words about advertising because, unlike most if not all the themes discussed in this book, it cannot be tied down to one spot in our presentational scheme. In one sense advertising contributes to the protection of consumers. That is to say it has an informational role, and clearly, if consumers are to extract the maximum satisfaction or utility from their limited incomes, then they need an adequate flow of information about price and potential performance of rival goods and services. Economists have of course always drawn attention to the other aspect of advertising, namely its persuasive element. In our earlier discussion of the operation of the market mechanism as a means of determining what will be produced we painted a picture of consumer sovereignty. The consumer is king – he casts his money votes and the production system conforms to his wishes. Advertising in its persuasive aspect modifies the picture in that enterprises, private and public, are trying to persuade the consumer to like what they are disposed to produce rather than the reverse. It is of course easy to become too excited about this problem. The great mass of consumers are arguably not so gullible as to be repeatedly persuaded to buy things they really do not want. Having said that, the persuasion problem does highlight the importance of education, and consumer education in particular.

Advertising is also significant because of its potential effect on the competitive process. Heavy levels of advertising may deter new entrants to a market.[4] Here we are thinking about the big outlay that may be needed to establish a new brand of a product. This barrier to entry gives those already in the market the power to raise price above cost, and thus to make excessive profits, without provoking entry. The role of advertising is however far from clear-cut. Thus the protagonists of advertising would argue that advertising can be seen as discharging a powerful pro-competition role. The quickest way to introduce a superior new product, and displace obsolescent products, is to advertise!

Economists also tend to predict that in markets where the number of competitors is small price competition will be avoided and competition will tend to take a non-price form, with heavy, indeed excessive, advertising outlays that merely cancel each other out. The market as a whole may not expand. (This is not likely to be general but is a distinct possibility in consumer, as opposed to capital, goods markets.) There is indeed some evidence of this tendency. In Chapter 4 below we shall see that both the Monopolies Commission, in its detergents report, and more recently the Price Commission, in its report on sanitary products, took this view.

Advertising also appears in another context. Consumer protection more conventionally defined concerns itself about advertising because of the possibility that advertisers may make untrue or deceptive statements about their goods and services. This may also give rise to unfairness as between suppliers. Suppliers passing off their goods as better than they really are gain an unfair competitive advantage as compared with those suppliers who really do produce commodities of the quality claimed. We should also recognize that some of the reasons for regulating advertising do not relate to deception and unfair competition but are connected with protecting people from dangers connected with smoking, drinking, etc.

We could hardly conclude this introductory chapter without offering a definition of what *we* understand by the term 'consumer'. There are many definitions of that word, and we have to select a definition that is appropriate to the scope of this work. It is quite clear that we would include the purchasers and users of consumer goods as normally understood in economics, and this would include the domestic users of the products and services of nationalized industries. (Space precludes us from delving into the extremely interesting subject of the pricing problems of nationalized industries.) We are not including individual consumption of services provided by national and local government such as health, eduction and social security. Nor is it possible to deal with the subject of house and land purchase, which is subject to a different sort of legal regulation. Finally, we are not concerned with the problems of the business as a purchaser of such things as raw materials and equipment.

2 Institutional Background

INTRODUCTION

Before we actually proceed to a discussion of the various ways in which consumers are protected, it would seem appropriate to sketch in for the reader's benefit the institutional background. In other words, who is responsible for what in this general field of activity? We shall begin with the international dimension and then move on to our own domestic institutions.

THE EUROPEAN COMMUNITIES COMMISSION AND COURT OF JUSTICE

Now that the UK is a member of the European Economic Community (EEC), founded by the Rome Treaty 1957, the European Coal and Steel Community (ECSC), founded by the Paris Treaty 1951 and the European Atomic Energy Community, founded by a separate Rome Treaty 1957, we have to take account of the impact of Community law. In practice it is the law springing from our membership of the EEC that is of prime concern to us in the present context, although we shall encounter some provisions that have originated under the Paris Treaty.

Under the treaty creating the EEC it was the task of the European Community Commission[1] (EC Commission) located in Brussels to see that the objectives laid down in 1957 were ultimately achieved. Since the end of the treaty transition period (31 December 1969) the Community has from time to time set itself further objectives. These have been defined at the summit meetings of the heads of state and government – get-togethers that have been dignified under the title of the European Council. Again, it is the task of the Commission to see that these further objectives are achieved. The Commission is in fact the civil service of the Community. At its head are the top commissioners, thirteen in number, one of whom is the president. The commissioners are nominated by the member states, the larger countries putting up two names, the smaller states one each. Although nominated by the states, the commissioners must act with complete independence. The staff of the Commission is divided into directorates-general, over one or more of which a particular commissioner will preside. Antitrust policy, discussed in Chapter 3, is the responsibility of Directorate-General IV. The harmonization of standards discussed in Chapter 5 falls to Directorate-General III. There is a separate Environment and Consumer Protection Service.

In its task of seeing that the objectives laid down are achieved the Commission makes proposals to the Council of Ministers (the latter should not be confused with the European Council). In approaching the Council of Ministers the Commission feeds it with draft regulations and draft directives. An approved regulation is of general applicability and is directly binding on all nationals. An approved directive is addressed to governments and places upon them the obligation to introduce the appropriate legislation at national level that will ensure the achievements of objectives set out in the directive. When we come to consider the regulations that have been introduced to give effect to EEC antitrust policy, we should remember that those legal instruments arose out of the above machinery. Likewise, this is true of Community product harmonization activities.

However, the Commission not only helps to create Community law; it also plays a major role in implementing it. We shall see that in dealing with antitrust transgressions the Commission has the power to issue formal decisions that can, for example, prohibit certain forms of business behaviour and may also impose financial penalties. Companies or individuals can appeal against such decisions to the Court of Justice. The latter is a final arbiter and its judgments are the ultimate authority in determining the stance of Community law in respect of particular forms of business arrangement or conduct. The Commission can also go to the Court of Justice to force states to come into line. For example, the Commission could take a member state to the Court if that state refused to take the action required by a directive.

DEPARTMENT OF PRICES AND CONSUMER PROTECTION

We turn now to our own domestic institutions. Pride of place must go to the Department of Prices and Consumer Protection (DPCP). The establishment of this department to look after consumer affairs generally came after the Labour victory in the election of 1974, although it had been foreshadowed in the previous administration by the allocation of consumer matters within relevant departments to junior ministers. Sir Geoffrey Howe had been Minister for Trade and Consumer Affairs at the former Department of Trade in 1972 and it was a logical step to split that department when it became apparent that the consumer interest could best be served by a separate department with its own secretary of state. The prices policy initiated by the Conservative administration and continued by the Labour government[2] has tended to bring the Secretary of State for Prices and Consumer Protection into the centre of political discussion, and the Department is now firmly established in Whitehall and in the public eye.

The Department is responsible for the making of policy on consumer affairs and related topics and must now look after the major legislation in the consumer field. For example, the Weights and Measures Act 1963, the Trade Descriptions Act 1968, the Fair Trading Act 1973, the Consumer Credit Act 1974, the Resale Prices Act 1976, the Restrictive Practices Act 1976 and the Consumer Safety Act 1978 all come under the aegis of the Department. It is also responsible for a number of agencies concerned with consumer interests, the more important of which include the Office of Fair Trading, the Consumer Protection Advisory Committee, the Price Commission and the Monopolies and Mergers Commission. Although references to the Restrictive Practices Court come from the Office of Fair Trading, the Court is, of course, entirely independent. Additionally, the Department must deal with independent bodies who are partly or wholly dependent upon the government (through the Department) for financing, notably the National Consumer Council and the Citizens' Advice Bureaux service.[3]

THE OFFICE OF FAIR TRADING

The Fair Trading Act 1973 may prove to be the most significant piece of consumer legislation for many years. If it should turn out in that way it will be noteworthy for its emphasis on protection by a national, government-financed body with coercive powers, rather than on the creation of further criminal offences or civil law rights which may be utilized by a consumer on his own personal initiative.

The Office of Fair Trading (OFT)[4] resulted from that statute. It is now one of the primary bodies for safeguarding the interests of consumers. The leading official is the Director-General of Fair Trading. The first holder of the office was Sir John Methven, who took up his office on 1 November 1973, and he was succeeded by Professor G.J. Borrie who is the present incumbent.

The Director-General (aided by his Office) fulfils his protective function in the following ways.

(a) He has a broad duty *to keep under review* the carrying on of commercial activities in the UK that relate to the supply to consumers of goods and services. He does so in order to become aware of practices that may adversely affect the economic interests of consumers.[5]

(b) He has to *receive and collate* evidence of practices that may adversely affect the interests of consumers – here the remit is not limited to practices that affect the economic interest of consumers but also covers their health, safety or other matters.[6]

(c) He may make references to the Consumer Protection Advisory Committee leading to the possible imposition of criminal sanctions by the Secretary of State in respect of consumer trade practices that adversely affect the economic interests of UK consumers – see below. Alternatively, he may report directly to the Secretary of State under Section 2 of the Fair Trading Act 1973.

(d) Where a person carrying on business has persisted in a course of conduct that is detrimental to the economic interests, health or safety of consumers, or is otherwise unfair as defined by the statute, the Director-General can require that assurances be given that that course of conduct will be discontinued. If this does not succeed he may bring proceedings against the person concerned in the Restrictive Practices Court.[7]

(e) The Director-General also has the power to encourage trade associations to prepare and circulate to their members codes of practice for guidance in safeguarding and promoting the interests of consumers in the UK.[8]

(f) He can also publish information and advice for consumers.[9]

(g) On the antitrust front he can refer agreements restricting competition to the Restrictive Practices Court. He also has the power to make references to the Monopolies and Mergers Commission. Both of these are discussed further below and in Chapter 4.

One of the important features of the Office is the independence enjoyed by the Director-General. This is well illustrated in the case of monopolies. At one stage these were the subject of ministerial references – in the earlier days the President of the Board of Trade exercised that role. However, following the Fair Trading Act 1973 the Director-General was given the power to refer monopolies to the Monopolies and Mergers Commission on his own initiative. Thus the implementation of competition policy in respect of monopolies was in some degree taken out of the political sphere. As we shall see later this independence does not exist in the case of merger references.

THE CONSUMER PROTECTION ADVISORY COMMITTEE

Having discussed the role of the Director-General and his Office we now consider the role of three other institutions to which he can make references: the Consumer Protection Advisory Committee, the Monopolies and Mergers Commission and the Restrictive Practices Court. We shall see however that the Director-General does not necessarily have a monopoly of reference-making. We first turn to the Consumer Protection Advisory Committee. This was established by the Fair Trading Act 1973[10] as the independent advisory body to the Secretary of State for Prices and Consumer Protection. The Committee is to consist of at least ten but not more than fifteen members appointed by the Secretary of State who will have regard to the necessity of including on the Committee at least one person who is experienced in the supply of goods or services to consumers; at least one person who has experience in the enforcement of the Trade Descriptions Act 1968 or the Weights and Measures Act 1963, and at least one person who is experienced in consumer groups or activities.[11] These restrictions are fairly minor and the Secretary of State is free to exercise his patronage in making appointments to the Committee.

Although independent, and advisory, the Committee is left no scope for initiative by the statute since its activities are defined solely in relation to references made to it by the Director-General, the Secretary of State or another minister. Its activities are entirely dependent upon such a reference being made.

Two types of reference are possible under the Fair Trading Act, but both types are concerned with the same basic question, namely whether a consumer trade practice (as defined by Section 13) specified in the reference adversely affects the economic interests of consumers in the UK. Such a question may be put by any of the persons detailed above, and the reference of that question obliges the Committee to consider the matter and make a report to the person making the reference. In compiling the report the Committee may require the Director-General to make available information that he possesses and to render any other assistance necessary to enable the Committee to make an investigation of the matter under consideration.[12] A 'consumer trade practice' for the purposes of the Act means:

> any practice which is for the time being carried on in connection with the supply of goods (whether by way of sale or otherwise) to consumers or in connection with the supply of services to consumers and which relates –
> (a) to the terms or conditions (whether as to price or otherwise) on or subject to which goods or services are or are sought to be supplied, or
> (b) to the manner in which those terms or conditions are communicated to persons to whom goods are or are sought to be supplied, or
> (c) to promotion (by advertising, labelling or marking of goods, canvassing or otherwise) of the supply of goods or the supply of services, or
> (d) to methods of salesmanship employed in dealing with consumers, or
> (e) to the way in which goods are packed or otherwise got up for the purpose of being supplied, or
> (f) to methods of demanding or securing payment for goods or services supplied.[13]

It will be observed that this definition covers the whole transaction or potential transaction from advertising and packaging through to the demand for payment. There is no stage of the process of supply of goods or services to a consumer that is not capable of being a consumer trade practice under the terms of the Act.

The second type of reference is the more significant and can only be made by the Director-General himself. The scope is slightly more restricted in that the Director must be of the opinion that a consumer trade practice is likely to have the effect of:

(a) misleading consumers as to their rights and obligations under relevant consumer transactions, or withholding information about such rights, or an adequate record of them; or
(b) otherwise misleading or confusing consumers with respect to any matter; or
(c) subjecting consumers to undue pressure to enter into a transaction; or
(d) causing the terms and conditions of a transaction to be so adverse to the consumer as to be inequitable.[14]

The restriction is only slight because the second ground in particular is phrased in the most general terms, allowing any practice that misleads or confuses to be the subject of a reference.

The significance of the second type of reference lies in the fact that the Director-General may decide to include in the reference proposals for recommending to the Secretary of State that the trade practice should be the subject of his power to impose criminal liability. In these circumstances the Committee must consider the reference and proposals and report on them within three months of the date of the reference. The report should state whether the Committee concludes that the consumer trade practice does adversely affect the economic interests of consumers in the UK; whether they agree that it is likely to have the effect that the Director-General is contending; and whether they agree with his proposals or agree with modified proposals, or completely disagree.[15] If the Committee agrees with the proposals or a modified form of them, the Secretary of State may, on receipt of the report, prohibit the consumer trade practice in question by statutory instrument. The instrument is subject to affirmative resolution by both Houses of Parliament. Though this procedure affords legislative powers to the Secretary of State, he has little discretion in the form of the instrument (having to give effect to the proposals in the report) and it may be thought that the enactment of a statute to curb every adverse trade practice would be unnecessarily cumbersome and time-consuming.

The reports of the Committee that have led to the prohibition of certain trade practices will be considered at the appropriate point in the text, but they have included *Disguised Business Sales*,[16] *Rights of Consumers*,[17] and *Prepayment for Goods*.[18]

THE MONOPOLIES AND MERGERS COMMISSION

This again is a body to which the Director-General can make references, although like the Consumer Protection Advisory Committee he does not have a monopoly of reference-making.

The Monopolies and Mergers Commission was first created under the Monopolies and Restrictive Practices (Inquiry and Control) Act 1948. The various alterations of title are described in Chapter 4 where we discuss its work in detail. The present role of the Commission is defined by the Fair Trading Act 1973. Without going into detail we can note that its task is to investigate monopoly and merger situations in the UK. It assesses their impact by reference to public interest criteria laid down in the 1973 Act. It does not initiate references or take the action necessary by way of remedy – those roles are discharged by other bodies.

The Commission itself consists of between ten and twenty-seven members, one of whom is the chairman, who are appointed by the Secretary of State for Prices and Consumer Protection. The membership is made up of persons who by their practical or academic experience are capable of assessing the impact of industrial structures and changes therein upon the public interest. The Commission has a staff to assist it in its process of investigation and analysis.

In respect of monopolies we have already noted that the Director-General can initiate references[19] although the Secretary of State, or the Secretary of State and any other minister acting jointly, may also refer.[20] In order to make references the Office of Fair Trading has developed a screening process – we also discuss this in Chapter 4. The Director-General has a number of investigative powers that facilitate this process.[21]

Reports of the Commission are sent to the Secretary of State and also to any other minister who may have joined in the making of a reference. Where remedial action is taken the appropriate minister (this is usually the Secretary of State) acts by statutory instrument – the legislation provides for orders to be issued that control the activities of monopolists.[22] As an alternative the Director-General may be asked to obtain voluntary undertakings from the firm or firms concerned.[23] The monitoring of orders and undertakings is a job for the Director-General, although more recently that role in respect of prices and pricing behaviour has been passed over to the Price Commission, which we discuss below and in Chapter 5.

In the case of mergers the Director-General does not enjoy the same independence. Candidates for reference are identified through the operation of the Inter-Departmental Mergers Panel (see Chapter 4) which the Director-General chairs. It advises the Secretary of State as to the mergers that should be referred, but it is left to him to decide whether or not to refer.[24] Again, Commission reports are sent to the Secretary of State and he has an order making power although he may ask the Director-General to proceed by way of the obtaining of voluntary undertakings.[25] In respect of both monopoly and merger reports the Director-General is empowered to give advice to the Secretary of State and any other minister concerned and they are required to take it into account.[26]

THE RESTRICTIVE PRACTICES COURT

Here again the Director-General makes references, only in this case he has a monopoly of the reference-making activity. Under the original Restrictive Trade Practices Act 1956 the reference role was exercised by the Registrar of Restrictive Trading Agreements, but following the Fair Trading Act 1973 that role was vested in his successor the Director-General.

The Restrictive Practices Court to which he makes his references was created under the 1956 Act. In 1964 its work was added to by virtue of the Resale Prices Act. The 1956 Act related to restrictions of competition in relation to goods such as horizontal price-fixing. The 1964 Act dealt with individual resale price maintenance arrangements, i.e. the practice by suppliers of fixing the price at which, for example, retailers must sell their goods. (The various forms of restrictive practice are discussed at the beginning of Chapter 3 and specific UK policy is discussed in Chapter 4.) There have been various additional Acts that have strengthened and widened the 1956 Act, namely the Restrictive Trade Practices Act 1968 and the Fair Trading Act 1973, and all the provisions have been consolidated in the Restrictive Trade Practices Act 1976, as amended, while resale price provisions are consolidated in the Resale Prices Act 1976.

The Restrictive Practices Court constitution is currently governed by the Restrictive Practices Court Act 1976. The Court consists of five nominated judges and not more than ten appointed members. The latter lay element is of particular interest – the Act says that they shall be chosen by virtue of their knowledge of or experience in industry, commerce or public affairs. Three of the judges have to be puisne judges of the High Court nominated by the Lord Chancellor, one shall be a judge of the Court of Session nominated by the Lord President of that Court and one shall be a judge of the Supreme Court of Northern Ireland nominated by the Lord Chief Justice of Northern Ireland. The Lord Chancellor selects one of the judges to be president of the Court and also recommends the lay members.

At hearings and judgment the Court normally consists of the presiding judge and two other members. Matters of law are determined by the judge or judges sitting – otherwise all members have an equal role. It is the task of the Court to decide whether restrictive agreements referred to them are in the public interest or not. Appropriate orders are then made. The task of the Director-General in all this is first to keep a register of agreements – those participating in agreements have a duty to register their agreements with him. Second, the Director-General and his staff analyse and select agreements for reference, help to determine the case against them and brief the counsel and expert witnesses who will actually appear before the Court. The respondents of course brief their own counsel and expert witnesses in an endeavour to defend their agreement. The Director-General has a number of other roles, a particularly important one being to bring unregistered agreements on to the register. Powers in connection with the latter function are expressly provided.

The Secretary of State has a number of roles in relation to restrictive agreements.

(a) Since the Director-General has a duty to refer all agreements, he must get the approval of the Secretary of State if he wishes to be absolved from referring agreements of minor significance.

(b) The legislation does provide for agreements of national importance to be exempted – this role is discharged by the Secretary of State.

(c) The Secretary of State also makes the orders that determine which particular kinds of agreement, within a general class, are registrable – e.g. which particular kinds of agreement relating to services must be placed on the register.

THE PRICE COMMISSION

The Price Commission is a relatively new institution. The first body with that title was created by the Conservative Government in 1973. The present Commission owes its existence to the Price Commission Act 1977. The duty of the Commission is to restrain the price of goods and services, and the way in which it seeks to achieve that objective is discussed in detail in Chapter 5. The relevant legislation (including the Price Code, which lays down the ground rules of price control) is as we noted earlier the responsibility of the Department of Prices and Consumer Protection.

The Commission is composed of a full-time chairman and fifteen part-time members, three of them being deputy chairmen, and all appointed by the Secretary of State for Prices and Consumer Protection. The members of the Commission have diverse backgrounds, being drawn from business and commerce, trade unions, the academic profession and the consumer movement.

The Commission enjoys a significant degree of independence. The legislation requires certain categories of business to pre-notify price increases but, unlike the other three bodies, the Commission decides which cases to investigate. However this by no means excludes the Secretary of State from the control process. The Commission, having investigated proposals, has to report to the Secretary of State and he is responsible for any implementation by way of either voluntary undertaking or order. Also, the Secretary of State can require the Commission to investigate the prices charged in particular sectors of industry and can, if recommended by the Commission, restrain prices in the sector examined.

OTHER GOVERNMENT DEPARTMENTS

There are other government departments that also have a protective role, although it may only represent a small element in their total activity. One is the Department of Health and Social Security, which is responsible for the Medicines Act 1968. Under its provisions the labelling, advertising and above all composition of drugs are regulated. In discharging these roles it is assisted by a number of bodies including the Committee on Safety of Medicines. This protective activity is discussed in Chapter 5. That Department shares a responsibility with the Ministry of Agriculture, Fisheries and Food for the implementation of the Food and Drugs Act 1955. Regulations (but also codes of practice) are drawn up in respect of standards of composition (including additives and contaminants), labelling, advertising and hygiene. These two departments also link together in the supervision of control over pesticides and veterinary medicines. This general area of activity is discussed in Chapter 5. The Department of Industry also discharges a protective role notably by its surveillance of the insurance industry under the Insurance Companies Act 1974. Its remit also extends to insurance advertisements. Again this is discussed in detail in Chapter 5. We should also note that the Home Office exercises a consumer protection role in its supervision of products such as firearms, dangerous drugs and poisons – for the statutory provisions see Chapter 5.

LOCAL AUTHORITIES

Local government reorganization led to the allocation of consumer protection functions to county councils and metropolitan and London boroughs. (Hereafter the phrase 'local authority' will be used to comprehend all those institutions, and the Regional and Island Councils in Scotland, and the Department of Commerce in Northern Ireland.) The appropriate department is usually labelled the Consumer Protection Department or the Trading Standards Department and discharges all of the obligations that were the responsibility of Weights and Measures Departments. Statutes as diverse as the Food and Drugs Act 1955, the Weights and Measures Act 1963, the Trades Descriptions Act 1968 and the Consumer Safety Act 1978 – the latter being a successor to the Consumer Protection Acts – fall to their lot. They do not necessarily have a complete monopoly. For example, hygiene matters are dealt with by district council Environmental Health Departments – see Chapter 5.

Local conditions dictate how active these consumer protection departments are and how much emphasis is placed upon the advisory role of the department. Their preventive role in regulating business practices in the local area has never been in doubt, but there has

INSTITUTIONAL BACKGROUND   31

recently been political controversy over the extent to which the department should assume an *advisory* role. Encouraged by central government, both verbally and financially, a number of local authorities established Consumer Advice Centres[27] which were intended to provide pre-shopping information for consumers, price comparisons and quality comparisons as well as being a 'front' for the Consumer Protection Department for the reception of complaints about shoddy goods and dubious trade practices. When government financial support for these centres became less generous, some local authorities reviewed their policy and closed down the centres. It is rather unfortunate that the provision of consumer information has become a political issue in some areas of the country, but this may have been inevitable once the local authorities had to decide whether they were prepared to pay for the centres largely out of the rates without a large measure of government subvention. Some critics would identify the closure of centres as the first signs of an end to the consumer protection boom.

Local consumer protection officers (or trading standards officers) work closely in liaison with the Department of Prices and Consumer Protection, the Office of Fair Trading and local agencies at work in the area. It is often from information supplied by local officers that the Office of Fair Trading can establish a case for taking action against traders or trade practices under their own powers. Additionally, the officers must report prosecutions under the Trade Descriptions Act 1968 and the Fair Trading Act 1973 to the Office of Fair Trading together with information about consumer complaints in their area collected with the assistance of the Citizens' Advice Bureaux and other consumer groups.

THE NATIONAL CONSUMER COUNCIL

The National Consumer Council was established early in 1975 as a non-statutory group with a membership appointed by the Secretary of State for Prices and Consumer Protection. (Also sitting on it are the chairmen of the Scottish, Welsh and Northern Ireland Consumer Councils.) Its genesis was in a White Paper published in 1974[28] which gave the Council four specific tasks:

(a) to represent the consumer view to government, the Director-General of Fair Trading, industry and to any other specific group;
(b) to be available for consultation by those requiring a consumer view on policies and proposals;
(c) to provide representatives for national and international bodies;
(d) to review the arrangements for the representation of the consumer in the nationalized industries.

In addition it may respond to requests for information and advice on particular issues, and it has already published several important reports and discussion papers.[29]

The most significant development in its role has been a recent attempt to become a strong force in the formulation of government economic policy. The present chairman of the NCC, Mr Michael Shanks, envisages a directly political role for the Council and has spoken out in favour of some sort of a federal scheme in which the Council would achieve the same type of influence as the TUC and the CBI on economic and social issues. It is interesting to note that the predecessor to the NCC, the Consumer Council, was abolished by the Conservative Government in 1970 after a life of seven years. The statement issued by the Department of Trade and Industry at the time said that 'the Government have concluded that an adequate advancement and presentation of the consumer's interests no longer requires the maintenance of the Consumer Council at public expense'.[30] One hopes that the political initiatives taken by the NCC will not result in its being made a sort of political football which will be kicked backwards and forwards by parties in Government and Opposition.

The NCC does not consider that it ought to receive complaints from the individual consumer but it has taken a very wide interpretation of its brief and a very liberal definition of 'consumer',[31] so that there should not, on the evidence so far, be many fears that it will fail to investigate areas which may give rise to concern.

THE CONSUMERS' ASSOCIATION (CA)

The CA is a remarkable phenomenon in the field of British consumer affairs. It began in 1957 as a small organization publishing a magazine containing the results of comparative testing of aspirins and

INSTITUTIONAL BACKGROUND 33

kettles, and has since then grown into a multi-million pound operation with a large research department exercising considerable influence over the manufacturers and retailers of products as well as over those who are responsible for the formulation of consumer policy.

The basis of the CA was comparative testing. Published results of such testing had been available in the United States for some years,[32] but it was a struggle to mount the same operation in Britain with the feared obstacles of the laws of defamation and the disinterest of the consumer in the information offered. No such difficulties now exist. The growth in subscribers to the CA monthly magazine *Which?* reached a peak of over 700,000 in 1975, and even after a price rise in that year there are still some 600,000 regular subscribers. The marked increase of interest in consumer matters may owe much to the success of the magazine. It is now accepted as a good indication of quality and value and its recommendations are undoubtedly acted upon by thousands of people.

The Association has branched out into specialist areas and publishes separate quarterly magazines concerned with money matters, cars and motoring, holidays and do-it-yourself. In addition it publishes a number of books and pamphlets designed to help the consumer find his way about in places as diverse as Britain's restaurants, its County Courts and its family planning clinics.[33] A diverse view of consumerism! An additional service now exists in the provision of legal advice for members on their individual consumer problems. A separate subscription is paid for this service.

After twenty-one years of comparative testing and reporting, and the provision of information on all sorts of topics, the Consumers' Association finds itself at an interesting stage of development. The income of the CA in 1978 was around £6.26 million, and the receipt of that sort of money causes some discussion over the proper role of the Association. It is undoubtedly the case that the objectives of the Association permit it to take up causes on behalf of consumers in general, and the portion of the budget that is allocated to 'campaigns' has risen to £250,000; but there is a strong feeling in the Association that it should carry on doing what it was intended to do – disseminating information to its members about the products it has tested. It is hard to escape the comparison with the National Consumer Council which the government has appointed to speak on behalf of the consumer. Should the Association be doing that job?

One significant factor that might militate against the assumption of such a role is the apparent unwillingness of the subscribers to the magazine to get involved in the administration of the Association itself. The Association is a company and membership is open to people with three years' continuous subscription to the magazine who are willing to pay an additional annual subscription of 50p. Despite the huge numbers of subscribers to the magazine, however, there are only 2,000 members of the company who have the right to vote at meetings and decide the policy of the company. On that evidence, could the Association truly claim to speak on behalf of the consumer? Would it even be right to spend its members' money on doing so, when it appears that the vast majority of the subscribers are simply looking for the sort of information about products that the Association has customarily provided?

Mr Peter Goldman, the Director of the Association for the last fourteen years, has said that one of the ways in which the Association might develop is in the presentation of the viewpoint of the UK consumer in Brussels as the EEC takes an increasing interest in consumer affairs. It will certainly be interesting to see what role is eventually selected for the second biggest consumer organization in the world.

THE CITIZENS' ADVICE BUREAUX

Out of wartime necessity has emerged peacetime provision of advice by a network of local agencies operating to nationally defined standards and principles. It was in 1938 that a combined operation by the Ministry of Health, the National Council for Social Service and the Family Welfare Association established an advice service which was to be activated in the event of an emergency, and the outbreak of war provided the emergency the following year. The host of wartime regulations made life complicated, and the community was grateful to receive, and some of them to be trained to give, the information necessary in the prevailing conditions. The major part of the cost involved in setting up a national, regional and local structure was met by central government.

At the end of the war government assistance was withdrawn and those local bureaux that had been established were left to scrape along on what money they could raise from local authorities and other sources. Many of the 1,000 bureaux established during the war folded up, and despite unstinting efforts by the volunteer advisers less than half the bureaux remained open at the end of the 1950s. It was then that the government appreciated the potential of the service, and payment was resumed to the central office in 1960. The Molony Committee on Consumer Protection[34] was strongly in favour of the service and recognized its potential:

> The aggrieved consumer needs an accessible local service to which he can take his troubles and where he will receive a realistic appraisal, a measure of help in presenting his case, or a pointer to the next step. This need cannot better be filled than by the Citizens' Advice Bureaux.[35]

Government money has continued since then and at present the National Association of Citizens Advice Bureaux, the central organizing body, receives a substantial grant from the Department of Prices and Consumer Protection.[36] This grant is used not only to provide central facilities which all of the 700 bureaux now established can utilize, but also to subsidize new developments in areas not well provided for and to help bureaux who cannot meet their financial obligations on the grants given by local authorities and others.

The bureaux are staffed primarily by volunteers under the supervision of an organizer, and they operate to standards and principles laid down by the central organization. The fulfilment of the accepted criteria is marked by the registration of a bureau, and registration carries with it a right to participate in the services provided nationally.

The bureaux provide a generalized service; they are not concerned exclusively with consumer matters, but in those areas where no provision is made by the local authority for consumer advice (particularly where it has existed but has been withdrawn) the local bureau will often find that a high proportion of all inquiries concern consumer problems. In the last year for which figures are available (1977–78) 3,100,000 inquiries were dealt with, of which 526,000 related to consumer matters.[37] Quite apart from providing the sort of advice that the Molony Committee advocated, the local bureaux usually develop a close liaison with the consumer protection officers of the local authority and also co-operate in the provision of information for the Office of Fair Trading concerning undesirable trading practices.

A relatively recent development in the service has been the employment of full-time salaried solicitors by some of the larger bureaux.

These qualified persons can give specialist advice on the spot and may also take steps actively to assist a client in pursuing a claim. Indeed, the whole service appears to be growing more active in pursuing clients' interests rather than in the simple furnishing of advice and information.

A final advantage enjoyed by the bureaux in their relationship with the public is the demonstrable independence of any central or local government influence. The money provided nationally is not referable to particular policies or a particular programme and it is obviously helpful for a member of the public to perceive the complete independence of the service. It is also interesting to note that the bureaux will often pick up a range of problems that are associated with one incident or set of circumstances. A generalist agency is better placed to recognize that what is ostensibly a court case about failure to repay hire-purchase instalments may involve failures in financial planning, failure to claim social security benefits, unfair salesmanship and other associated problems. Most advisers would confirm that troubles rarely come singly!

THE ADVERTISING STANDARDS AUTHORITY AND THE CODE OF ADVERTISING PRACTICE COMMITTEE

All the agencies we have discussed so far in this chapter have been directly connected with, or have received financial support from, the government or have been the creation of the consumers themselves. Now we come to an example of a particularly English phenomenon, the self-regulating agency. The cynic would suggest that the motive for self-regulation is almost always the fear of governmental regulation, and in the field of advertising there are certainly international precedents for intervention by the executive in the form and content of advertising.[38] So far in this country we have relied on the industry itself to ensure that proper standards are maintained.

The Advertising Standards Authority (ASA) was established by the Advertising Association in 1962 to supervise the British Code of Advertising Practice. The Code is actually administered by the Code of Advertising Practice Committee which is composed entirely of representatives of advertising and the media, and the ASA exists as a kind of public face to receive complaints direct from the public. At least half of the members of ASA including the chairman are drawn from outside advertising circles.

The Code contains general provisions relating to qualities demanded of all advertisements and specific provisions relating to the more contentious areas of advertising. The basic principles, specifying the general obligations of the advertiser are set out in a preamble:

1.1. All advertisements should be legal, decent, honest and truthful.
1.2. All advertisements should be prepared with a sense of responsibility to the consumer.
1.3. All advertisements should conform to the principles of fair competition as generally accepted in business.
1.4. No advertisement should bring into disrepute or reduce confidence in advertising as a service to industry and the public.[39]

Although it is not possible to concentrate further on the detailed provision of the Code it is interesting to note that in the interpretation section the following injunction is to be found: 'This Code is to be applied in the spirit as well as in the letter.'[40]

A brief glimpse of what the Code is intended to achieve will immediately raise questions about allowing self-regulation in as important a field as advertising. As we shall see, the criminal and the civil law apply to advertisements as much as to any other form of statement, but the very nature of an advertisement makes it difficult to prove the degree of deception necessary to found a civil or a criminal action. Should the law be tightened, or should we allow the arguments of the ASA to convince us that self-regulation is satisfactory?

The Authority would argue that self-regulation has three virtues.[41] It can enforce 'the best professional standards' as decided by those who are at work in the industry. It can enforce the spirit of the Code as well as its letter, resisting attempts to circumvent it by devious ingenuity. It can maintain standards in areas which would defy legal definition – good manners and taste. These three arguments sound like three variants of the same basic premise, that the law is not a suitable instrument to enforce advertising standards. Against that argument one can point to other jurisdictions in which the problems have been overcome and advertising subjected to a rigorous legal code.[42]

Although it appears that advertising might eventually be brought under legal control in this country as a result of European developments,[43] the current practice is to allow self-regulation to suffice with minimal interference from government. The ASA launched a campaign in 1975 to bring its role to the attention of the public and that resulted in a considerable increase in the number of complaints, but the system currently lacks a pre-publication scrutiny committee for all advertisements and substantial sanctions for advertisements that do not meet the Authority's professional standards.[44]

Rather more legal provision is made for the control of advertising on television, and the Independent Broadcasting Authority Act 1973 imposes certain obligations upon the IBA who have overall responsibility for the programmes put out by the networks and by independent local radio. The IBA maintains two separate committees to advise on the general aspects of advertising and on the advertising of medical products and toiletries, and the principles that it adopts are then subject to scrutiny by the government. Apart from the form and content of the advertising that is broadcast the IBA must also take steps to ensure that it is demonstrably different from the programmes and not occupying an excessive amount of airtime.[45] The principles adopted by the IBA are reinforced by their ability to reject scripts on the ground of unsuitability or return them for amendment. The IBA has a stricter control over advertising in the media than the ASA could possibly have over advertising generally.

THE NATIONALIZED INDUSTRY CONSUMER COUNCILS

The economic importance of the nationalized industries alone should lead to special arrangements for taking into account the consumer interest in their operation and the level of service provided. Apart from the usual parliamentary scrutiny of the management and pricing policies of these industries the consumer interest is represented on advisory councils relating to them.[46]

The effectiveness of these councils has been doubted,[47] and one may wonder whether they serve a purely cosmetic purpose, but there is a considerable amount of money expended on them each year and they do receive complaints from the public. However, with respect to the nationalized industries the most significant control is likely to be political and parliamentary.

CONSUMER GROUPS

Our account of institutions would not be complete without reference to local consumer groups. They discharge a valuable function at the grass-roots level by encouraging interest in consumer matters and by assessing local services and products. Apparently there are now upwards of sixty such bodies, the first having been established in 1961. The co-ordinating body is the National Federation of Consumer Groups, which was set up in 1963. The latter is partly financed by the Consumers' Association and has links with the Department of Prices and Consumer Protection and the Office of Fair Trading. The National Federation campaigns on national issues – in Chapter 11 we shall see that in 1978 it joined with the National Consumer Council and the Consumers' Association in commenting on the government's consultative document on monopolies and mergers policy.

THE LAWS AND THE REGIONS

We should emphasize that overwhelmingly the laws discussed in this book apply to the UK as a whole, i.e. to England, Wales, Scotland and Northern Ireland. All citizens and companies in the UK are subject to the Rome Treaty. Equally, EEC regulations apply to all UK persons and companies while EEC directives would require the appropriate governmental authorities (including those with devolved powers) to amend statutes, etc., appropriately to give effect to the intent of the directives. The vast majority of the statutes that we discuss apply to the UK as a whole. This is, for example, true of the Fair Trading Act, the Restrictive Trade Practices Act, the Trade Descriptions Act, the Price Commission Act and the Medicines Act, to mention but a few. That does not however rule out limited modifications and exceptions to take account of local circumstances. However there are a few local statutes, the most important of which relate to food. Thus there is the Food and Drugs Act 1955, which relates to England and Wales, and there are separate acts for Scotland (1956) and Northern Ireland (1958), which have the same philosophy as the 1955 Act. In respect of such local statutes the reader should also be aware that enforcement will reflect the devolvement of powers.

3 Competition Policy – Creating a European Market

INTRODUCTION

In this chapter we recognize that the protection of the British consumer begins with the opening up of the UK market to foreign suppliers. Tariffs against goods and services produced in other member states of the European Communities have been totally removed. It was however recognized at the outset, when the Communities were in process of formation, that the removal of tariff barriers would be frustrated if businessmen created other compensating non-tariff barriers. Such barriers might be antitrust in character. Instead of selling into each other's markets competitively, businesses might collude as to the prices to be charged. Alternatively, they might allocate markets to the national groups located therein. Producer groups in particular national markets might seek to impose restrictions upon national dealers that prevented the latter from accepting supplies from without. A firm dominant in a national market might seek to protect that dominance by indulging in predatory and exclusionary practices designed to prevent imports entering that national market. For example, a dominant firm might seek to impose exclusive dealing terms upon dealers. Mergers might also frustrate the process of creating a Community market. A firm in one state might take over a competitor in another state who had begun to make competitive incursions. When the EEC was in its early stages of development Hans van der Groeben, who was the first Brussels Commissioner responsible for competition policy, put the problem to the European Parliament in the following terms:

> It is ... beyond dispute – and the authors of the Treaty [i.e. the Rome Treaty] were fully aware of this – that it would be useless to bring down trade barriers between Member States if the Governments or private industry were to remain free through economic and fiscal legislation, through subsidies or cartel-like restrictions on competition, virtually to undo the opening of the markets and to

prevent, or at least unduly to delay, the action needed to adapt them to the Common Market.[1]

But the problem was not likely to be one that would arise only during the period in which tariff barriers were being reduced. It would continue to present itself as businesses sought to regulate trading relationships between the member states. Moreover, from time to time structural changes would occur which would generate pressure for solutions involving restrictive business practices. There is no better example of the latter than the scheme devised by the major European synthetic fibre manufacturers collectively to restrict output capacity. Thirty per cent of the industry's capacity in 1978 was estimated to be unused, and as a result price competition was extremely intensive and losses were piling up. In circumstances where the market is international domestic solutions are of little avail. If producers in one member state were to take plants out of production the price level in the domestic market would still be eroded by low-priced supplies stemming from the remaining excess capacity in the rest of the Community.

Because of this kind of problem both the Rome and Paris Treaties had specific antitrust rules written into them. In addition the Paris Treaty led to rules being laid down as to how competitive pricing was to operate. These antitrust and pricing rules, and the cases they have given rise to, form the main substance of this chapter.

Before we turn to the law we need to review briefly the various antitrust phenomena to which the law addresses itself. This review will also serve as an introduction to the discussion of UK antitrust policy that follows in Chapter 4.

It is traditional to treat the antitrust problem under two main headings. There are restrictive business practices, and there is what may for convenience be called the concentration problem. This is a useful distinction, although there is in practice an element of overlap which complicates the picture somewhat. As a first approximation we can say that restrictive business practices are arrangements between otherwise independent firms that are designed to concert their activities in the market. They may also take the form of the imposition (individually or collectively) of restrictions upon the market activity of other firms. The arrangements may be horizontal or vertical. The most common form of horizontal collusion is the price-fixing agreement which may take the form of an undertaking to charge a common price (discounts, etc., have also got to be regulated) or to charge a minimum price below which the parties will not sell although they will be free to sell above. Within the original Six it has not been uncommon for prices to be fixed by a common selling syndicate – a company owned by the producers to which they assign their output. The syndicate eliminates competition between the producers, sets the price for their combined output and pays them in proportion to their deliveries to it. Price in the market may be manipulated by collective agreements to restrict output. A more radical approach may be adopted which requires parties to take plant out of production. Prices can also be manipulated by market-sharing (geographic or by type of customer), which may confer on individual sellers a monopoly in a particular segment of the market. All these arrangements may be accompanied by enforcement practices designed to make parties toe the line. Concealed price cuts, sales beyond agreed limits and incursions into markets allocated to others may lead to carpetings, fines or even expulsion from trade associations. The latter may have serious consequences in terms of loss of access to markets – see below.

Paradoxically, the more effective such devices are the more they are likely to attract interlopers. It has therefore been common practice for price-fixing and similar arrangements to be buttressed by exclusionary practices. These take several forms. One is collective exclusive dealing, in which a group of suppliers persuades a group of dealers to sell the suppliers' goods only – if the group of suppliers is also bound to sell only through the group of dealers then the arrangement would constitute reciprocal exclusive dealing. Collective boycotts – a collective cutting off of supplies – can be applied to dealers who renege on their undertakings. Another device is the deferred or loyalty rebate – here an additional discount is given at the end of a period of trading to those dealers who have not bought from outside suppliers. Aggregated rebates may also be employed in which dealers enjoy a progressive rebate scale which is related to their purchases from the group as a whole. This tends to induce dealers to concentrate their orders on the group at the expense of outsiders.

Arrangements may also be vertical. Producer groups may collectively fix the prices at which their goods are to be resold by dealers – we call this collective resale price maintenance (rpm). Alternatively, individual suppliers may prescribe the price at which individual dealers will resell their products – this is individual resale price maintenance. Both devices may be enforced by threats to cut off supplies. Individual rpm can be facilitated by what is called a non-signer clause. This takes various forms but the objective is the same in all cases, namely to bind the dealer contractually in the absence of a specific contract. In the UK a legal provision was introduced which in effect declared that if a dealer had been notified of the appropriate resale price he was contractually bound to charge that price. Mention at this point must also be made of the vertical practice of sole or exclusive dealing since this is of particular relevance in the EEC context. When conducting sales in a particular domestic territory, or abroad, suppliers may undertake to restrict their supplying at the wholesale stage to an appointed sole dealer. Such an arrangement may be accompanied by territorial protection or what is sometimes called a no-poaching provision. That is to say, other dealers will, as a condition of their appointment, be required not to supply the retail trade in the territories of other concessionaires.

Our earlier reference to arrangements relating to prices, output and investment were examples of agreements to charge certain prices, to sell certain quantities, etc. But in addition we have to take account of information agreements. In such cases the parties do not, for example, *agree* about prices to be charged but merely inform each other about prices that have been charged, are being charged or will be charged. These arrangements can of course lead to results similar to collusion. For example one firm may act as a price-leader and the rest may follow. There may indeed be collusion as to prices, although the parties may seek to pass off the uniformity of prices as being the result of an information agreement. Those who have operated agreements have justified them as being necessary in order to deal with phantom competition, i.e. the quotation of false low offers by customers, or as being necessary to prevent the excessive laying down of productive capacity in conditions where investment plans might otherwise be matured in secrecy.

Not all agreements are necessarily motivated by a desire to restrict competition even though they may incidentally have that effect. Here we are thinking about various forms of what may be called efficiency-promoting agreements. In the case of specialization agreements firms may agree not to produce a full range of products but to concentrate on certain lines and thus to enjoy more fully the economies of long runs. They may nevertheless supply each other with their specialisms in order to be able to offer customers a full range of products. In joint research and development agreements firms may agree to develop a new product or process jointly rather than to duplicate development expenditures. Firms may also conclude capacity adjustment agreements. Where there is a chronic excess of productive capacity such an agreement may prove to be the quickest and least painful method of bringing supply and demand into a better balance.

The most obvious phenomenon under the concentration problem head is monopoly – although in practice a true monopolist, who has significant market power, is a relatively rare phenomenon. The reason for this is that the conditions required are quite rigorous – there must be only one supplier in the market, and there must be no close substitutes to which consumers can switch if the monopolist tries to raise price. More common is market dominance, which arises when a firm is responsible for a preponderant part of total supply. Again, in order to exercise market power – i.e. to be able to exercise a significant effect on the level of price – the dominant firm must produce a good or service with no close substitutes. In practice it is not just the structural condition, i.e. the share of the market, that may be significant. Also important in circumstances of monopoly and dominance is the restrictive practice dimension – the reader will recollect that he was forewarned that our analysis is complicated by overlaps. Firms with market power may employ various predatory and exclusionary practices in order to maintain their position in the market. New competition may be driven out by heavy (and temporary) price cuts. Dealers may be pressurized into dealing exclusively. Tie-in arrangements may be insisted upon – as a condition of being supplied with certain goods customers may also be required to acquire their supplies of other goods from the same supplier.

In practice the predominant structure of most manufacturing industry and mining in modern Western economies is characterized by neither monopoly nor market dominance but by oligopoly. The latter structure is one where there are a few suppliers, between which there is a rough parity of influence in the market. It is not immediately obvious why such a structure should be regarded as giving rise to an antitrust problem. Quite the contrary: the existence of a number of independent centres of initiative in the market suggests that a competitive outcome should be expected. In practice, the fewness factor tends to make the firms highly interdependent – price strategies have to take account of a rival's reactions. Because of this firms may seek a *modus vivendi* in order to establish some stability in their relations. Fewness facilitates forms of collusion that are difficult to detect. Alternatively, price leadership may emerge. As a result of either of these devices price may be raised above the competitive level. However the latter is possible on a sustained basis only to the extent that there are barriers to entry – control over vital technology via patents, control of key facilities, pronounced economies of scale, heavy advertising and product differentiation. The last two involve heavy initial expenditures which may deter entrants.

Mergers are clearly a relevant phenomenon. The most obvious problem arises in connection with the horizontal variety where firms at the same stage in the process of producing a particular good or service amalgamate. Mergers do not of course necessarily produce a monopoly. Only when the last two producers in a market decide to come together does that happen. But obviously a merger reduces the number of competitors – it can thus make an existing oligopoly yet tighter. To that extent it may facilitate collusion and price leadership. Vertical mergers, where a firm takes over other firms further back or further forward in a particular production–distribution chain, can also pose problems. These may take the form of a denial of supplies to non-integrated competitors. Alternatively, a vertically integrated firm may operate a price squeeze, enhancing the price of raw materials supplied to non-integrated producers and depressing the price of the subsequent product. However, to be successful such a vertical practice does require conditions of horizontal dominance on the part of the firm exercising the squeeze. A vertically integrated firm may also foreclose outlets to non-integrated producers. In recent years much attention has also been directed towards conglomerate mergers. A pure conglomerate merger is an amalgamation of firms with different product lines. Because of this it is not too immediately obvious why they should be a problem. Possible, and we emphasize the word 'possible', anti-competitive effects may arise. To cite just one example, the conglomerate may use the monopoly profits obtained in one market to make, or threaten to make, competitive forays in other markets in which it operates. This may confer upon a conglomerate a dominating position in those other markets.[2]

Finally, we should note the existence of joint ventures where two companies decide to set up a joint subsidiary instead of each establishing separate companies. Here the antitrust significance is that there is a sacrifice of potential competition. We should also note that co-ordination of behaviour can occur not by ownership, as in the case of a merger, but by virtue of interlocking directorates – i.e. cross-membership on the boards of companies who might be apparent competitors.

THE EEC ANTITRUST RULES

The Rules on Restrictive Practices

The key provisions are to be found in Rome Treaty Articles 3(f) and 85. Article 3 lays down the general objectives of the Rome Treaty – internal tariffs shall be eliminated; there shall be a common external tariff against the rest of the world; there shall be a common agricultural policy; etc. Article 3(f) calls for the creation of conditions that guarantee that competition in the common market is not distorted. It is however in Article 85 that the substantive law is to be found. That article, which is in three parts, is reproduced in the Appendix to this chapter. We will look at each of these parts in turn. However, before we do so we should note that differences exist as between antitrust systems in their approach to restrictions of competition. Some laws regard the preservation of competition as paramount. A restriction of competition is *per se* (in and of itself) illegal and no mitigating arguments will be accepted. The task of the antitrust enforcement agency is merely to satisfy those sitting in judgment that collusion exists and an adverse decision automatically follows. Other laws initially prohibit or condemn agreements but then provide for the possibility of exemption in certain defined circumstances. Some laws adopt a neutral position: they declare neither in favour nor against restrictions of competition but provide for investigation and enable prohibitions to be handed down when abuse is found to exist. Some countries simply do nothing. As we shall see, the EEC law is of the second category.

Article 85(1) contains the basic prohibition while Article 85(2) goes on to declare that prohibited agreements are null and void. The latter implies that it would be illegal to operate them or seek to enforce them in the courts. Just exactly when an agreement becomes null and void depends on the circumstances, and we shall briefly discuss the relevant administrative provisions later. Article 85(3) defines the circumstances under which an agreement, which would otherwise be prohibited, can in fact be exempted.

The Article 85(1) prohibition applies to restrictions of competition not only in selling but also in buying. It applies to services as well as to goods. The prohibition applies to agreements, the decisions of associations of enterprises and to concerted practices. An agreement obviously relates to those undertakings that can be contractually enforced in the courts. But it can also apply where not all the characteristics of a civil law contract are present. In the *Franco–Japanese Ballbearings* case there was an agreement in which the central feature was an exchange of letters between the French and Japanese trade associations which led the latter to raise their export prices in the French market.[3] In the *Quinine* case the Commission's adverse decision quite explicitly addressed itself to, among other things, a gentlemen's agreement which consisted of a written document that was not signed.[4]

A decision of an association of enterprises covers the possibility that a firm being part of an association might conveniently claim that it did not agree with this or that particular association decision. However, the individual firm will usually be obligated to adhere to association decisions and will thus be caught. It should be noted that a decision of an association of enterprises also covers a situation where a trade body makes a recommendation to members in which there is no obligation to comply. This was so in the *VCH* case, where the Court of Justice argued that the recommended prices were not devoid of effect in that they permitted the parties involved to foresee with reasonable accuracy what the behaviour of their rivals was likely to be. There was, it should be added, an obligation to make a profit.[5] In this particular context it is perhaps as well to note that the list of restrictions cited in Article 85 (which list is illustrative and not exhaustive) includes the indirect as well as the direct fixing of prices.

The concept of concerted practice is of particular interest because it requires us to recognize that there are a variety of ways in which behaviour in the marketplace can be concerted. Obviously a written document, signed and witnessed, is one. But altogether less formal arrangements[6] can also be the means of achieving a similar objective. One firm may make a representation to another; such representation may, for example, be an indication of the price it intends to charge in respect of a particular transaction or class of transactions. The representation is intended as an inducement to the other firm to charge the same price, and the other firm realizes this and signals its willingness to conform by falling into line. Over time there may indeed emerge a sustained pattern of behaviour in which successive representations are made which successively induce matching responses. A parallelism of action emerges without there being a formal agreement. It is situations like this that have inspired the need for concepts such as the concerted practice and they enable antitrust authorities to deal with situations where the more formal kind of collusion may not be admitted or indeed may not exist. The concept was first used in the *Aniline Dye* case, where on three occasions nine or ten of the most important suppliers of dyes in the EEC introduced equiproportionate price increases within a few days of each other. Although agreement was not admitted by the parties, the Commission did point to circumstantial evidence of collusion and the firms were found guilty of being involved in a concerted practice. For this fines were imposed.[7] The parties to the arrangement appealed to the Court of Justice and in the proceedings the Commission offered the following definition of a concerted practice:

> In order that there should be a concerting, it is not necessary that the parties should draw up a plan in common with a view to adopting a certain behaviour. It suffices that they should mutually inform each other in advance of the attitudes they intend to adopt, in such a way that each can regulate its action in reliance on its competitors behaving in a parallel manner.[8]

The Court upheld the Commission's decision and in doing so observed that a concerted practice was 'a form of co-ordination between undertakings which, without going so far as to amount to an agreement properly so called, knowingly substitutes a practical co-operation between them for the risks of competition.'[9] It added that parallelism of action was not to be identified with a concerted practice although it constituted a strong indication of such a practice, particularly when it led to prices above the equilibrium level expected from competition. This point is largely valid. Markets that are perfectly competitive, and can indeed, in terms of the absence of market power, be said to be the very acme of competition, will exhibit a uniformity of price. But even markedly different structures, such as oligopoly, may also have the same quality. In such a market price uniformity could in certain cases be said to be a product of commercial prudence rather than of conspiracy. Thus if a firm raised its price above the going level its sales would fall drastically, particularly if the products were not greatly differentiated. Such an increase might not therefore be ventured. Equally, lowering price below the going level might provoke a matching cut which would render the initiating price reduction not worthwhile. For a more recent application of the concerted practice concept see the *Genuine Vegetable Parchment* case.[10]

Article 85(1) also goes on to declare that the object of the agreement, decision, etc., must be to prevent, restrict or distort competition in the Common Market. The illustrative list of restrictions includes direct and indirect fixing of selling and buying prices, limits on production, the sharing of markets, the application of discriminatory conditions and tie-ins. Particularly interesting is the point that the prohibition applies to restrictions of competition in the Common Market and not to restrictions operated by Common Market firms only. This has led the Commission to claim an extra-territorial jurisdiction for Community antitrust law. At this point we should note that the antitrust laws of some countries (notably the US) claim to be able to exert a jurisdiction not only over companies located on their territories but also over companies located outside, who by their actions have effects on those states. This is basically what is known as the 'effects doctrine'. It is of course one thing to claim such a jurisdiction and another to carry it into effect. Can the foreign company be compelled to come into court? Is there any way of effectively imposing a fine?

As we have seen in the *Aniline Dye* case companies involved in concerted practices were fined. Since ICI, a company incorporated under British law, was one of the firms fined, and this was prior to UK membership, an extra-territorial jurisdiction appeared to be claimed. Indeed, the Commission has always been firm on this point. In the *Aniline Dye* case it observed: 'This decision is applicable to all the undertakings which took part in the concerted practices, whether they are established within or outside the Common Market.'[11] This gave rise to an appeal by ICI to the Court of Justice. The Commission could of course have addressed its prohibition merely to ICI's subsidiaries in the EEC, in which case a claim to an extra-territorial jurisdiction would not have arisen. In its appeal ICI did in fact plead that the prohibited behaviour was that of its subsidiaries and not of itself. The Court argued otherwise: the fact that the subsidiaries were distinct legal personalities did not dispose of the possibility that their behaviour could be imputed to the parent company. The subsidiaries being controlled by the parent, it was indeed reasonable to argue that what the former did was what the latter told them to do. In defence of this argument the Court observed as follows:

> The telex messages relating to the 1964 increase which the applicant [i.e. ICI] had addressed to its subsidiaries in the Common Market, determined, in a manner binding on their addressees, the prices and other conditions of sale which they must impose in relation to their customers.[12]

Although the point that subsidiaries do what parents tell them to do was a convenient way of justifying the imposition of a fine on the parent, and was consistent with a claim to an extra-territorial jurisdiction, it fell short of an unqualified application of the effects doctrine. What was needed was a case where a company, of a non-member state, that had no subsidiaries in the Common Market participated in an outside association that had restrictive effects upon the Community market. This is indeed what occurred in the *Genuine Vegetable Parchment* case.[13] A Finnish company, Serlachius, was a member of the Genuine Vegetable Parchment Association, an international trade association which had its headquarters in Sweden. There was no evidence in the Commission's decision that the Finnish company had any presence within the EEC; nevertheless it was fined for its participation in concerted practices affecting the EEC internal market.

It is also an important feature of Article 85(1) that the preventions, restrictions, etc., must be such that they 'may affect trade between Member States'. Obviously agreements that directly regulate trade will fall due for investigation, as for example a group of firms in one member state agreeing on their export prices in sales to other member states. But other indirect effects are caught. For example, an exclusive dealing agreement between producers and dealers in one member state, although it would not involve the direct regulation of imports, would have the effect of inhibiting or even totally precluding the entry of supplies from without. In the *VCH* case the central concern was a Dutch cement trade association which was not involved in regulating import prices – a separate international cartel was concerned with that issue. The VCH merely fixed or recommended the price at which merchants should resell home and imported supplies. Nevertheless, it was regarded as having an effect on interstate trade, the point apparently being that the VCH determined prices across the board and this prevented low-cost Belgian and German cement supplies from increasing their share of the Dutch market at the expense of Dutch production.[14] All three of these are examples of arrangements that cut down trade. But arrangements that artificially stimulate trade can also fall foul of the law. For example, in the *Cimbel* case Belgian cement producers regulated prices at home to a degree that enabled them to subsidize exports to other members of the Community and this was also condemned.[15] Thus the important point is that trade should not be distorted one way or the other. The interstate clause also implies that the Rome Treaty competition rules have only a limited scope in protecting the consumer. There is still a role for domestic antitrust laws in maintaining competition. Some commentators have seen some more recent decisions and judgments as indicating a whittling down in the significance of this clause,[16] but for all that it seems likely that restrictions that are local in their effect will not attract the attention of Brussels. Not least is this so because the Commission staff is severely limited in size.

It is when we come to Article 85(3) that we encounter the exemption aspect. In order for, say, an agreement to qualify for exemption four cumulative conditions must be met. (a) The agreement must contribute 'to improving the production or distribution of goods or to promote technical or economic progress'. (b) Then the consumer has to be considered – he must be allowed a fair share of the resulting benefit. Benefit may be a fall in price. In some specialization agreement cases (see the *Clima–Chappé–Buderus* case[17]) the Commission has recognized that specialization would lower costs of production and has assumed that the competition still remaining would guarantee that the reduction of costs would be passed on in whole or part to the consumer. But benefit may also take other forms, such as a more rapid and easy availability of goods (see *Jallatte–Voss–Vandeputte* case[18]) or an improvement of quality and technical performance (see *Fabrique Nationale d'Armes de Guerre–Cartoucherie Française* case[19]). The consumer has been interpreted by the Commission to include purchasers next in line as opposed to the final consumer. Thus in the *ACEC–Berliet* case[20] the operators of buses were regarded as recipients of the benefit derived from a co-operation and joint research and development agreement in the field of bus construction. (c) The agreement, in achieving the improvement and the fair sharing, must not impose restrictions that are not indispensable to the attainment of those objectives. (d) The agreement must not allow the parties to eliminate competition in respect of a substantial part of the products in question.

Mention should also be made of the fact that quite early on the Commission decided that competition has to be restricted to a noticeable or appreciable extent for Article 85(1) to be invoked. This idea was first enunciated in the *Grosfillex* case[21] and was confirmed by the Court in *Volk* v. *Vervaecke*.[22] This was followed in 1970 by a Notice on agreements of minor importance[23] which established a *de minimis* rule. Under the current provisions[24] if firms participating in an agreement have a market share that is not more than 5 per cent in a substantial part of the Common Market, and the aggregate annual turnover does not exceed 50 million units of account, then the agreement does not fall under the Article 85 prohibition. Some flexibility above these limits is allowed. Also we should note that the control of a subsidiary by a parent does not fall within the scope of the Article 85(1) prohibition – this was the essential point in the *Christiani and Nielsen* case[25] and it has been reaffirmed since.

Enforcement

In the light of our interest in the protection of the consumer, an obviously important question is, who is responsible for enforcing these competition rules? Is it the consumer, or does someone act on his behalf? In this instance, as is usually the case in antitrust law, enforcement is a specialized task which is largely in the hands of an official agency. The application of Article 85 (and Article 86, to which we turn later) lies primarily with the European Communities Commission, although its formal decisions to prohibit, etc., are subject to appeal to the European Communities Court of Justice.

To aid it in locating agreements the Commission has established a system of notification,[26] although unlike the British system notified agreements are not open to public inspection. Notification is clearly of assistance to the Commission in locating violations, but it is also helpful to businessmen in that it enables them to discover what is and what is not allowed. Although notification is not a duty, there is a strong incentive for companies to notify, since if they do not do so within any time limits that have been set there can be no question of their agreement being exempted. For example, in the *Quinine* case the parties were advised to notify but deliberately chose not to do so. Subsequently they were caught by the EC Commission (having previously been attacked by the US antitrust authorities) and, not having notified, they were denied the possibility of an exemption hearing and were indeed heavily fined.[27] The actual status of agreements in relation to notification is variable.[28] Old or existing agreements, i.e. agreements that were in force at the time when the notification rules were established, that were notified in due time enjoy a provisional or temporary validity until the Commission renders a formal decision upon them. In the interim the agreements can be enforced in the courts and the parties to them are immune to private suits. But once the Commission issues a decision to the effect that they are prohibited (exemption not being possible), then it would be an offence to continue them and financial sanctions could be applied. But new agreements formed since the issuing of the notification rules do not enjoy the same protection. In their case it is prudent for those involved to clarify their position by notifying them to the Commission. The point is that, if an agreement is operated prior to notification and then it is prohibited, it would be invalid from the date of its introduction until the date of the application for a negative clearance or exemption. The parties would have been operating the agreement at their peril and could be fined.[29]

It is now necessary to explain that when a proper notification has been made, a number of different consequences can follow. The Commission may issue a negative clearance. This is granted when the Commission finds that the contents of an agreement are not such as to render it subject to Article 85 – the Commission finds no reason to intervene. It should be emphasized that before such a decision is issued the parties to the agreement may have had to modify it, stripping it of offending matter. Alternatively, agreements may (and this could include cases where some stripping has been attempted) offend under Article 85(1). In that case the only hope of the parties is to qualify for exemption under Article 85(3). If they succeed they can continue to operate the agreement. If exemption cannot be accorded then the agreement has to be dropped if sanctions are to be avoided. Parties may choose to abandon a hopeless case rather than press it to the point where a formal prohibitory decision has to be issued.

We turn now to the other enforcement powers enjoyed by the Commission, and in so doing we emphasize that they also apply to the task of dealing with the abuse of dominant positions covered by Article 86. The Commission has other means of detecting transgressions. It keeps its eyes and ears open. A complaints procedure has been established in order that possible infringements can be submitted to the Commission. Such complaints can be submitted by member states, or by natural or legal persons provided they can show a legitimate interest. Presumably a consumer, as opposed to an industrial user, could exercise this right, although in practice it seems that it is firms, rather than the man in the street, who make complaints. A supplier may find himself excluded from a dealer network by a collective exclusive dealing agreement. A dealer may be boycotted because he has not honoured a reciprocal agreement not to deal in the goods of suppliers outwith the agreement, or he may have been fined because he sold below the price stipulated by suppliers. Producers may suspect that they are paying prices for materials that are inflated by monopolistic devices. Complaints tend to be of these kinds. When a complaint is made but the request for action is dismissed by the Commission, in whole or part, the complainants have a right to institute proceedings in order to protect their legitimate interests. Such an appeal would be heard by the EC Court of Justice (see as an example the *Metro–SB–Grossmarke* case).[30]

The Commission has a fourth avenue of information. It carries out sectoral investigations where the flow of trade between states is suspiciously small or in some way distorted. Recent inquiries have centred on the supply of naphtha and of jet fuel. Earlier studies concerned the lack of intra-Community exchanges of margarine and beer. It should also be emphasized that Commission officials are empowered to enter firms, inspect books and call for information. Financial sanctions can be levied if firms do not comply.

In most instances, before the Commission arrives at a decision hearings will be held at which the parties concerned and also third parties, provided they have sufficient grounds (which could imply that consumers are included), have an opportunity to be heard. A draft decision is then submitted to the Advisory Committee on Restrictive Practices and Monopolies (this is drawn from member state experts), and then promulgation takes place.

The Commission has substantial powers to fine firms involved in transgressions. For example, in respect of the offending elements in the *Sugar* case a collective fine of 9 million units of account was imposed although this was significantly reduced on appeal to the Court to 1,590,000 units of account.

Restrictive Practice Cases

When in 1972 the first report on competition policy emerged it was implied, in the light of experience to that date, that horizontal cartels concerned with price-fixing, output restriction and market-sharing were not likely to be exempted.[31] De Jong in 1975, analysing thirty-two horizontal cartel cases between 1964 and 1973, noted that there were no exemptions.[32] (It was of course possible that by failing to notify exemption was precluded – as in *Quinine* and *Aniline Dyes*.) The position in 1978 does not justify any significant departure from these assessments of the Commission's stance.

Price agreements have been consistently attacked. For example, in the *Glass Containers* case the Commission dealt with an international arrangement operated by the International Fair Trade Practice Rules Administration, an organization registered in Liechtenstein. Manufacturers of bottles, jars and flasks in Germany, France, Italy, Belgium and the Netherlands were parties to the arrangement. The latter was quite comprehensive since it involved a common method of calculating prices, the general adoption of a delivered price system, exchange of information on prices and, perhaps most significant of all, the fixing of export prices on the basis of the domestic prices in the country of destination. The 'natural price leader' in a domestic market informed foreign producers as to his prices, and if they supplied in his market they charged his price. A restriction of competition and an effect on interstate trade were all too evident. No benefit accrued to the consumer and so an exemption could not be accorded. The parties were therefore ordered to bring the infringements to an immediate end.[33]

We shall treat common sales syndicates as a form of price agreement and in so doing shall note that the Commission has consistently attacked them also. Arrangements of this kind have usually been encountered in markets where products are homogeneous and price-cutting activity could be fierce – i.e. fertilizers, cement, sulphuric acid, etc. Several early cases concerned fertilizers. In for example, the *CFA*[34] and *Cobelaz*[35] cases the arrangements covered both home and export sales, but modifications had to be made so that sales to other EEC countries were carried out independently by individual manufacturers. In these instances prior to the decision significant market power had existed and the granting of negative clearances was possible only when the arrangements had been modified to exclude a direct effect on interstate trade. More recently in the *Necomout* case Dutch malt exporters operating a common sales syndicate were brought into line without the need for a formal decision.[36] Occasionally sales syndicates have been granted negative clearances as they stood. This was so in the *SAFCO* case, which concerned a common selling agency operating on behalf of French exporters of canned vegetables. Without modification, the Commission granted a negative clearance because its supply represented such a small part of the market. For example, in West Germany (a major area of its export activity) it supplied, on average, only 1 to 2 per cent of canned vegetable production, and this of course ignored the existence of fresh vegetable supplies.[37]

There is a long line of cases in which the Commission has struck down market-sharing arrangements. For example, in 1965 it dealt with an agreement between Belgian and Dutch producers of detergent (the *Savon Noir* case). Under the agreement the Belgian parties were forbidden to sell their detergent on the Dutch market and the Dutch producers entered into a reciprocal arrangement. In order to buttress the arrangement all parties undertook, on pain of penalties, to prohibit any reselling by buyers that might prejudice the division of the market. We shall return to this latter aspect later. The Commission declared the agreement prohibited, exemption not being warranted.[38] More recently the Commission brought about the abandonment of a long-term agreement between a British and a Belgian producer of industrial sand. British Industrial Sand Ltd (BIS), a subsidiary of Hepworth Ceramic Holdings Limited, and Sablières et Carrières Réunies (SCR) had, for certain kinds of sand, assigned the UK market exclusively to BIS and the rest of Europe to SCR. Two other aspects of the case are of particular interest, namely the agreement not to supply machinery, or excavate, in each other's territories and an exchange of directors in order to maintain close contact and to supervise the undertakings.[39]

Quotas and output restrictions have been a feature in several actions; often however they have been encountered alongside other restrictive devices as in *Quinine* and in the *VCH* case — the latter involved large numbers of German cement producers who had completely eliminated competition between themselves in the Benelux, and particularly the Dutch, market.[40] Such output controls relate to the physical quantity supplied. However some controls may restrict the range of available products. For example, in 1977 the Commission secured the termination of certain clauses in agreements between manufacturers of video cassettes and video cassette recorders. The parties were the Dutch firm Philips and seven German firms including Blaupunkt and Bosch-Siemens. These firms had undertaken not to manufacture or sell any such equipment other than that conforming to the system licensed by Philips. The arrangement was in fact underpinned by the cross-licensing of patents. If a firm broke the agreement it forfeited its licences under the patents of the others but they kept their rights under those of the terminating party.[41]

The Commission also has to its credit a long line of successful actions against exclusionary practices, notably collective exclusive dealing. The earliest case concerned the Pottery Convention involving Belgian dealers in, and layers of, wall and floor tiles on the one hand and tile manufacturers in Belgium, the Netherlands and Germany.

The manufacturers could deliver only to approved customers party to the agreements, and the latter could not purchase goods from outside manufacturers – the arrangement was therefore reciprocal. Competition was clearly restricted, interstate trade was equally affected and the Commission saw no grounds for exemption under Article 85(3). The exclusion of outside suppliers from the Belgium market was obvious. The manufacturing parties argued that outsiders could apply to join the Convention but the Commission retorted that admission needed unanimous approval – the implication being that there was no guarantee that the approval would necessarily be forthcoming.[42] Quite recently the Commission attacked a reciprocal exclusive dealing system operated by a Dutch pharmaceutical association. The latter controlled some 80–90 per cent of the pharmaceuticals sold in the Netherlands, 70 per cent of which were imported mainly from other member states. The Pharmaceutische Handelsconventie also imposed resale price maintenance on all products, including imports. An indication that it was unlikely that exemption would be granted was sufficient to bring about a voluntary termination.[43]

In the *German Wall and Floor Tile* case a group of German producers had instituted an aggregated rebate arrangement. The rebate was payable only on purchases from the group and progressively increased with the volume of orders. The effect of this was to induce purchasers to concentrate their orders on the German group, and outsiders had to make significant price concessions in order to draw custom away. The effect on interstate competition was clear. The Commission *inter alia* objected that the rebates should relate to purchases from individual producers, in which case they had the possibility of reflecting actual savings. Moreover, if the aim was to favour tiles relative to substitute products, then purchases of foreign tiles ought to be taken into account. The arrangement was not capable of exemption.[44] Like exclusive dealing aggregated rebates have been a common device, hence the importance of this particular decision.

The Commission has encountered a number of important cases of information exchange. There was an element of this in the *Glass Container* case discussed earlier and in the *Dutch Sporting Cartridges* case[45] where the agreement was informally terminated following an intervention by the Commission. Part of the latter arrangement consisted of a reciprocal collective exclusive dealing arrangement which in the light of the decision in the *Pottery Convention* case indicated a violation under Article 85. Additionally the suppliers (they covered all the major brands) notified their prices to a central committee. This provoked the Commission into the following observation:

> Although each supplier could fix his own prices, the obligation to notify prices and price changes to a suppliers' committee had the consequence of inhibiting price changes and, generally speaking, of reducing the effects of price changes on competition.... The suppliers would be less inclined to change their prices, knowing that their major rivals would be immediately informed and could therefore react. The system of price notification could thus fully achieve its aim of ensuring, through the prompt reciprocal prior notification of price changes, that any price change triggered off another, and thus of encouraging the parties to the system to maintain their prices.

More recently, the Commission has investigated a pure information agreement, operated by enterprises in the UK, France and West Germany that supply metal and plastic paper machine wire. In its original form the agreement required the parties to supply to the Secretariat-General of the International Association of Paper Machine Wire Manufacturers (a) price lists and terms within two to three weeks of their becoming effective, and (b) copies of all invoices for deliveries (except to the US) within ten days – the invoice to specify the name of the customer, the type of wire, the price and any other relevant terms. The Secretariat-General was authorized upon request to communicate the price paid by any particular customer to any national association or member firm, the object being to prevent customers playing one supplier off against another. The Commission saw this interchange as being inconsistent with a competitive relationship. Following the Commission's intervention, the parties agreed to cease the exchange of price lists, to supply copies of invoices without identifying the customer and to use the latter purely for the purpose of preparing statistics.[46]

The Commission's clean sheet in resisting any temptation to exempt cartels with significant market power was in some jeopardy in 1978. This arose in connection with the problems of the European synthetic fibre manufacturers that we discussed earlier. The Industrial Commissioner, Viscount Etienne Davignon, is reported to have been favourable to a capacity adjustment cartel that within a year would have cut EEC capacity by 15 per cent and then have frozen it until 1981. It is difficult to see how such an arrangement could have been squared with the requirements of Article 85(3) – notably the need to guarantee that the consumer should share in the benefit. To the consumer there would have been no immediate gain – only a rise in price. Article 85(3) also requires that the parties to the agreement should not be able to eliminate competition in respect of a substantial part of the product in question. In this case the eleven firms who actually went ahead and signed the agreement had 80 per cent of the market between them. It would therefore have been necessary to side-step these difficulties by referring to Article 87, which does allow the Council of Ministers to define in various sectors the degree to which Article 85 (and 86) are to apply. In fact the plan was rebuffed when considered by the Commission.[47]

When in the early sixties the Commission began to hand down restrictive practice decisions, its initial concern was not with the major horizontal cartels but with distribution arrangements. In particular it concentrated much effort on (vertical) sole or exclusive distribution agreements. Indeed, the first occasion on which it exercised its power of prohibition was in connection with such an arrangement in the *Grundig–Consten* case. This was to prove to be a key case since it led to a regulation for the block exemption of certain forms of sole distribution agreement. In addition the philosophy lying behind the case influenced the Commission in formulating its position in respect of a variety of other situations.

In the *Grundig–Consten* case the West German firm Grundig appointed Consten, a Paris firm, as its sole dealer in France at its particular stage in the distribution chain – i.e. importer/wholesaler. Grundig also banned all its sole dealers in other states from delivering Grundig goods into the French market and thus undermining Consten's position. This is referred to as territorial protection although, as we noted earlier, the lawyers prefer to call it the no-poaching rule. In order to buttress Consten's position Grundig assigned to it the use of the trade mark GINT (*G*rundig *Int*ernational). In fact a rival French firm UNEF obtained supplies from German wholesalers and a preventative legal action was then commenced by Consten which, given its importance for Community law and the need for clarification, brought the Commission into action. The Commission in fact prohibited the entire agreement,[48] but an appeal was made to the Court of Justice with a number of member states joining in. In the upshot the sole distribution aspect was upheld, the offence being narrowed down to the element of territorial protection.[49] The latter buttresses the sole dealer's monopoly in the chain of distribution and, by compartmentalizing the Common Market, gives rise to differences in prices for the same goods in the different member states. Goods that have entered into trade must be allowed to move freely across frontiers in the hope that interstate price differences will be ironed out. Sole dealers must be allowed to poach.

The Commission followed this up by a number of decisions in which pure sole distribution agreements were exempted.[50] In other words, they do offend against Article 85(1) but because they have advantageous effects in helping competitors to penetrate markets, etc., they are capable of exemption. Moreover, being pure — i.e. there being no territorial protection — parallel imports are possible, which prevents the undesirable effects that would stem from compartmentalization of national markets. The Commission was in fact paving the way for the block exemption of this type of agreement. Regulation 19 of 1965 provided for block exemptions, and under Regulation 67 of 1967 bilateral sole dealing agreements (between enterprises in two states), unencumbered by devices such as territorial protection, were accorded block exemption status.

Earlier we said that the philosophy of *Grundig–Consten*, as narrowed down by the Court, has informed other decisions. This is well illustrated in the more recent *DCL* case.[51] This was concerned with the liquor distribution arrangements of The Distillers Co. Ltd. The company had originally inserted in its seller's conditions of sale a clause that forbade UK customers of DCL subsidiaries from reselling its goods outside the UK. This arrangement was buttressed by another requirement, namely that goods could not be taken out of bond without excise duty being paid. If sold in other member states of the Community, for example, that excise duty was non-refundable. This ruled out the possibility of any such resale since sole distributors in Community countries were supplied with liquor under bond at zero duty and local excise was applicable in both cases. Both elements were notified, and (not surprisingly in the light of previous cases) at the request of the Commission the first clause was redefined to cover countries outside the EEC and the second was dropped. Later DCL introduced price terms for the UK, although these were not correctly notified. These granted from the gross price very significant discounts, rebates and allowances provided the liquor was not to be sold outside the UK. Certain UK companies in fact bought whisky at the lower discounted UK price and resold it in France and Belgium. DCL came to know of this and refused to supply them, except at the higher gross price. The companies in question complained that the application of the gross price made parallel exports impossible. The Commission refused exemption. Exemption was indeed ruled out because of the notification point referred to earlier, but the Commission indicated that even in the absence of that problem it would not have changed its position. Here again we find the Commission attacking a practice that can maintain different prices in the various national markets of the EEC.

Article 85 has also been invoked in cases involving industrial property. For example, it is clear from the *Grundig–Consten* and *Sirena–Eda*[52] cases that trademark rights cannot be used to prevent goods circulating freely over the whole territory of the Community.

So far the Commission has been presented as a guardian of competition. However there is another side to the Commission's activities where certain forms of co-operation can be viewed in a favourable light. In 1968 the Commission issued a *Notice on Co-operation*, which indicated that it was anxious to encourage certain forms of collaboration. In the notice certain competitively innocuous practices were approved of but the Commission also indicated that it intended to address itself to situations where there was some restrictive effect but where counterbalancing gains in efficiency and progressiveness might be expected to accrue. A number of favourable decisions followed concerned with activities such as specialization and joint research and development. Specialization can be beneficial by spreading fixed costs over longer runs and thus lowering unit costs. It is on the other hand restrictive of competition, since the number of competitors is reduced. There may however be enough competition left to guarantee that some of the efficiency gain is passed on to the consumer in the form of lower prices. Good examples of cases where exemptions have been accorded for specialization arrangements are the *Jaz–Peter*[53] and *Clima–Chappé–Buderus*[54] cases. In the latter a French and a German producer of air-conditioning equipment agreed to rationalize their production – each undertook to produce only certain types of equipment. In order to offer a full line to customers, each supplied the other with equipment they had ceased to produce themselves. The fact that each was to be an exclusive distributor in its own home market constituted a restriction of competition, but this was not thought to be a significant drawback, given the intensity of competition remaining in each domestic market.

Decisions such as these paved the way for another block exemption regulation. Regulation 2821 of 1971 provided general powers to block-exempt standardization, joint research and development and specialization agreements. Regulation 2779 of 1972 provided a specific power for the latter. Current limitations require that the market share in a substantial part of the Common Market must not exceed 15 per cent and the annual aggregate sales must not exceed 300 million units of account.

Joint research and development can also economize in resources by eliminating duplication of expenditure. On the other hand, there is a sacrifice of potential competition. However, arrangements of this kind may have a stimulating effect on competition. It might be that an agreement would enable smaller or less well entrenched suppliers to offer more effective competition to those more fully established. A good example of this is the recently approved agreement between Vickers and the French firm Sopolem for the joint development of microscopes.[55] The European market for microscopes is dominated by German and Japanese producers, while the collaborating parties had only a small share and had not been able to break out of their home markets on any scale. The agreement also envisaged rationalized use of their distribution networks and possible specialization in production.

DOMINANT FIRM RULES AND CASES

Article 86, the text of which is reproduced in the Appendix to this chapter, is concerned with dominant firm behaviour. There are three important elements in this article. First, there must be a dominant position. Second, the existence of dominance is not sufficient for a prohibition to be invoked: it is also necessary that the position be abused. Third, and similar to Article 85, there must be the possibility of an effect on trade between the member states. The first two call for further comment.

A dominant position has two aspects. In the first place, there is a geographic dimension since the undertaking (or undertakings, since two or more firms may be involved) must have a dominant position in either the Common Market or a substantial part of it. No indication of what the word substantial means is given in the Rome Treaty. If therefore we wish to know how small a part of the Community may be deemed substantial we have no alternative but to refer to past cases for guidance. The territory of one member state has on several occasions been deemed large enough – it was West Germany in the *GEMA*[56] and *Continental Can*[57] cases, it was Belgium when the Court of Justice dealt with a copyright dispute (*BRT–Sabam* case[58]) and it was the UK when the Commission dealt with the cutting off of supplies by a manufacturer of cash-register spares (*Lipton–Hugin* case[59]). In the *Sugar* case the Commission treated Holland on its own and Belgium and Luxembourg as substantial parts of the Common Market.

The second aspect, where economic analysis is highly relevant, is that for dominance to exist in a geographic sector it is necessary to define the relevant product market. The point here is that we are concerned with the degree, if any, of market power enjoyed by the firm(s) in question. For example, it might be that a firm is deemed to be in possession of market power because it controls the whole supply of a particular product. But it may be that there are close substitutes to which consumers can turn if the price of the product in question is raised. In other words, to have market power a firm must have total or substantial control over all the products that are reasonably interchangeable. Actually, to enjoy any permanence of power there must also be some barriers to the entry of competitors who might otherwise be attracted to the market by the high price enjoyed by the possessor of the market power.

The *Continental Can* case, although concerned with a merger, illustrates this type of approach. That case concerned the activities of the Continental Can Company Inc., a large US multinational manufacturing metal containers, other packaging materials and machines for the manufacture and use of containers. It acquired a majority shareholding in a large West German producer of light-metal containers, Schmalbach-Lubeca-Werke AG of Brunswick. Continental Can then transferred its holdings in Schmalbach to a holding company, the Europemballage Corporation. It also agreed to make an offer for the shares of the large Dutch can producer, Thomassen and Drijver-Verblijfa NV of Deventer – actually the offer was made by Europemballage. This was accomplished and thus control of both Schmalbach and Thomassen came to be vested in the one holding company created by Continental. The EC Commission then intervened. It saw the acquisition of Schmalbach as being a violation of Article 86. This was a controversial interpretation of Article 86 since it was being applied to a merger.

Essentially the Commission was arguing that Schmalbach had a dominant position in the West German market for light containers for preserved meat and fish, and metal caps for preserve jars. The Commission also argued that the extinguishing of Thomassen's competition, via the acquisition, was an abuse within the meaning of Article 86. An effect on interstate trade was likely in that Thomassen would not now sell competitively in the West German market, nor for that matter would Schmalbach sell in the Benelux market. The case is instructive since much turned on the question of whether Schmalbach really had a dominant position in West Germany.

The Court in fact found against the Commission. In doing so it did not invoke any particular market share as being critical but pointed to the existence of other sources of ongoing or potential competition, such as containers made of plastic or glass and suppliers of metal containers for other goods who could turn their attention to the meat and fish-container market. It also noted that food packers could manufacture their own containers.

Identifying the relevant market is of course only a first step on the road to proving the existence of dominance. It still leaves us with the question of what proportion of the relevant market has to be attained in order to be dominant. In the *Continental Can* case no particular percentage was specified but the Court did emphasize as a test the idea that 'the remaining competitors could not constitute an adequate counterweight'. Obviously an absolute monopoly, as in the *GEMA* and *Liptons–Hugin* cases, will qualify since in such cases there is no counterweight whatsoever. In the *Sugar* case Raffinerie Tirlemontoise, with 85 per cent of the Belgian–Luxembourg market, was on this test also not surprisingly regarded as dominant. However the figure can sink much lower than that. In the *Chiquita* case[60] the share of the banana market (consisting of Belgium, Denmark, Germany, Luxembourg and the Netherlands) enjoyed by United Brands (UB) was only 40 per cent. However in justification of this relatively low figure the Court also took account of certain other structural features, namely the fact that even the largest of UB's competitors were small (i.e. Castle and Cooke 9 per cent, Del Monte 5 per cent) and that barriers against new entrants were high (there was a need for large investments and numerous sources of supply; penetration costs were considerable; scale economies were present).

We have already noted that the sin is not to have a dominant position but to abuse it. A number of examples are given but these are merely illustrative. They are: directly or indirectly imposing unfair purchasing or selling prices or other unfair trading conditions; limiting production, markets or technical development to the prejudice of consumers; applying dissimilar conditions to equivalent transactions with other trading parties, thereby placing them at a competitive disadvantage (this obviously refers to price discrimination); and making the conclusion of contracts subject to acceptance by other parties of supplementary obligations, which, by their nature or according to commercial usage, have no connection with the subject of such contracts (clearly this refers to tie-ins).

In actual cases, one of the main forms of abuse encountered has been the granting of fidelity rebates. In the *Sugar* case two large West German sugar producers had in concert offered rebates that were conditional upon buyers taking all their supplies from them. In a recent case the Commission took Hoffman–La Roche to task for a similar practice in respect of supplies of vitamins for bulk use in medicines, foods and feeding stuffs.[61] The Commission observed: 'Whether to compensate for the exclusivity or to encourage a preferential link, the contracts provided for fidelity rebates based not on differences in costs related to the quantities supplied by Roche but on the proportion of the customer's requirements covered.'[62] Moreover, Roche was able to extend its power to products where it was not dominant, since the rebates were not calculated separately for each particular group of vitamins but were aggregated across all purchases. A fine was imposed.

The Commission has also attacked the practice of refusal to supply. This arose in the *Commercial Solvents* case. Commercial Solvents, a monopolist of a raw material needed to produce a particular drug, decided (through its subsidiary) not to supply the raw material to an existing producer of the drug. The Court of Justice stated that an undertaking that is in a dominant position in the supply of a raw material, and is thus in a position to control the supply to producers of products manufactured from that material, cannot refuse to supply such a customer with the effect of eliminating all competition therefrom.[63]

In the *GEMA* case the Commission objected to the activities of a performing rights society which in fact enjoyed a monopoly of the German market. GEMA was established to protect the rights of member composers, authors and publishers. Rights were assigned to it and it exploited them in return for royalties. GEMA had imposed unduly restrictive terms on its members: they had to assign to it all existing and future rights in all respects and in all countries, for a minimum period of six years. The Commission objected to the universality of the assignment required of members. It felt that they should be free to assign only a part of their rights and be able to retain the other part for individual exploitation. The Commission also singled out for criticism the exclusion of non-residents – a provision that was apparently designed to consolidate the market power of other national societies.

A not dissimilar instance of the imposition of unduly onerous terms arose in the *Eurofirma* case in 1973, which was settled without the need for a formal decision. A company, on behalf of six national railways, invited tenders for the development and supply of passenger carriages. The company inviting the tenders inserted a provision giving it unrestricted rights to use the designs, patents and so forth that arose from the execution of the contract. The Commission took the view that the company had a dominant buying position and that the unrestricted right of sole exploitation was an abuse.[64]

More recently, the Commission has attacked the practice of charging different prices in different parts of the Common Market for the same product. This was the central issue in the *Chiquita* case. In the appeal proceedings the Court of Justice took the view that price should be related to cost and should not be set at the various levels that the different national markets would bear.

Mergers

Explicitly the Rome Treaty contains no article that deals with mergers. However the Commission has since at least 1965 maintained that Article 86 does apply. It was of the view that, if a dominant firm took over another and so established a monopoly, that was an abuse within the meaning of Article 86. The view that Article 86 does apply to mergers was put to the test in the *Continental Can* case which we have discussed. As we have seen, the Commission lost the specific case but the Court did accept that Article 86 could be applied to mergers. It reasoned that if this was not so the Treaty would be undermined. If control of a market via collusion between independent companies was blocked by Article 85, that Article could be side-stepped by those companies amalgamating. Article 86 is however less than perfect as an instrument of merger control since it cannot be activated until a dominant position exists, whereas it might be desirable to prevent such a position from emerging in the first place. The Commission has therefore proposed an amendment to the Treaty which would provide a specific controlling power in respect of all kinds of mergers and would require certain kinds of amalgamations to be pre-notified. This has not yet been adopted.

THE PARIS TREATY RULES

The Paris Treaty deals with both antitrust and pricing. Article 65 bears some resemblance to Article 85. All agreements, all decisions of associations of enterprises and all concerted practices tending either directly or indirectly to prevent, restrict or distort competition in the common market for coal and steel are prohibited. The Article lists various forms of restriction such as price-fixing, allocation of markets and control of production, investment and technical development. There is no interstate trade clause. However as an exception to this proscription, and in contrast to the Rome Treaty, the Commission is required to authorize agreements, etc., that involve specialization or joint buying or selling, provided three cumulative conditions are fulfilled: (a) the arrangement must substantially improve production or distribution; (b) the practice must be no more restrictive than necessary; (c) it must not give the participants the power to determine prices or control output in a substantial part of the production in question in the Common Market. Benefit to the consumer is not a requirement. Some quite generous exemptions have been granted, notably in the German steel industry in 1976.

Article 66 relates to dominant firms and mergers. The Commission has a power to address recommendations to firms in a dominant position in a substantial part of the Common Market who are using the position for purposes contrary to the Paris Treaty. As far as mergers are concerned (horizontal, vertical and mixed), beyond a certain size limit they are subject to prior authorization by the Commission. The Commission has to allow them provided certain effects will not result. These negative criteria are that the concentration will not have the power in the field of ECSC products:

to influence prices, to control or restrain production, or to impair the maintenance of effective competition in a substantial part of the market for such products; or

to evade the rules of competition resulting from the application of the present Treaty; particularly by establishing an artificially privileged position involving a material advantage in access to supply or markets.

In short, mergers must be assessed according to their effect on competition and no exemption on grounds of efficiency is allowed. The process of authorization implies that the Commission can forbid a merger (and this also applies to joint ventures) if it fails to meet the above test.

Rules are laid down that govern the pricing offers that can be made. These rules call for price publicity. Prices must also be related to a geographical basing point and quotations to customers take the form of the published basing point price plus transport costs (the latter are supposed to be transparent — i.e. publicized and thus known to all possible suppliers) from the basing point to the customer. There is however considerable scope for competition. Under conditions of boom steel firms will probably be able to charge the full basing point price plus transport cost. But if there is a recession in sales they can indeed align them down to *match* the lowest delivered price which any other producer within the Community could offer. Such an offer does not have to be made — it is sufficient that it *could* be made. In other words, knowing all the basing point prices of all other producers and knowing the transport charges of all other producers to the customer in question, any particular producer can push his quotation down to the lowest of those theoretically possible delivered prices. It is of course always open to a producer to notify a cut in his own basing point price, in which case he can make lower offers. Equally well, if some producers notify cuts in their basing point prices, then other producers have more scope to align down to match them. Here we are referring to internal alignment — competition against other Community offers. In addition Community producers can align down to meet (actual) offers from non-Community sources. This is referred to as external alignment. During recessions affecting the Community, and particularly during world recessions, the Community steel industry has proved to be highly competitive. List prices have been cut and the alignment possibility has been used to the full as Community producers scrambled to obtain a share of diminished Community orders; this has been particularly noticeable when the export market has been depressed. They have also competed vigorously against non-Community offers, which in depressed world market conditions have come in at low, even artificially low, price levels.

In conditions of manifest crisis the Commission can step in and fix prices, production quotas, etc. In other words, although price competition, subject to rules, is to be the order of the day, if it gets out of hand intervention is possible with a view to limiting the price fall. Given that before the Second World War the European steel industry was cartelized and had little experience of competition, it is hardly surprising that, when faced with the prospect of free competition, it should have been felt prudent that a safety net be provided.

It should be noted that the pricing rules, allied to the relatively open nature of the Community steel market, have been responsible for the existence of a highly competitive market. So much so that since 1974 the Community industry has indeed been in difficulties. The recession in the Community and in world markets has led to intensified internal competition and the Community has had to contend with low-priced offers from countries such as Japan. As a result the edge of competition has had to be blunted. In 1976 the Commission involved the steel industry in a voluntary plan to cut back deliveries in order to raise prices. In 1977 compulsory minimum prices were introduced in respect of some products and guidance prices were issued in respect of others. Minimum import prices were also imposed.

APPENDIX

ARTICLES 85 AND 86 OF THE ROME TREATY

Article 85
1. The following practices shall be prohibited as incompatible with the common market: all agreements between undertakings, all decisions by associations of undertakings and all concerted practices, which may affect trade between Member States and the object or effect of which is to prevent, restrict or distort competition within the common market, and in particular those which amount to:
- (*a*) the direct or indirect fixing of purchase or selling prices or of any other trading conditions;
- (*b*) the limiting or controlling of production, markets, technical development or capital investment;
- (*c*) the sharing of markets or sources of supply;
- (*d*) applying, in relation to customers in the trade, unequal conditions in respect of equivalent transactions, placing them thereby at a competitive disadvantage;
- (*e*) making the conclusion of contracts subject to acceptance by the other parties of supplementary obligations, which, by their nature or according to commercial practice, have no connection with the subject of such contracts.

2. Any agreements or decisions prohibited pursuant to this Article shall automatically be null and void.

3. The provisions of paragraph 1 may, however, be declared inapplicable in the case of:
- – any agreement or category of agreements between undertakings,
- – any decision or category of decisions of associations of undertakings, and
- – any concerted practice or category of concerted practices,

which contribute to improve the production or distribution of goods or to promote technical or economic progress, whilst allowing consumers a fair share of the resulting benefit and which does not:
- (*a*) impose on the undertakings concerned restrictions which are not indispensable to the achievement of the above objectives;
- (*b*) afford such undertakings the possibility of eliminating competition in respect of a substantial part of the products in question.

Article 86

It shall be incompatible with the common market and prohibited, in so far as trade between Member States is liable to be affected by it, for one or more undertakings to exploit in an improper manner a dominant position within the common market or within a substantial part of it. Such improper practices, may, in particular, consist in:
- (*a*) the direct or indirect imposition of unfair purchase or selling prices or of other unfair trading conditions;
- (*b*) the limitation of production, markets or technical development to the prejudice of consumers;
- (*c*) applying in relation to like parties unequal conditions in respect of like transactions, placing them thereby at a competitive disadvantage;
- (*d*) making the conclusion of contracts subject to agreement by the other parties to make additional payments, which, by their nature or according to commercial practice, have no connection with the subject of such contracts.

4 Competition Policy – The Domestic Market

INTRODUCTION

In the last chapter we were concerned with laws designed to root out restrictions of competition that inhibit the flow of competitive trade across the frontiers of the EEC. However, as we saw in Chapter 3, restrictions covered by Article 85 may be tolerated if counterbalancing advantages are deemed to accrue and the consumer is expected to share in the benefits. In this chapter the focus is still on the antitrust problem, but in this case our concern is with our own competition laws. In the main these address themselves to restrictions of competition by British companies that directly affect the domestic market. It is true that the UK laws can be applied to behaviour that affects foreign markets, but this will not be a matter for concern in this book. *Alienus caveat emptor!*

It is also important to note that, although we are viewing antitrust laws as devices that can protect the consumer, the motivation that has lain behind their enactment has on some occasions been mixed. There have been other considerations in the minds of legislators besides the protection of the consumer. Not surprisingly therefore we shall see that the laws themselves do not dwell exclusively on the need to appraise restrictions of competition by reference to their impact on buyers. It should however be added that, although the consumer interest as such is not always explicitly referred to, the need to serve it, among other things, may nevertheless be recognized implicitly.

In the UK consumer protection in the form of antitrust law is a relatively recent development. As we shall see in the next chapter, modern laws concerned with the adulteration of food and drink go back to 1860. Modern weights and measures legislation began in 1878, and what has been described as the consumer's charter, the Sale of Goods Act, dates from 1893. Antitrust law in the UK began in 1948 with the Monopolies and Restrictive Practices (Inquiry and Control) Act. It is true that a Committee on Trusts reported in 1919, but no legislation emerged. Equally, there were three long-standing common law doctrines that could in principle have been applied to restrictions of competition – they are the doctrines of monopoly, conspiracy (both civil and criminal) and contracts in restraint of trade. In practice none of them proved to be the basis of a thoroughgoing attack on competitive restrictions.

The problem with the doctrine of monopoly was that monopoly tends, as we have seen, to have a very restricted meaning. It applies when an individual controls the total supply of a product. This is an unlikely situation and in practice the doctrine proved of little use.[1]

Much the same could be said of the doctrine of conspiracy. Originally conspiracy was an act that was otherwise lawful but that became unlawful if two persons combined to take action with intent to do injury to a third party. That doctrine was laid down in a trilogy of cases[2] at the end of the nineteenth century, of which the *Mogul* case is the most celebrated, and was summed up by Lord Cave in the case of *Sorrel* v. *Smith*.[3] The upshot of these cases was that, however severe the effect on a third party of the action of a combination in forwarding or defending their trade interests, no legal liability attached. Only if the object of the combination was wilfully and maliciously to damage the third party was the case actionable. Proving that the purpose of the combination was to further the interest of the parties was easy; but proving that it was malicious was a much more formidable task.

The doctrine of restraint of trade did appear to be more promising. The modern doctrine was laid down by Lord Macnaghten in the *Nordenfelt* case.[4] He maintained that all restraints were void but stated that there were exceptions to this rule where such restraints were held to be reasonable — 'reasonable that is, in the interests of the parties and reasonable in the interests of the public'. The latter aspect looks promising since it takes explicit account of the public interest. In reality the doctrine did not live up to its promise. The balance was loaded very much in favour of the parties. It was easy to prove 'reasonableness' *inter partes*. But the onus in proving that an agreement was injurious lay with the person making the allegation and, to quote another case, the onus was 'no light one'.[5] Stevens and Yamey have also observed that the courts, by equating the public interest with reasonableness between the parties to the contract, excluded judges from concern with their economic impact.[6] In further pursuit of this point it should be noted that the doctrine of restraint of trade has in more recent years been employed against forms of restrictive practice.

For example, the courts have attacked the practice by petrol suppliers of tying retailers exclusively to their supplies — the so-called solus contracts.[7] However, in so doing the main preoccupation of the courts has been the reasonableness of the behaviour of one party towards the other rather than the fact that such contacts could restrict new entrants, and by reducing competition could deny the community the economic benefits thereof.

RESTRICTIVE PRACTICES

The attack on restrictive practices began in 1948 with the Monopolies and Restrictive Practices (Inquiry and Control) Act. Although this was to prove to be a landmark in the development of competition policy, the protection of consumers did not bulk large in the argumentation that eventually gave rise to the Act. The arguments that carried the day were these. First, restrictions of competition were deeply entrenched in British industry, and there was also impressive evidence of British involvement in international cartels. Some of the work that established these facts was actually carried out during and immediately after the Second World War[8] when some seminal thinking also took place about how to tackle the problem. Some of the restrictions were due to the existence of trade associations, which had been called into existence by the state in both world wars in order to help to organize the war economy. During the thirties the state had in some instances actually insisted on the introduction of restrictive arrangements, designed to help to raise prices to profitable levels, as a condition for the conferment of tariff protection. Second, the prime objective of postwar economic policy was full employment. This goal was enshrined in the 1944 White Paper on *Employment Policy*.[9] This was a quite crucial document since it can be argued that the pursuit of full employment has been the overriding aim of postwar policy, and that fact explains a great deal and is not without significance for the consumer. The White Paper referred to the need to maintain a surveillance of, and indeed to control, monopoly in all its guises. It argued that what was needed was expanded output (and therefore high employment), whereas those who enjoyed market power might prefer to restrict output (and therefore employment) in order to enjoy higher prices and profits. But underlying the White Paper there was a deeper argument. During the war British industry had been run down and foreign markets had been lost. Industry had to be revitalized if those markets were to be regained and high employment assured. Moreover our foreign investments had been sold off to help to pay for the war. Therefore the import of raw materials, fuel and food required a massive export drive, since we would have to earn the necessary foreign currency that way given that our foreign investment income had been wiped out. British industry had to be revitalized for this task and it was crucially important that restrictive practices should not be allowed to impede the process.

The 1948 Act related to the supply of goods and to the application of processes to goods. A 'monopoly' was defined as a situation where at least a third of the supply of a class of goods (or the application of a process to goods) in the UK (or a substantial part thereof) was supplied by (a) one person, or (b) by two or more persons being interconnected bodies corporate or (c) by two or more persons who restricted competition by agreement or otherwise. Obviously (a) and (b) were monopoly or dominance situations and we shall look at that aspect later. It was (c) that is relevant in this context. Where the one-third of supply criterion appeared to be satisfied, the Board of Trade, as it then was, could refer the matter to the Monopolies and Restrictive Practices Commission for investigation. In making such a reference the Board could merely require the Commission to state whether a 'monopoly' situation defined by the Act did indeed exist and what the cartel enjoying that 'monopoly' did by virtue of it or to preserve it. In addition, the Board could require the Commission to state whether the conditions found to exist operated against the public interest. A cursory glance at the Act makes it all too apparent that, in terms of the spectrum of possible approaches discussed in Chapter 3, the UK law at this stage did not embody a *per se* approach, nor did it initially presume agreements to be contrary to the public interest. Rather, the law adopted an essentially uncommitted and pragmatic approach in which industrial situations could be examined to see if they were contrary to the public interest. The Commission then, as now, was not responsible for redress. That power lay with the Board or the relevant Ministry, and they were not obliged to do what the Commission recommended. If they did take action it might be by statutory order but more usually it was by securing voluntary undertakings.

A glance at the public interest criteria (see below) indicates that the need to be concerned with the effect on consumers was not explicitly identified. The desirable aims were efficiency and full employment. Nevertheless, the consumer could stand to gain from greater efficiency and his interest was glimpsed at in guideline (a):

> [Public interest guidelines under the 1948 Act Section 14]
> ... regard shall be had to the need, consistently with the general economic position of the United Kingdom, to achieve
> (a) the production, treatment and distribution by the most efficient and economical means of goods of such types and qualities, in such volume and at such prices as will best meet the requirements of home and overseas markets;
> (b) the organisation of industry and trade in such a way that their efficiency is progressively increased and new enterprises encouraged;
> (c) the fullest use and best distribution of men, materials and industrial capacity in the United Kingdom; and
> (d) the development of technical improvements and the expansion of existing markets and the opening up of new markets.

We described the 1948 Act as a landmark in the evolution of consumer protection policy. It was a landmark not because it achieved a great deal in rooting out competitive restrictions, thus helping the consumer, but because it acted as a reconnaissance. The 1944 White Paper had recognized that more needed to be known about the detailed effects of competitive restrictions, and it is here that the painstaking analyses of the Commission performed a signal service. The reconnaissance established that they were widespread and entrenched. The Commission also concluded that in the main they were deleterious to the public interest. In this latter conclusion it was obviously thinking about their effect in inhibiting efficiency and adversely affecting our foreign trade potential. There is however no doubt that it also saw the consuming interest as suffering, and equally there is no doubt that the press and public opinion drew that conclusion.

The late Alex Hunter summarized the Commission's appraisal of the effects of price-fixing as follows:

> It can be concluded that for any 'competitive' industrial structure the Commission's opinions are in line with orthodox economic thinking. Price competition is found to be a useful element in the process of competitive adjustment making for a better allocation of resources between different products within the industry, the encouragement of the efficient and the elimination of the inefficient

producers, lower prices to the consumer, etc. Agreements to fix prices restrict this adjustment, and therefore the presumption is that they operate against the public interest. Only in a few special cases have exceptions to this rule been made.[10]

However it was really the report on Collective Discrimination[11] that was the final and key influence. Under the 1948 Act it was possible to refer classes of practice (as opposed to 'monopoly' situations) to the Commission for investigation. The Collective Discrimination report of 1955 dealt with the exclusionary practices – e.g. aggregated rebates, collective exclusive dealing, etc. The Commission found them to exist in a large number of trades and decided that generally they were harmful to the public interest. The majority of the Commission also felt that such practices, clearly defined, should be prohibited. A new criminal offence should be created – this point was not however taken up. Exceptions might however be granted.

The effect of all this, together with a substantial press campaign against restrictive practices, was the 1956 Restrictive Trade Practices Act which changed the posture of the law. A more hostile approach was now adopted. *This approach continues to operate under the provisions of the current Restrictive Trade Practices Act 1976, as amended.*

The Act required that all agreements between two or more parties carrying on business in the UK in the production of, supply of or application of processes of manufacture to *goods* had to be registered with a newly created officer, the Registrar of Restrictive Trading Agreements. Such registered agreements were open to inspection by the public. *Under the Fair Trading Act 1973 this and other functions of the Registrar were vested in the Director General of Fair Trading (DGFT) in consort with his staff at the Office of Fair Trading (OFT).* Agreements were defined as the acceptance by two or more parties of restrictions relating to such things as prices to be charged, quantities to be supplied, processes of manufacture to be applied, persons or areas to be supplied.

The important thing about the 1956 Act, and thus the current consolidating Act of 1976, was the status of such restrictions. It was assumed that they are contrary to the public interest. However, the Act did not, save for one exception which we shall discuss later, adopt a *per se* approach. The Act provided that the parties to agreements could bring forward defences. But the Act did not allow the parties total freedom of action in seeking to justify themselves. Rather, seven types of pleading (known as 'gateways') were originally provided. They are set out below.

(a) that the restriction is reasonably necessary, having regard to the character of the goods to which it applies, to protect the public against injury (whether to persons or to premises) in connection with the consumption, installation or use of those goods;
(b) that the removal of the restriction would deny to the public as purchasers, consumers or users of any goods other specific and substantial benefits or advantages enjoyed or likely to be enjoyed by them as such, whether by virtue of the restriction itself or of any arrangements or operations resulting therefrom;
(c) that the restriction is reasonably necessary to counteract measures taken by any one person not party to the agreement with a view to preventing or restricting competition in or in relation to the trade or business in which the persons party thereto are engaged;
(d) that the restriction is reasonably necessary to enable the persons party to the agreement to negotiate fair terms for the supply of goods to, or the acquisition of goods from, any one person not party thereto who controls a preponderant part of the trade or business of acquiring or supplying such goods, or for the supply of goods to any person not party to the agreement and not carrying on such a trade or business who, either alone or in combination with any other such person, controls a preponderant part of the market for such goods;
(e) that, having regard to the conditions actually obtaining or reasonably foreseen at the time of the application, the removal of the restriction would be likely to have a serious and persistent adverse effect on the general level of unemployment in an area, or in areas taken together, in which a substantial proportion of the trade or industry to which the agreement relates is situated;
(f) that having regard to the conditions actually obtaining or reasonably foreseen at the time of the application, the removal of the restriction would be likely to cause a reduction in the volume or earnings of the export business which is substantial either in relation to the whole export business of the United Kingdom or in relation to the whole business (including export business) of the said trade or industry; or
(g) that the restriction is reasonably required for purposes connected with the maintenance of any other restriction accepted by the parties, whether under the same agreement or under any other agreement between them, being a restriction which is found by the Court not to be contrary to the public interest upon grounds other than those specified in this paragraph, or has been so found in previous proceedings before the Court.

The task of the Registrar was to refer registered agreements to the newly created Restrictive Practices Court. The Registrar would bring forward arguments as to the deleterious effects of the agreements in question which the respondents would seek to rebut. The respondents would seek to justify their agreements by trying to get the agreement through one or more gateways and the Registrar would argue against. If the parties failed to get through a gateway then the agreement fell, since the Act contained a presumption against and no counterbalancing claim had been substantiated. If the parties succeeded in getting through one or more gateways they were still not in the clear. At this point a tailpiece balancing process came into operation. The Court had to decide whether the advantages proved outweighed the detriment. If not, the agreement fell. If they did the agreement was upheld. When the Act became operational it was not necessary for the parties to agreements to go through this long and expensive procedure. They could decide not to contest the case. An Order would then be made declaring the agreement contrary to the public interest and the parties would undertake not to operate them or ones to the like effect.

It was also the task of the Registrar to see that agreements were brought on to the register. In this task he was aided by complaints made by the general public. The enforcement problem has been highlighted in recent years. It has come to the attention of the DGFT that important agreements have been concealed. We shall discuss this point in Chapter 11.

To what extent, we may ask, was the Restrictive Trade Practices Act a piece of consumer protection legislation? There is no doubt that the press campaign that led up to the Act envisaged this as an element. Indeed, the press had something of a field day citing as it did cases such as the Birmingham retailer who sought to cut the price of tea to old-age pensioners and had his supplies cut off. In Parliament too the opposition championed the need for legislation on the grounds that monopoly practices restricted supply and raised prices to the consumer. Servants of the consumer who had been chastised by trade associations were also referred to. Foremost among these was a Mr Mendelsohn, a motor accessory dealer from Stockport, who was hauled before a private court because he sold below the list level. In ministerial speeches however we search in vain for any observations to the effect that the curbing of restrictive practices would benefit the consumer with greater efficiency and lower prices. Ministers seemed to be preoccupied with the pure mechanics of the proposed Act. It may be that this ministerial preoccupation was partly designed to avoid playing into the hands of the opposition — reference to the deleterious effects of cartels on consumers would have been useful ammunition for their opponents on the other side of the House. In the Act the public interest is referred to but is not defined in terms of such things as serving the consumer. Rather, it is initially presumed merely that restrictive agreements are contrary to the public interest — in other words that the creation of competition is in the public interest. Somewhat ironically, when the consumer does appear it is in connection with the grounds upon which exemptions from competition may be accorded — i.e. gateways (a) and (b). The reader will also note that the 1956 Act did not, and the present Act does not, regard the creation of competition as being uniquely valuable. Other objectives are also deferred to including the prevention of regional unemployment (gateway(e)) and the supporting of export activity (gateway (f)).

The contribution of an Act however ultimately depends on what it actually does and not what it is claimed it will do. Looking at the Act in this fashion there can be no doubt that, subject to one qualification which we shall discuss later, it was a major piece of consumer protection legislation. In support of this view we can cite the effect that it had in undermining restrictions of competition, although, as we shall see, the battle was long drawn out. The success of the Act was reflected not so much in terms of the agreements that the Court struck down as in the number of associations who decided not to contest. Between 28 November 1957 and 30 June 1969, 2,600 agreements were registered. However by the latter date 1,240 had been abandoned, another 960 had been varied (i.e. offending clauses had been dropped, etc.) and 90 had lapsed. Much of this was due to the severe attitude of the Court in early cases. Seven of the first 8 agreements judicially considered were struck down. Thereafter, it is argued, a subtle modification of attitude on the part of the Court occurred in which a less clear-cut approach was adopted. Nevertheless, between 1958 and 1968, out of the 33 cases where agreements were defended for the first time, only 10 got by.

A major factor in explaining the wholesale abandonments was the fate of the Yarn Spinners' Agreement.[12] This was an agreement of great significance since it was a key arrangement in a major industry. What happened to that industry was bound to be taken notice of by British industry generally. In practice the Registrar, ably assisted by his economist witness Professor S. R. Dennison, was able to persuade the Court that the minimum price agreement kept prices higher than they would be under free competition. The agreement contributed to inefficiency by keeping high-cost firms in production. Also, a more compact industry was called for but the agreement kept excess capacity in existence. These sources of inefficiency also impeded the industry's export performance. In reply the respondents were able to persuade the Court that if the agreement was abrogated there would be a serious adverse effect on employment in Lancashire. More hesitantly, the Court was persuaded that the unemployment problem would be persistent. The respondents had thus passed through a gateway and the Court was called upon to perform the tailpiece balancing process. The Court concluded that the detriments arising from the absence of competition within the industry more than outweighed the forecasted unemployment. The agreement was struck down. This had a powerful effect on industrial thinking. The conclusion drawn was that if such an agreement could not get by then the prospects for many others were bleak. Large-scale voluntary abandonments followed and there can be no doubt that the Yarn Spinners' judgment was a landmark on the path to a more competitive economy.

Once the existence of a significant restriction of competition was established, a lot of argument before the Court was naturally concerned with the attempts of respondents to get off by seeking first to pass through a gateway or gateways. As we have seen, in a few cases they were able to do so and to prove that the advantage of their agreement outweighed the detriment. In the *Water-Tube Boilers* case[13] the agreement was unsevered – that is to say it was a bid-fixing agreement which applied to home as well as to overseas sales. The respondents did succeed under the export gateway (f) and got by. In the *Sulphuric Acid* case[14] a pool had been formed by acid-making manufacturers in order collectively to purchase imported sulphur from the dominating supplier Sulexco, an American export combination. This too got by, in this case by first passing through gateway (d), which relates to the need to countervail a preponderant supplier. These gateways do not of course involve the consumer in a direct way. On the other hand gateways (a) and (b) do, and it is particularly instructive to see how the Court appraised the consumer interest. We should perhaps note that gateway (b) includes industrial and public sector purchasers, and of course if they benefit the man in the street may also benefit although indirectly.

The gateway (a) argument, which is concerned with the avoidance of injury, was relatively little used. Where it was deployed it seemed to be prone to failure. Gateway (a) featured in the first case heard before the Court – the *Chemists* case.[15] This concerned the restriction of the sale of proprietary medicines to licensed chemists shops on the ground that this reduced the risk of injury through ignorant self-medication. The Court was not impressed, partly because no examples were given to show the existence of such dangerous medication and partly because even if such a risk was a reality it was difficult to see how the system of retailing in question would prevent it. Gateway (a) also featured in the *Tyre Trade Register* case.[16] This was concerned with an agreement between the association of tyre producers and six associations of distributors to the effect that trade terms should only be accorded to those tyre shops whose names appeared on a specially kept register. Standards were laid down for inclusion on the register and these included the presence of a 'qualified' tyre fitter. The respondents argued that their restriction was necessary in order to prevent accidents arising from incorrect fitting. Neither the Registrar nor the Court was particularly impressed by the arguments deployed. The Registrar noted that the safety provisions had been introduced only after 1957, thus leaving the Court to infer that the original and true purpose was merely to restrict entry into fitting. Even if a qualified fitter was present there was no way of guaranteeing that he did the fitting. The Registrar also contended that incorrect fitting was not a serious factor in road accidents and that enforcement was not adequate in that traders not on the register were in fact able to obtain trade terms.

Gateway (b) was much more popular, no doubt because of its broad character. Here the Court did indicate its attitude towards the relationship between competition and the consumer interest. In the *Yarn Spinners'* case the Court was quite clear in its preference for price competition as opposed to the stability of prices under the agreement when it observed:

> What we have to consider is whether price stabilisation as an alternative to a free market is a benefit to the purchasing public in the circumstances of this particular case. We cannot think that as a general rule it is a benefit; if we were to hold that we would be going contrary to the general presumption embodied in the Act that price restrictions are contrary to the public interest. There may be particular cases where price stabilisation confers a peculiar benefit

sufficiently great to outweigh the loss of a free market, but this is not one of them. We cannot find that in the circumstance of this case stabilising the price of yarn confers any benefit on the purchasing public that is not outweighed by the loss of the chance of reductions in price that might be secured under free competition.[17]

In the *Scottish Bread* case price fixing and stabilization were seen as being likely to 'prevent or retard the introduction of progressive methods in industry and thus operate positively against the interests of the consumer'.[18] In the *Phenol* case[19] the Court saw the rigidity of a fixed price as a disadvantage to purchasers.

In a number of cases the respondents argued that price restrictions benefited consumers by diverting competition into the maintenance and improvement of quality and service. This point was made in the *Yarn Spinners'* case and was rebutted as follows:

> Competition in quality is no doubt a benefit, but the removal of the restriction would not prevent it. If there was no restriction the spinner would have a choice between giving better quality at the same price or the same quality at a lower price.[20]

The Court dealt likewise with this argument in a number of other cases including those of the *British Bottle Association*,[21] the *Linoleum Manufacturers' Association*[22] and the *Federation of British Carpet Manufacturers*.[23]

An allied contention was that price-fixing inhibited debasement. If price competition was introduced it would cause manufacturers to reduce their costs by debasing the product and the consumer would be the oser. This was a critical element in the argument put forward by the Federation of British Carpet Manufacturers and it was decisively rejected by the Court. It was rejected in a number of other instances including the *Associated Transformer Manufacturers' Agreement* case where the Court observed: 'no manufacturer, who proposed to stay in business, would prejudice his good name or run any risk of doing so in this matter of quality'.[24] Of course if this was generally true it would cast doubts on the grounds for much consumer protection activity. The Court was however aware that the purchasers in this instance were public authorities 'well qualified to scrutinize quality and specify for it . . . .'.[25]

But the Court did not conclude that competition was universally the consumer's best friend. On an admittedly very limited number of occasions restrictions of competition were justified in the interest of the consumer or user. In the *Glazed Tile* case,[26] where the man in the street was quite clearly in the picture, a price agreement and a standardization agreement were conjoined. It was argued that standardization led to economies in production and that the resulting lower costs were passed on to the consumer in the form of lower prices. The standardization was buttressed by the price agreement since by discriminating against non-standard tiles it concentrated demand on the standardized variety. In the *Permanent Magnets* case[27] the consumer was concerned more indirectly, since the man in the street did not purchase the product in question directly but rather as components of various electrical consumer durables. The Association claimed that its arrangements gave rise to a high level of beneficial technical collaboration but this would cease if the price-fixing agreement was struck down. Firms would not reveal their secrets if these secrets were used by others to undercut them. The Court was persuaded that the detriments of the agreement were small since prices and profits were reasonable and that the collaborative benefits to consumers outweighed them.

The *Black Bolt and Nut* case[28] concerned a price-fixing arrangement operated by forty-four firms who were responsible for about 90 per cent of the industry output. The ordinary consumer did not figure directly here since the sales were made to other firms. Nevertheless, an argument was developed that had a potentiality in situations where the man in the street was concerned. The prices were fixed on the basis of costing samples. The system was however far from ideal. The respondents made their bid under gateway (b) but all their arguments in favour of fixed prices failed – except one. The Court was persuaded that the user did not have to 'go shopping'. He knew that prices were the same over more or less the whole industry and he did not have to waste time and money approaching various suppliers in order to discover who was offering the lowest price in respect of thousands of types and sizes. The main purchasers also agreed that this was a benefit which saved them money and enabled them to work on a lower margin. The reader may well think this an odd inversion of consumer logic – is not selective shopping an indispensable feature of the competitive system? The Court seemed to have at the back of its mind the extravagant assumption that competition would work only if all offers were considered. Clearly some economy in shopping is necessary, but this does not imply that there should be zero choice in respect of price. The respondents were able to persuade the Court to uphold the agreement. The same argument was deployed in the *Glazed Tile* case but it failed on the grounds that there were not many manufacturers.

We should also note that an indirect benefit to the ordinary consumer in the form of lower prices was established under gateway (b) in the *Cement* case.[29] The Court accepted that the absence of competition reduced risk and thus the industry was content to accept a lower rate of return on its capital.

Earlier we observed that, although the 1956 Act helped to create a more competitive economy, the battle was long and drawn-out. This was so because industry found ways around the Act. Price leadership, but above all information agreements (usually pre-notification arrangements relating to price), were the main loophole. These were often introduced before the formal price-fixing agreements were terminated. If the evidence of Loughborough University's study[30] is any guide, perhaps half the industries in which restrictions were terminated introduced information agreements. Unfortunately the 1956 Act did not explicitly address itself to the information agreement problem. The latter is an unfortunate example of an incapacity to learn from the experience of other countries – the US had begun to encounter the information agreement problem as early as 1911! It is true that the word 'arrangement' as used in the 1956 Act could be interpreted in a way that enabled the Act to be brought to bear on information agreements (see *Galvanised Tank* and *Tyre Mileage* cases,[31]) but a new Act was needed in order to bring the law into head-on opposition to information agreements. This was achieved by the Restrictive Trade Practices Act 1968.

The 1968 Act required registration of information agreements relating to prices, terms and conditions, quantities supplied, processes applied, persons and areas supplied and costs. It was left to the Department of Trade and Industry to decide which categories should be placed on the register, and in 1969 agreements relating to prices and terms and conditions were in fact called up. A new gateway was added. It states:

> (h) the restriction does not directly or indirectly restrict or discourage competition to any material degree in any relevant trade or industry and is not likely to do so.

This was clearly designed to apply in information agreement cases (although it was not intended to be solely tied to them). The point of the gateway is that an information agreement might have no restrictive effect yet as we have seen it would fall if no gateway could be satisfied. It might be thought that gateway (b) was wide enough to deal with the matter, but the decision to introduce gateway (h) seems to indicate that any benefit arising from an information agreement might be too small to qualify under (b).

The 1968 Act is important for two other reasons. First it was felt necessary to tighten up on enforcement. The registration requirement needed to be backed by greater sanctions. The Act made registration a statutory duty. An unregistered agreement is void, and it is illegal to give effect to or enforce it. Any person (and this apart from complaints is the only point at which the individual consumer can play a role) who is harmed by such an agreement can bring an action for damages. The DGFT can also approach the Court and ask for an Order restraining the parties from operating or enforcing such an agreement. How effective these sanctions are we shall discuss in Chapter 11.

Second, the 1968 Act embodied some retrogressive features. Certain agreements could be exempted from registration. This applied to agreements of importance to the national economy and agreements for holding down prices – the latter being a response to the needs of prices and incomes policy which we discuss in Chapter 5. A number of conditions were laid down in respect of the former which mean that this power of exemption is not likely to be generously used. An agreement has to be calculated to promote an industrial or commercial project of substantial importance to the national economy. Its main objective must be to promote efficiency or create or improve productive capacity. The objective must not be capable of being achieved within a reasonable time except with the aid of the agreement. No restrictions must be accepted other than those reasonably necessary to achieve the objective. The agreement must on balance be expedient in the national interest and the latter involves consideration of its effect on consumers.

We noted earlier that the 1948 and 1956 Acts applied to goods. The supply of services was not brought into the picture until 1965, when the Monopolies and Mergers Act was placed on the statute book. Services both commercial and professional could be referred to the Monopolies Commission under the one-third rule. Then in 1973, by virtue of the Fair Trading Act, restrictions relating to commercial services (including information agreements) were made referable to the Restrictive Practices Court (professional services were left for reference to the Commission). In 1976 an order was made calling up on to the register service agreements (other than information agreements) giving rise to restrictions relating to prices, terms and conditions, quantity, form or manner, and persons and areas to be supplied. Some services were however exempted from registration and some of these are of concern to the consumer. They include agreements between insurance companies relating to the provision of insurance services and agreements between building societies relating to interest rates. Agreements arising in connection with government control of building societies, and indeed financial institutions generally (this obviously includes the banks), were also exempted from the call-up.

It should also be noted that the 1973 Fair Trading Act remedied some other deficiencies. Under the 1956 Act, some forms of agreement were exempt from registration. One was the patent licence. This gave rise to a considerable loophole since patents owned by a group of competitors could be pooled and identical restrictions could be imposed on all who drew upon the pool. The 1973 Act did not attack patent licensing as such, but where three or more parties contribute patents (or designs) to a pool, and the agreement imposes restrictions on prices, quantities to be produced and so on, then the agreement has to be treated in the same way as any other agreement. In short, it is registrable and actionable before the Court. Another type of agreement that was exempt under the old Act related to the recommending or suggesting (as opposed to the fixing) of resale prices by a group of firms. This too was, by virtue of the 1973 Act, made registrable and actionable according to the customary processes. On the other hand bilateral exclusive dealing was exempted under the 1956 Act and has remained so.

Earlier we asserted that the 1956 Act was undoubtedly a potent instrument of consumer protection. However we admitted that there was one qualification, and it is to this that we now turn. The 1956 Act dealt with resale price maintenance (rpm). The collective variety was registrable and actionable before the Court. Collective enforcement, as for example by collective boycott, was declared illegal *per se*. The position on individual rpm however marked a step backward in an area that was quite unambiguously of concern to the consumer. In the Parliamentary debates leading up to the Act considerable play was made of the beneficial effects of individual rpm. It was pointed out that women's organizations had expressed a preference for fixed retail prices on the grounds that it enabled them to budget more accurately for their shopping! The present-day consumer, ever watchful for the biggest discount off the recommended price, would almost certainly regard this type of argument as exhibiting a high degree of economic *naiveté*. Nevertheless this and other arguments persuaded ministers to strengthen the position of individual rpm. A non-signer clause was provided for, whereby a retailer was regarded as being contractually bound provided he had been informed of the prescribed retail price.

Subsequently the tide of opinion moved against individual rpm. It was argued that it restricted the shoppers' choice. Ideally it ought to be possible for retailers who wished to pursue a cash-and-carry policy to be able to cut margins while those who wished to provide personal service, delivery and credit could apply a larger margin. The structure of shopping would respond to the relative size of the demands for these two approaches. Under the rpm system the low price policy was frustrated and new lower cost methods of retailing were inhibited. Significant savings to the consumer were also forecast if rpm was abolished. In 1964 a virtual *coup de grâce* was delivered in the form of the Resale Prices Act. Individual rpm was initially declared void and unlawful. Classes of goods to which rpm applied were made registrable and actionable before the Restrictive Practices Court. Certain suitable gateways were devised, as follows. If individual rpm was dropped:

(a) the quality of the goods available for sale, or the varieties of the goods so available, would be substantially reduced to the detriment of the public as consumers or users of those goods; or
(b) the number of establishments in which the goods are sold by retail would be substantially reduced to the detriment of the public as such consumers or users; or
(c) the prices at which the goods are sold by retail would in general and in the long run be increased to the detriment of the public as such consumers or users; or
(d) the goods would be sold by retail under conditions likely to cause danger to health in consequence of their mis-use by the public as such consumers or users; or
(e) any necessary services actually provided in connection with or after the sale of the goods by retail would cease to be so provided or would be substantially reduced to the detriment of the public as such consumers or users.

The reader will note that in all cases the interests of consumers are paramount. This point was emphasized in the *Chocolate and Sugar Confectionery* case.[32] Megaw J. pointed out that resale price maintenance could not be upheld because of the possibility that hardship would be experienced by manufacturers or dealers if it was abolished. The Court had to confine itself to effects on consumers. If however effects on suppliers and dealers also had adverse consequences for consumers then the Court would give considerations to those effects. The reader should also note that the tailpiece balancing process, introduced in 1956, was also employed in the 1964 Act.

In some trades, such as groceries, rpm had already largely broken down. With few exceptions grocery manufacturers had ceased to take action against retail price cutting. Out of just over 150 classes of goods originally registered only three were proceeded with as far as a Court hearing. The confectionery and branded footwear manufacturers fought and lost. The pharmaceutical industry however won. In respect of both ethicals (obtainable on prescription from a doctor) and proprietary medicines (advertised and purchased at chemist outlets) the practice was approved. Pharmaceuticals and books (the Net Book Agreement was upheld under the 1956 Act) are the only two products where individual rpm is now legal. The *recommendation* of retail prices is of course still permitted. However it should be noted that under the provisions of the Price Commission Act 1977 if the Commission, having been asked to examine a sector of commerce by the Secretary of State for Prices and Consumer Protection, finds that recommended prices are spurious the Secretary of State can ban their use in that sector or ban their use by retailers in double pricing.

It should also be noted that where rpm has not been expressly approved it is unlawful for suppliers to employ back-door measures in order to maintain resale prices. For example, it is unlawful for a supplier to withhold supplies from a dealer or to discriminate against him because the dealer has been or is likely to cut prices. From time to time the DGFT has had to warn suppliers of these points, and if necessary he or individuals can enter into civil proceedings in order to obtain the appropriate relief. Having said that, it should be added that the 1964 Act made it lawful for supplies to be withheld if the supplier had reasonable cause to believe that in the previous twelve months the dealer had been using the goods (or similar ones) as loss leaders. The act of loss leading was defined as resale not for the purpose of making a profit but either (a) for attracting customers likely to purchase other goods or (b) for advertising the business of the dealer. The legal provisions relating to rpm have more recently been consolidated in the Resale Prices Act 1976.

MONOPOLY

By taking over the restrictive practice element the 1956 Act left the Monopolies Commission (currently referred to as the Monopolies and Mergers Commission (MMC)) with the task of dealing with the unitary 'monopolist'. It will be recollected that such a firm was one that controlled a third or more of the supply of goods (or the application of a process to goods) in the UK market (or a substantial part thereof). The investigation of monopoly situations in the supply of exports was a part of its role, and the MMC still discharges that task. We have also seen that the investigation of monopoly situations in services was given to the Commission as a result of the Monopolies and Mergers Act 1965 but that following the Fair Trading Act 1973 its service remit was whittled down to professional services. In the 1973 Act the old monopoly criterion of one-third was reduced to 25 per cent.

We should also note that the 1948 Act applied where two or more firms controlling the requisite monopoly supply restricted competition *with or without* an agreement. The task of looking at agreements was, as we have seen, shed in 1956, but the possibility that firms might indulge in various forms of parallel action without the existence of the kind of agreements covered by the 1956 Act has continued to be a Commission concern. Obviously in oligopoly situations prices may move in line by virtue of devices such as price leadership. Under the 1973 Act this is referred to as a complex monopoly situation.

The MMC still retains the power to look at specific forms of practice and has done so on several occasions. Some of these have been of direct concern to consumers as, for example, in the case of the reports on the public interest consequences of recommended prices, refusal to supply, professional services and parallel pricing.

The 1973 Act also indicated a greater concern for the consumer interest. This is revealed in the new public interest guidelines which now specifically emphasize the role of competition and the importance of promoting the interests of consumers. The new guidelines are as follows:

[Public interest guidelines under the 1973 Act (Section 84)]
 . . . the Commission shall take into account all matters which appear to them in the particular circumstances to be relevant and, among other things, shall have regard to the desirability
 (a) of maintaining and promoting effective competition between persons supplying goods and services in the United Kingdom;

(b) of promoting the interests of consumers, purchasers, and other users of goods and services in the United Kingdom in respect of the prices charged for them and in respect of their quality and the variety of goods and services supplied;
(c) of promoting, through competition, the reduction of costs and the development and use of new techniques and new products, and of facilitating the entry of new competitors into existing markets;
(d) of maintaining and promoting the balanced distribution of industry and employment in the United Kingdom; and
(e) of maintaining and promoting competitive activity in markets outside the United Kingdom on the part of producers of goods, and of suppliers of goods and services, in the United Kingdom.

The 1973 Act is also important because of the change it brought about in respect of the actual making of references. Under the 1948 Act this function was firmly placed in the hands of the Board of Trade. This was unfortunate because it involved a possible conflict between the Board's role as a sponsor of industries (it was also obviously open to pressure from other ministries who were sponsors) and its role as the body responsible for the policing of monopoly. Under the 1973 Act the DGFT can make monopoly references independently of ministers. This independence which he and his office enjoy arguably is a thoroughly welcome development.

In this area of policy, as in the case of restrictive practices, the role of the individual consumer is very limited. Now, as under the original Act, it is possible for the ordinary citizen to make suggestions as to the industries that ought to be referred and such suggestions are listed in the annual reports of the OFT. The OFT has in fact evolved a screening process in order to sift out possible candidates for reference. Three sets of criteria are applied — conduct indicators, performance indicators and information concerning previous investigations. The conduct indicators include (a) data on the number of consumer and trade complaints made to the Office; (b) evidence or allegations of price leadership or price parallelism; (c) the advertising-to-sales ratio in those industries employing advertising; (d) data on takeovers, etc. The performance indicators relate to the return on capital (as a sign of the exercise of market power) and the degree to which the industry seems to contribute to inflation. The previous investigation criterion is designed to highlight the fact that if an investigation has taken place recently yet another one would be ruled out in the absence of strong evidence of major changes in conduct or performance. The results derived from these criteria help to identify relatively broad product groupings which can then be broken down into smaller product markets for a closer look. Possible candidates may then emerge although a reference would still await upon interdepartmental discussions.

It is important to re-emphasize that the MMC machinery under the 1973 Act is still based on a case-by-case pragmatic approach. Monopoly is not presumed to be against the public interest in the way that restrictive practices are: rather, when faced with a reference it is the task of the MMC to say whether what it has found operates, or may be expected to operate, against the public interest. The slant is important; i.e., monopoly exists and the MMC has to say whether it has adverse consequences – the legislation has never put the matter the other way round, i.e. that a monopoly exists and to justify its continuance it must have proved to be positively beneficial.

If the MMC discovers that there are adverse public interest consequences it can in its recommendations adopt either a structural or a regulatory approach. The first approach would, as the phrase suggests, involve changing the structure of the industry. The mischiefs uncovered might be deemed to be an inescapable consequence of a highly concentrated structure. A policy of breaking the monopoly up into a series of competing firms, or at least of forbidding any further concentration via merger, could theoretically be adopted. The second approach would leave the structure alone and would seek to restrain the consequent conduct of the firm in question. Thus if a firm had the power to raise prices unduly and did in fact do so, the Commission could suggest the imposition of price controls. The Commission has shown a marked preference for the regulatory approach. In this remedial context we should note that the Monopolies and Mergers Act 1965 provided significant powers of the kind we have just discussed.

How then does the Commission go about its investigatory role? We noted earlier that the first task of the Commission is to verify that a monopoly position does exist. If it does then it can proceed to the full investigation. It is then required to report in whose favour the monopoly exists – that is, to say which firm or group enjoys the benefit of the monopoly position. Under the 1948 Act the next task was to report what were the 'things done' by virtue of, or to maintain, the monopoly. This has been redrafted and the MMC is now required to report what steps – i.e. uncompetitive practices, etc. – are taken to exploit or preserve the monopoly. Then the MMC is required to report any act or omission attributable to the monopoly. This is new. Finally, it has to come to a conclusion as to the effect on the public interest and to advocate remedies if any are called for.

A report usually begins with a review of the companies involved and their historical development. This is quite crucial since it throws light on how the monopoly came about. Was it the result of sheer competitive and innovative superiority or was it due to takeovers and to predatory and exclusionary practices? Obviously a review of the current pricing structure helps to highlight possible ongoing discriminatory and exclusionary factors. The Commission is also concerned about productive efficiency and about the adequacy of management and the organizational structure. The record of technological progress is clearly highly relevant. The report usually includes crucial data on the rate of return on capital as compared with industry generally.

In some instances the MMC has found monopolies not to be against the public interest – indeed, to be efficient and highly progressive. In flat glass[33] Pilkington, with over 90 per cent of the market, had some remarkable technological achievements to its credit which major producers in the rest of the world were adopting. Nor did the MMC think that Pilkington had exploited its market position by extracting high profits. A similar finding of progressiveness was made in the case of the cigarette filter rod inquiry,[34] and the rate of return of 50 per cent on capital was regarded as a reasonable reward for innovatory skill. In the investigation of cigarette making machinery,[35] Molins was found to have a market share of getting on for 60 per cent of the market but this was due not to monopolizing behaviour but to the fact that it was so much better at its job than its rivals.

In other reports however monopolists have been found to have abused their position by making unduly high profits. A good example is the report on chlorodiazepoxide and diazepam.[36] In this instance Roche Products was estimated to be making 70 per cent on its capital. The Commission, adopting a regulatory stance, recommended price reductions of between 25 and 40 per cent. It also considered that the company should repay some of its excess profits. In the breakfast foods report[37] the Commission did not go quite so far. It noted that the return on capital had been as high as 70 per cent but had declined to 37 per cent. A reduction was not recommended. Instead the MMC, noting that the return was not excessive, but might become so, recommended that profits be kept under review and that government approval should be given before the price of breakfast cereals was

COMPETITION POLICY – THE DOMESTIC MARKET   93

increased. We shall see in the next chapter that this kind of situation is clearly one to which the Price Commission, under the 1977 Price Code, addresses itself and in that respect it and the MMC are complementary. The Commission was concerned about the heavy level of advertising and sales promotion expenditure that it encountered in the detergents industry.[38] Here the MMC was dealing with a duopolistic structure and economic analysis suggests that in such circumstances firms may choose to compete not on price but by product differentiation heavily backed up by advertising. It would have been possible to break up the detergents industry into a series of smaller enterprises but the Commission once again preferred regulation. It recommended reductions in wholesale selling price and in selling expenses. It is perhaps worth noting that recently excessive selling expenses have also been attracting the attention of the Price Commission. This was the case in the recent report on sanitary products.[39]

The Commission has been particularly critical of predatory price discrimination designed to eliminate competitors. Cases of this kind have not been frequent. One of the best examples was afforded by British Oxygen,[40] which indulged in local price cutting to dislodge a new entrant. However in the case of Lucas, who had supplied ignition coils to car manufacturers at a loss for many years in order to discourage them from buying from A.C. Delco, the Commission did not condemn the practice.[41]

Other forms of practice designed to exclude entrants stand little chance of escaping unscathed. The Commission has been very consistent indeed in attacking such arrangements. This it did in respect of the exclusive dealing arrangements in wallpaper[42] and oxygen,[43] solus ties in the case of the major oil companies (together with their vertical integration forward in the form of petrol station ownership)[44] covenants binding competitors not to compete in asbestos products[45] and pricing arrangements which put new entrants at a disadvantage (the Rank Xerox Group Pricing Plan).[46]

MERGERS

Mergers were not brought within the ambit of antitrust control until 1965 when the Monopolies and Mergers Act was added to the statute book. The current merger control provisions are to be found in the

Fair Trading Act 1973, which reduced the market share from one-third to a quarter (as in the case of monopolies) and introduced new public interest criteria (as for monopolies).

The 1965 Act was a relatively low-key affair. Although there were grounds for regarding mergers as a possible loophole, alongside information agreements, in the attack on restrictive practices, in fact the ministerial speeches at the time that the Bill was going through Parliament showed no real awareness of this point. Nor was there any specific reference to the consumer dimension. The 1965 Act was indeed introduced during a period when opinion was by no means opposed to mergers. The then President of the Board of Trade, and for that matter his successors in both the main parties, tended to regard mergers as broadly beneficial. At that time only a minority were such as to be likely to give rise to adverse effects on the public interest. Reflecting this mood was the passage in the following year of legislation that created the Industrial Reorganization Corporation (IRC). This body was conceived as a device for restructuring British industry by means of mergers. In 1970 the Conservative government abolished it. Although the gradual strengthening of antitrust policy has been a matter on which the main parties have been united, devices such as the IRC have been exceptions to this accord.

The current provisions apply to horizontal, vertical and conglomerate mergers affecting the supply of goods or services. One of the parties to the merger must be a UK enterprise. A merger is caught if one of two conditions exist: (a) the parties to the merger control a quarter or more of the supply of goods or services of any description in the UK, or a substantial part thereof; (b) the value of assets taken over exceeds £5 million. The first criterion is relevant in horizontal merger cases; the second brings vertical and conglomerate amalgamations within the net.

In defining mergers the 1973 Act refers to situations where one or more undertakings cease to be distinct enterprises. This obviously includes cases where one company acquires total control of another. But the matter does not end here. The Act also bites where one company acquires less than full control, i.e. more than 51 per cent but less than 100 per cent of the voting stock. But it also applies in situations where a controlling interest does not exist (i.e. the holding is less than 51 per cent) but where none the less the company holding such an interest controls the other company or can materially influence its policy.

The process of reference to the Monopolies and Mergers Commission exhibits a significant contrast to that which applies in respect of monopolies. Reflecting the continuing political sensitivity of merger policy, the DGFT does not have the power to refer. Instead this is vested in the Secretary of State for Prices and Consumer Protection. In Chapter 11 we shall discuss this less-than-happy arrangement. The necessarily rapid process of screening mergers for possible reference is carried out by an Interdepartmental Mergers Panel of which the DGFT is chairman. Recommendations are made to the Secretary of State who may choose not to accept them. When mergers are referred to the Commission they may be stayed pending a report. Following an adverse recommendation remedial action lies with the Secretary of State. He may forbid mergers that have not been consummated. If already consummated he may order a divestiture or may impose controls on such things as prices charged.

When mergers are referred the method of assessment adopted is the same as that which applies in the case of monopolies. The law (as opposed to ministerial pronouncements) neither approves nor disapproves of them. Rather we once more encounter a pragmatic, case-by-case, approach. At the end of its investigation, with the public interest criteria in mind, the Commission has to decide whether the merger operates, or may be expected to operate, against the public interest. This involves a calculation of costs and benefits. On the one hand the Commission has to try to determine the competitive significance of the merger. For example, in the case of a horizontal merger, what will be the effect of a reduction in the number of firms? This obviously involves a consideration of what is the relevant market.[47] The effects on competition may also involve taking into account the effects of potential competition and countervailing power.[48] An adverse impact on efficiency is obviously important. In some reports the Commission has seen a merger as being likely to have a deleterious effect on an existing high-quality management.[49] In one case the managers quite explicitly indicate that if taken over they would leave. In another the Commission concluded that the morale of management would fall and some managers might leave — they were very specific and would be difficult to replace. On the other hand, mergers may give rise to large-scale economies or prompt a more effective and vigorous research and development effort. Perhaps a merger will lead to an injection of better management or will at least stimulate the existing management.[50] The effect on the balance of payments and on the regional distribution of economic activity are other dimensions where pros and cons may have to be assessed.

Where costs exceed the benefits the Commission will recommend against. Such would be the case if competition was likely to be adversely affected and gains in efficiency, etc., were small or non-existent.[51] If there were gains in, for example, balance of payments terms but the Commission was not unduly disturbed about the effect on competition the merger would probably be approved.[52] If, however, a merger was thought not to give rise to adverse effects on, say, competition and also had no real advantages to offer the public it would be allowed to proceed. We say this because proof of positive public interest benefit is not the test for acceptability. Rather, the law allows mergers to proceed unless they adversely affect the public interest.

5 Market Interventions

INTRODUCTION

So far our view of consumer protection has been confined to those laws that are designed to create and maintain competition. Competition was assumed to be a process that keeps costs and prices low – a point that successive price regulatory bodies such as the National Board for Prices and Incomes and, more recently, the Price Commission have readily admitted. It is also a process in which the highest rewards go to those producers who strive most successfully to produce existing goods, and to devise new ones whose design and performance best meet individual needs. Now we have to recognize that competition, beneficial though it is, has not been deemed a sufficient means of protection.

The Problem of Inflation

In the first place the state has from time to time decided that price determination should not be left to free market forces. That is to say, the control of the general price level and specific prices should not depend merely on a policy that consists of manipulating aggregate demand and seeking to create conditions of free competition. Rather, the government has chosen to step into the arena of price formation with a view to exercising a closer influence and control. This intervention may have been *indirect* – as for example when policy has been designed to counteract the pressure for increased incomes. As we noted in Chapter 1, increased incomes accompanied by less than proportionate increases in productivity tend, other things being equal,[1] to force up costs of production with the result that profit margins are squeezed. Businessmen then seek to restore their margins by raising prices – it is generally assumed that under conditions of market dominance and oligopoly this may not be difficult, although the degree to which it occurs will depend upon the buoyancy of the market.[2]

If the state introduces an incomes policy it seems to suggest that it has made one of three judgments as to the cause of inflation (although some combination of the three is possible). One would be that it is not the pressure of excess demand but the pushfulness (for increased incomes) of trade unions that is causing the upward movement of costs and prices. Trade unions exert their monopoly power and back it up with a willingness to strike.

The second is that it is the pressure of excess demand for goods that is the villain of the piece, in that it in turn generates an excess derived demand for labour. This causes businessmen to compete for labour by raising wages. Costs then rise and so do prices. This is essentially a demand-pull rather than, as in the first case, a cost-push explanation. The obvious retort to the second line of argument is to say that if this is the case then surely the answer lies in deflating demand. However, perhaps with the Phillips curve[3] in mind, the reply might be that the necessary degree of deflation of demand, and consequent unemployment, might, given the attachment to the desirability of maintaining high employment, be felt to be socially and politically unacceptable. It should also be added that such a policy is flying in the face of market forces in that the policy is designed to hold wages below the level to which they would rise in free-market conditions. Whereas in the trade union push situation the state is only (possibly a word of understatement) taking on the unions, in the demand-pull case it is taking on the unions, who see increases in prospect, and also the employers, who would be willing to offer them.

The third judgment might be that an incomes policy will help to dampen inflationary expectations. If significant inflation comes to be regarded as a normal state of affairs it tends to aggravate the problem of excessive wage claims. Workers realize that any increases in wages will be nullified by a subsequent rise in prices. They therefore add something extra to their wage claims in order to compensate for the expected rise in prices. If this starts to happen inflation will begin to escalate. Under such circumstances an incomes policy may be seen as a way of inducing wage-earners to take the view that inflation is going to be kept under control, thus preventing the perverse effect of expectations. The imposition of price controls would appear to be potentially an even more persuasive expectational device and this probably explains why on some occasions governments have chosen to operate wage and price controls simultaneously. The mixing of policies conveniently leads us on to another point, namely that, and as a modification of what we said earlier, it would be a mistake to imagine that governments, in seeking to control inflation, have put all their money on income or income and price controls. In practice they have usually adopted a policy-mix. Income, and possibly price, controls have been conjoined with deflationary demand policies (including control of the money supply). On occasions, as we shall see, governments have also resorted to subsidies; tax cuts have also been offered in the hope that wage claims would to that extent be abated. This policy-mix approach may reflect the judgment that there are several causes operating at one and the same time, although we cannot rule out the possibility that it may reflect an underlying uncertainty as to what is the true cause of rising prices.

Alternatively, as we have just noted, the intervention may also be *direct* as when controls have been placed on price increases and various products have been subsidized. The commitment to controlling prices may vary. In some instances, for example in the 1973–77 Price Code, which we discuss below, the attack on prices was across the board and basic to the assault on inflation. In other cases the control of prices has been in some degree cosmetic. Price controls have been introduced so as to induce trade unions to accept limitations on their right to bargain freely. In other words, social justice has required that profits and dividends as well as wages and salaries should bear, or appear to bear, some of the burden.

This then brings us to the question of the extent to which policies to control inflation are in fact forms of consumer protection and the extent to which they are motivated by that consideration. We have to bear in mind the possibility that consumers may in fact be protected. For example, prices may be rising but so may incomes. Indeed, in the first two cases we have just considered the increase of costs and prices derives from an increase in wages. This being so it is not immediately obvious why any protection is needed since real wages – i.e. the purchasing power of money wages – may not be falling.

There is of course an obvious riposte that we can enter at this point. Inflation is a problem to the extent that it is unanticipated. For example, creditors can be adversely affected by inflation. X may be willing to lend money at 10 per cent per annum, assuming mistakenly that prices will be stable. Suppose however that they rise by 10 per cent per annum: then our creditor ends up with a money rate of interest that is indeed 10 per cent but a real rate of interest that is zero. That is to say he really requires £10 to reward him for parting with his liquidity and another £10 to restore the purchasing power of his money at the end of the year. If, of course, our creditor had known that inflation was going to occur he could have protected himself by demanding a commensurately higher money rate of interest. If prices rose by 20 per cent our creditor would have ended up with a negative real rate of interest. It needs no great elaboration on our part also to appreciate that in inflationary circumstances the debtor correspondingly gains – we have therefore a sectional redistribution of income. It is perhaps worth mentioning at this point that this factor has undoubtedly been important in recent years when retail prices have been rising at 25 per cent or more per annum but interest rates have not risen to anything like this level. We are of course also thinking in pre-tax terms. There is indeed a certain irony in all this when it is recognized that some economists would argue that the increase in the supply of money is the main if not the sole cause of inflation and all would agree that no sustained inflation can occur *without* an increase in the supply. Given that the state controls the money supply, it can be argued that it has connived in the inflation, yet some of its creatures, e.g. the Post Office, have offered miserably low rates of interest which were far below the rate of inflation.

In explaining the problem of inflation we should add that it is not just the failure to anticipate it but the inability to compensate for it that is important. Here we are thinking about people living on fixed incomes – not all pensions are index-linked! We are also drawing attention to the fact that not all those in employment have the advantage of strong trade unions who can use their industrial muscle to secure compensating increase in incomes. Those who do not have a trade union or have a weak one may therefore suffer. It should also be noted that inflation does not mean that in real terms some people can keep pace while others cannot. To the extent that the size of the national cake is given, if some get less others must get more. Some may therefore be said to have a vested interest in inflation.[4]

All this suggests that an anti-inflation policy is a form of consumer protection – at least for some. But we should note that the protection of the consuming interest is not the only reason for attacking inflation. In the postwar period a major motive has undoubtedly been a desire to maintain the competitiveness of our exports and thus to protect the balance of payments. Also, inflation may have a deleterious effect on economic growth by penalizing saving and thus starving the economy of capital funds for expansion.

Guaranteeing Standards and Preventing Injury

The second reason for market interventions is concerned with the fact that an uncontrolled system of competition may lead (a) to the production of goods that are either adulterated or that the consumer finds it difficult to appraise in terms of quality and performance, or (b) to the production of goods that give rise to injury. Our initial examples will relate to these two aspects although in the treatment that comes later we shall see that various forms of control, some statutory, have also been introduced in other areas including professional, financial and other services.

When in the 1860s and 1870s some of the first consumer protection Acts were introduced (we shall discuss these below), the main emphasis was upon adulteration which was then rife. The addition of water to milk and to beer was commonplace. Exhausted tea leaves were added to fresh tea, the exhausted leaves being glazed with black lead. Coffee had roast vegetable material, such as acorns, added to it. Bread was bulked up by inclusion of mashed potato and alum was added as a bleach. Mustard was adulterated by the addition of wheat flour, pea flour and much else. Sand was added to sugar. These are just a few examples chosen at random.[5]

Today such gross adulteration is no longer a problem, although it is interesting to note that the current legislation (Food and Drugs Act 1955) makes the adulteration of milk a specific offence (see Section 32). There are however products that by their very nature the consumer finds difficult to appraise in terms of quality. This is particularly true of foods although as we shall see later other products also exhibit this characteristic. For example, how much meat is there in meat pies, sausages and sausage rolls? How much fish is there in fish paste? How much fruit in preserves? In cases such as these the state has laid down standards that prescribe minimum contents. Such activities are of course to be distinguished from labelling, which does not of itself prescribe the quantity of ingredients to be incorporated but merely tells the prospective consumer what they are. It should perhaps be added that, apart from protecting the consumer, the objective of such activities (and this is a point of some generality) is to prevent unfair competition whereby those who produce sub-standard goods gain at the expense of those who try to produce better quality goods. On the other hand, desirable as such standards may be, they also can be disadvantageous to the public interest. If the regulations are tightly drawn and slow to change they may preclude advantageous substitution of ingredients by the manufacturer. For example, if an ingredient rises in price the manufacturer may be able to employ a cheaper substitute which is perfectly adequate, but the regulations may prevent him from benefiting the consumer in this way.

Protection from injury is a major reason why a system of uncontrolled competition cannot be tolerated. In the first place the pressure of competition will force manufacturers to seek ways of reducing costs. But some forms of economy will be undesirable. This would be so if those engaged in the production, transport, storage and sale of foodstuffs and in catering sought to economize on the maintenance of hygienic conditions. The not infrequent reports of food poisoning emphasize this ever-present danger. Those who wish to be reminded of the possible insanitary conditions of a free-enterprise food industry should read Upton Sinclair's *The Jungle*, which provides a horrifying picture of conditions in the Chicago meat-packing industry in the early years of this century.

Considerable danger could arise from the uncontrolled incorporation of additives and contaminants in food. Additives are substances added to food for purposes other than nutrition. There has in fact been an unparallelled rise in the use of additives in recent years, partly to meet the needs of modern technology and partly because of consumer pressure for novelty, improved quality, better appearance and convenience in preparation. There are several classes of additive. Preservatives are designed to prevent biological deterioration. For example, the nitrites and nitrates used in curing ham help to produce the popular pink colour but also have the more important function of preventing the development of *clostridium botulinum*.[6] (The unhappy fatal effects of the latter were illustrated by the poisoned salmon episode in the summer of 1978.) Colourants are also widely used; for example, chlorine dioxide and benzoyl peroxide are agents that are used to make bread white. Anti-oxydants, such as butylated hydroxyanisole, are incorporated in oils and fats to prevent them becoming rancid. Emulsifiers, such as inert cellulose, are added to some foods in order to prevent the separation of the liquid contents. In addition there are various solvents, flavourings and artificial sweetening agents. It is however necessary to recognize that, valuable as these substances are, they may be found to have harmful effects. The banning of the sweetening agent cyclamate on the grounds that it was a carcinogen is an apt example.[7] The use of the flour treatment agent agene (nitrogen trichloride) introduced in 1923 was abandoned in 1946 when it was found that dogs fed with agenized flour developed disturbances of the central nervous system.[8] In 1975 a food colourant orange RN was banned because of its hepatoxic potential demonstrated in laboratory animals.[9] The idea that the consumer can in such circumstances protect himself (*caveat emptor*) is wholly unrealistic.

In addition to additives there are contaminants. Some, such as a lead and mercury, can be allowed in limited amounts. There are also what are called unintentional contaminants, which may creep into food as residues left in crops and animals as a result of the application of pesticides and veterinary medication. Clearly these need to be controlled.

Injury may also arise in connection with drugs and cosmetics. There have been a number of disturbing instances of tragedies due to drugs, notably the deaths caused in 1937 in the US by the sulfa-based drug Elixir Sulfanilide, the malformation of babies caused by Thalidomide and the alleged effect of Chloromycetin in causing aplastic anaemia. In connection with cosmetics we can instance the case of hexachlorophane which, incorporated in excessive amounts in talcum powder, caused a number of deaths in France in 1972. Here again the *caveat emptor* principle has little to offer.

This kind of problem is not confined to food and drugs. It also arises in connection with durables and consumer goods generally. The design of such goods may lead to danger in use. In earlier years this was, for example, the case with paraffin stoves, which sometimes had lethal consequences when they were accidentally knocked over. Such fire hazards may not have been the result of a search for economy but merely the product of bad design. So concerned was the Molony Committee on Consumer Protection[10] about this potential source of hazard to life and limb that it issued an interim report[11] on the subject.

PRICE CONTROL – DIRECT AND INDIRECT

The Emergence of Control

Price control has in the past been a feature of wartime but not peacetime economies. Wars are by their very nature inflationary. The high level of economic activity puts a large quantity of purchasing power in the hands of the population but the supply of goods does not match it since much of the output is not available to soak it up but is sent on to the battlefield. Although the free market could solve the problem, it would be at the expense of a sizeable, possibly massive, inflation. The need to maintain morale, particularly among low-income groups, requires that prices be kept low. As a result war economies are usually characterized by price controls and, since at the sub-equilibrium price uncontrolled demand would exceed supply, supplies are rationed. The redundant purchasing power is siphoned off by taxation, exhortations to save, etc. But we would stress that such price control has been a *temporary* phenomenon. As we noted in Chapter 1, the postwar Labour Government eventually initiated a bonfire of controls and the succeeding Conservative Government finished the process off. A kind of free-market philosophy then took the stage. The emphasis on controlling the price level lay in the use of monetary policy. With some delay the force of competition was progressively introduced – we noted its evolution in Chapter 4. Incomes policy was also in abeyance. The short-lived wages freeze of 1948–49 was not repeated.

However, as we shall see this was not to be a permanent state of affairs. The turning point was the early sixties. Increasingly thereafter indirect control over prices, in other words the concept of incomes policy, began to take on the appearance of a permanent feature of economic policy – even though political parties might from time to time genuinely think that they could get along without such a device or might find it convenient to reject it for short-term electoral purposes. Price control also began to make a comeback, although it is still too early to make a firm judgment as to whether that policy, in any really thoroughgoing fashion, is likely to be a more or less permanent feature of the economic landscape.

The change in thinking about policy can be pinned down to 1961. The Conservative Government had earlier created the Council on Productivity, Prices and Incomes as an advisory body. In the early reports there was no sign that the so-called 'three wise men' had any attachment to incomes policy, but in the fourth report, in 1961, perhaps reflecting a somewhat changed membership, it was apparent that the Council had come round to the view that some effort should be made to relate the rise of incomes to changes in overall productivity, for

> hitherto the United Kingdom has chiefly depended on a rise in the flow of spending for stimulation of its growth. So long as that is so, restraints on spending will always disappoint the expectation on

which growth depends . . . today that rise [i.e. in money incomes] has a capacity for self-propulsion which restraint of demand by itself seems unlikely to hold back without creating heavy unemployment.[12]

More or less simultaneously two external reports, one for the Organization for European Economic Cooperation[13] and one for the Bank of International Settlements,[14] laid emphasis on the role of wages in inflation. The way was being paved for an incomes policy.

At this point we should point out that an incomes policy involves the fixing of a norm increase. If cost stability across the board is to be achieved the norm has to be set at the level of the average increase in productivity. The basic theory then runs as follows.[15] In some industries productivity gains may exceed the average, in which case costs will fall (assuming the prices of imported raw materials, etc., remain stable). Competition should ensure that prices fall commensurately, although this will depend on keeping a tight rein on demand.[16] On the other hand some sectors will generate little or no productivity increase but, in so far as they receive the norm increase, their costs and thus their prices will tend to rise. The protagonists of incomes policy point out that these latter price increases will be compensated for by the former price decreases, thus leaving the overall price level stable.

During the sixties policy had a twofold aspect. Attempts were made to increase production and productivity. Hence the National Economic Development Council (NEDC) – a Conservative creation – and the Economic Development Committees ('Little Neddies'). The NEDC went on to produce a growth plan for the period 1961–66. The subsequent Labour administration also produced a National Plan and a new ministry, the Department of Economic Affairs, to be concerned with planning for faster growth. The expectations upon which the plan was based were quickly undermined by severe deflationary policies in 1966 and the new Department ultimately disappeared.

The other aspect of policy was the attempt to keep incomes in line with whatever growth emerged. The Conservatives made only limited headway here. They introduced a 'pay pause' in the public sector (it also covered Wages Council occupations) in July 1961. This ended in March 1962. Just prior to this they had published a White Paper, *Incomes Policy: The Next Step*,[17] which proposed that annual pay increases should be limited to the likely annual expansion in productivity which was put at 2–2½ per cent. In the meantime the NEDC had been created and in the light of the assumptions in its programme of growth 1961–66 it persuaded the government that it would be possible to raise the figure to 3–3½ per cent. The government adopted this as its 'guiding light' which, as the phrase implies, was merely for guidance. The government followed this up by creating the National Incomes Commission (NIC), an independent body 'to provide impartial and authoritative advice' on the matter of incomes. The government could refer pay claims and settlements to it for consideration – it did not deal with particular increases in prices or profits. The government took no powers to enforce the findings of the NIC. It will be apparent that at this point incomes policy was very much a kid gloves affair. In fact the NIC had no great impact. In the words of one commentator, 'Its establishment was opposed by the TUC and it received no co-operation from any trade union at any time.'[18]

Incomes Policy 1965–70

The return of a Labour government saw the emergence of incomes policy as a central feature of economic policy. In truth, the policy was described as a *prices* and incomes policy, and indeed the decision of the trade unions to sign in December 1964 the *Joint Declaration of Intent on Productivity, Prices and Incomes* in concert with the government and employers' organizations would not have been possible if this deference to social justice had not been evident. The policy was therefore a step on the road to direct control of prices.

The policy prescribed a norm for annual wage and salary increases of 3–3½ per cent.[19] Exceptional circumstances were defined where an increase above this norm could be allowed. They were as follows: where employees made a direct contribution to increasing productivity; where it was essential in the national interest to secure a redistribution of manpower; where there was a general recognition that pay had fallen too low to maintain a reasonable standard of living; where there was widespread recognition that pay had fallen seriously out of line with that given for similar work and it was in the national interest that it be improved. The policy therefore envisaged some flexibility.

The price increase criteria were less clearly defined – there was no norm. There was an overriding criterion that pricing should have the aim of ensuring that the general level of prices in the economy should remain stable. Enterprises were expected not to increase prices except where (a) output per employee could not be increased sufficiently to allow for the wage or salary increases permitted under the incomes criteria or (b) there were unavoidable increases in non-labour costs (e.g. raw materials, power) or capital costs. In both these cases there was the further proviso that price increases were allowed only if no offsetting reduction was possible in, for example, the return sought on investment. The other ground for a price increase was that an enterprise was, because of its lack of profits, unable to raise (internally or externally) the capital needed to meet home or overseas demand, having made every effort to reduce costs.

Enterprises were required to reduce prices in the opposite circumstances or where profits were excessive because of the existence of market power. These price criteria were not significantly changed throughout the life of the policy, whereas the wage and salary criteria were significantly changed in the various phases.

In the initial phase (1965–66) the policy was voluntary in character although this did not preclude ministerial persuasion. It was hoped that the publicity given to the policy, and the fact that the two sides of industry had given their assent to it, would have the desired influence on collective bargaining and pricing decisions. However, in order to strengthen the policy an independent body, the National Board for Prices and Incomes (NBPI), was established.[20] In 1965 it was created as a Royal Commission; in 1966 it was reconstituted on a statutory basis. Its task was to examine particular cases of price or wage and salary increases referred to it by government in order to advise whether they were in accord with the national interest. The Board also went on later to study various factors that affected renumeration and could increase efficiency, such as payment by results systems, job evaluation and productivity agreements.[21] It should also be mentioned that at the end of 1965 an early warning system[22] was introduced, whereby the government was notified in advance of nearly all important wage and price increases. This was in order to give the government time to consider such increases before they were put into effect and if necessary to have the benefit of a reference to the NBPI. This was operated on a voluntary basis by the TUC and CBI although the government intimated its intention to seek statutory powers.

It should also be emphasized that in the voluntary phase, and indeed when powers of wage and price and control were taken, the

NBPI was not itself responsible for implementing policy. Any persuading or controlling was left to government departments.

The policy was a failure in that actual wage increases were about twice the norm. In the first half of 1966 the British economy got into difficulties, notably with the balance of payments. As a result in July 1966 severe deflationary measures were introduced and in addition under the Prices and Incomes Act 1966 a freeze on prices and incomes was announced. Peacetime statutory control had emerged.[23] The Act provided, for example, that a trade union or person who took action (including strike action) with a view to compelling, inducing or influencing an employer to contravene regulations was himself liable to legal action. During the first six months (the period of standstill) a zero norm was imposed on wages, salaries and dividends. The exception criteria for increases above the norm (see above) were suspended. There were also severe limits on price increases. During the second six months (the period of severe restraint)[24] the zero norm for wages, salaries and dividends was retained but for pay certain exceptions were restored and slightly less severe restrictions were placed on prices.

In the third period (July 1967–March 1968) the Prices and Incomes Act 1967 introduced 'the period of moderation'.[25] The pay norm was zero but the exception criteria were restored. The policy at this stage, and later, has been described as voluntary but the government had the power to delay increases. It could impose a thirty-day standstill while it examined a proposed pay or price increase. If it referred the increase to the NBPI a further delay of three months could be imposed. If the NBPI reported adversely yet a further three-month delay could be required. This made for a maximum possible delay of seven months.

In the fourth phase (March 1968 to the end of 1969), following the 1967 devaluation, a tight policy was called for.[26] The pay norm was zero and a ceiling of $3\frac{1}{2}$ per cent was placed on those wage and salary increases that met the exception criteria. However, certain increases were allowed above the ceiling for significant productivity and wage restructuring agreements, and for low-paid workers as part of a settlement that did not, taken as a whole, breach the ceiling.[27] The power to delay price and pay increases was extended by increasing the maximum possible delay to twelve months. The Prices and Incomes Act 1968 also gave the government a new power – it could now order price reductions (as opposed to delays of increases) on an NBPI recommendation.

The fifth and final phase began at the beginning of 1970 and it signalled a watering-down of policy. The norm was edged up to $2\frac{1}{2}$–$4\frac{1}{2}$ per cent and the maximum delay period was reduced to four months. Other powers lapsed.[28]

Incomes Policy 1970 onwards

A change of government followed. The Conservatives were vehemently opposed to wage controls. The NBPI was disbanded. Wage increases accelerated in 1970. In 1971 the government began to backtrack when it adopted the $n-1$ strategy in the public sector where settlements were running at 10 per cent per annum. The idea was that each settlement in the public sector should be 1 per cent less than the last. The policy had some success with the postmen who settled for 9 per cent. But early in 1972 the policy was broken by the miners who secured 25 per cent, and other unions demanded and received generous treatment. An attempt was made to secure a voluntary policy but it failed, and in November 1972 statutory wage controls were introduced. Since that date wages and salaries have been subject to incomes policies of one sort or another. Sometimes the policy has been statutory; on other occasions the government has been able to agree policies with the TUC (and CBI). There has been at least one occasion when the absence of a voluntary agreement would have led to the imposition of statutory controls. We shall not discuss the various phases at length but the basic details are summarized in Table 1. Dividend control has also been a feature of policy.

Not all the phases of policy described in Table 1 can really be regarded as incomes policies where pay controls were helping to hold down prices. The reverse seems to have been true of stage three of the Heath policy and of the Social Contract. In both cases domestic inflation was given a massive push by among other things an explosion of world commodity and oil prices, and the wage arrangements were not in their conception capable of holding the line.

The Price Code and Price Controls

A few months after the Conservatives had introduced statutory wage control they also introduced a Price Code which embodied a system of statutory price control.[29] In other words, instead of attacking inflation indirectly the Heath Government decided to make a direct assault on prices and in a more thoroughgoing way than ever before in peace-

TABLE 1 *Incomes Policy 1972–78*

Time span	Basic norm	Compulsory/voluntary	Other details
30 November 1972–31 March 1973 (Stage One)[a]	Freeze	Compulsory	Pay Board to operate the Pay Code. A twelve-month rule for increases.
1 April 1973–6 November 1973 (Stage Two)[b]	Limit £1 per week plus 4% with a maximum of £250 per annum per person	Compulsory	
7 November 1973–(Stage Three)[c]	Limit £2.25 per week	Compulsory	Settlements were to be spaced at twelve-month intervals. Special exceptions to the ceiling were allowed to help those engaged in low-paid or unpleasant or dangerous jobs. Threshold agreements (indexation) could be negotiated giving an extra 40p per week for every 1% rise in retail price index above 6% from October 1973 level. The miners demanded a large increase which was resisted and led to a strike and to three-day working in industry. This was followed by the Conservative loss of the election in February 1974.
February 1974–31 July 1975	Loose guideline that wage claims should be moderate – see across	Voluntary – the Social Contract	The Pay Board and statutory pay controls were abolished in July 1975.[d] The Social Contract had been negotiated between trade unions and Labour Party in 1973. Labour promised social and industrial policies to the taste of the unions while the unions promised to moderate wage claims. The TUC wage guidelines (June 1974) were as follows: (a) the objective of wages deals was to ensure that real incomes were maintained (pay should keep up with prices); (b) all major rises were to be twelve months apart; (c) exceptional treatment was to be allowed for productivity deals, pay structure reforms, awards for those earning less than £30 per week, the elimination of low pay for women and improvements in job security.
1 August 1975–31 July 1976 (Phase One)[e]	Limit of £6 per week. No increase for those over £8,500 per annum	Agreement with TUC – but see across	During the Social Contract wage increases escalated. The 1975–76 policy was designed to restore control by bringing wage rises down – hourly wage rates (February 1975) were up 29% on the level of 12 months earlier. Failure to agree on the wage guidelines would have led to their statutory imposition.

1 August 1976–31 July 1977 (Phase Two)[f]	Limit of 5% subject to not less than £2.50 per week for lower paid and a maximum of £4 per week	Agreement with TUC
1 August 1977–Autumn 1978 (Phase Three)[g]	Limit of 10% per annum	Voluntary. A looser arrangement, which was not agreed by the TUC. Exceptions were allowed to the 10% limit as follows: (a) those designed to deal with anomalies – the flat rate increases of previous policies had eroded differentials; (b) self-financing productivity deals. Sanctions applied to employers breaching the pay ceiling.
August 1978– (Phase Four)[h]	Limit of 5% per annum	Voluntary. Not agreed by TUC. Exceptions included productivity deals and reduction of hours (both of which had to be self-financing) and increases for low-paid workers. Pensions, sick pay and job security improvements were exempt from the limit. Conventions with respect to settlement dates had to be respected. Sanctions against employers were continued but were dropped in November 1978 following parliamentary disapproval. Later lower paid workers (i.e. those earning less than £70 per week) were allowed a choice between 5% or £3.50 per week increases.

[a] *A Programme for Controlling Inflation, The First Stage*, Cmnd 5125, HMSO, London, 1972; Counter-Inflation (Temporary Provisions) Act 1972.
[b] *The Programme for Controlling Inflation: The Second Stage*, Cmnd 5205, HMSO, London, 1973; Counter-Inflation Act 1973.
[c] *The Price and Pay Code for Stage 3*, Cmnd 5444, HMSO, London, 1973.
[d] Renumeration, Charges and Grants Act 1975.
[e] *The Attack on Inflation*, Cmnd 6151, HMSO, London, 1975.
[f] *The Attack on Inflation: The Second Year*, Cmnd 6507, HMSO, London, 1976.
[g] *The Attack on Inflation after 31st July 1977*, Cmnd 6882, HMSO, London, 1976.
[h] *Winning the Battle Against Inflation*, Cmnd 7293, HMSO, London, 1978.

time. The Price Code in one form or another has been a permanent feature of policy since 1973 and it continued to operate even when the government temporarily retreated from really active engagement in the pay arena.

The statutory basis of the Price Code and the independent Price Commission (the latter paralleled the Pay Board — see Table 1 above) was the Counter-Inflation Act 1973. We should emphasize that the Code changed over time. The 1973 Code was progressively modified and in 1977 a significantly different Code was introduced. The 1973 Code applied across the board — there was no question of it merely being invoked in cases of specific investigation. It was, particularly at first, a rigid system for determining what price increases were, and what price increases were not, acceptable. If increases did not conform to the Code the Price Commission could, and indeed did, reject them. For example, the Price Commission secured the cancellation, deferment or modification of over half the price increases notified to it in the first six months of operation.[30] As far as enforcement of this form of consumer protection is concerned it is all too apparent that it was (and still is) an official process — however, we shall see later that the consumer and his representatives have a role to play.

The 1973 Price Code had a threefold element. It will simplify matters if we concentrate on the rules relating to manufacturing and distribution. We will take manufacturing first. Price increases had to be pre-notified in certain cases and had to be based on the dual foundation of allowable cost increases and a reference profit margin. Each of these requires further elucidation.

Category I firms (manufacturers with annual sales exceeding £50 million) and Category II firms (those with annual sales between £5 million and £50 million) had to give the Commission twenty-eight days' notice of their intention to raise prices.[31] Category III firms (those with annual sales between £1 million and £5 million) did not have to pre-notify. Instead they had to keep records so that the Commission could see that they kept to the Code. There were a series of regional offices who made sample checks on such firms. Not all increases in costs could be passed on. Permitted price increases were limited to a demonstrated increase in allowable costs. The latter included items such as labour, materials, components, energy, rent and rates, interest and bought-in services. Allowable costs excluded selling costs, royalty and licence fees and at first even depreciation. It is however important to add that at the beginning only part of the labour cost increase was allowed. This gave rise to what was called the productivity deduction, and initially only 50 per cent of the increase in labour costs was allowed. The idea here was that the consumer should gain from the benefits of increased productivity. On top of allowable costs went a profit margin. The Code laid down that net profit margins should not rise above the reference level and this was the average of the best two trading years out of the five up to April 1973.

The arrangements for distribution were different. Distributors were divided into Category II (annual sales over £10 million) and Category III (annual sales between £0.25 million and £10 million). The larger firms were free to alter selling prices but their gross and net profit margins had to be kept at reference levels. Gross margins were not to exceed the margin made in the twelve-month period before April 1973. Net margins were determined in the same way as for manufacturers. Monitoring was done through quarterly returns. If the margins were found to be too high, distributors had to make price cuts and special offers to consumers to bring themselves back into line. The small class of distributor was bound by the same rules but from a control point of view was only obliged to maintain records.

Although the main role of the Commission was to check on the notified proposals for price increases, to vet the periodic returns concerning margins and to carry out sample checks among those who did not have to make any notification or return, the Secretary of State for Prices and Consumer Protection (SSPCP) could ask the Commission to collect information on costs, margins, prices and profits in specified sectors of industry and commerce. The Commission published over thirty such reports – their effect was however purely through publicity.

In its original conception the Code was a very rigid affair. The limitation on cost recovery (notably the productivity deduction) severely squeezed company profits and by 1974 had precipitated a company liquidity crisis.[32] The Code had therefore to be modified. The productivity deduction was reduced to 20 per cent and then in 1976 was abolished. Other changes included the introduction of profit safeguards, low profit relief, retrospective cost recovery and investment relief.

The attack on inflation was not conducted purely under the Price and Pay Codes. Subsidies were also introduced under the Prices Act 1974. This gave the SSPCP power to subsidize certain foods – this was a device for getting trade union agreement to a voluntary incomes policy. Subsidies under this, and later, legislation were paid on products such as bread, cheese, household flour, milk and tea. Coupled with this were statutory maximum prices (Prices Act 1974) for staple foods and an agreement on price restraint between the then SSPCP and the food manufacturers and retailers – the 'Price Check' scheme.

By 1977 it was recognized that a new Code was needed. Inflationary conditions had slackened and, as has been explained earlier, the depressed market conditions meant that some firms could not secure the increases allowed under the old Code. It was the force of competition rather than the Code that was increasingly restricting price increases. It was also apparent that, even though the old Code had been relaxed, its rigidities had led to a distorting effect on the allocation of resources and possibly some attenuation of the process of competition.[33] British industry was in favour of dropping price controls totally, but the need to secure continued wage restraint precluded the government from adopting such a policy. The government was indeed of the opinion that there existed a permanent case for government surveillance of prices and pricing practices. Even if on investigation particular price increases proved to be warranted it was desirable that companies should be required from time to time to explain and justify their pricing practices to a body acting on behalf of the public and the consumer. In reply to the criticism that the best protection for the consumer was competition, ministers advanced the following argument. It was admitted that competition laws existed, but it took a long time, sometimes years, before a particular industry investigation could be completed. What was needed, if inflation was to be checked, was an instrument of control that could act swiftly. In any case there were circumstances where the promotion of competition was impractical. Obviously oligopolies were one such situation – they might be justified in terms of economies of scale, but they could produce price parallelism which facilitated inflation.

The Price Commission Act 1977 inaugurated a new system. The Act described the duty of the Price Commission as being to restrain the price of goods and services 'so far as appears to be consistent with the making of adequate profits by efficient suppliers . . .'. In considering cases for price increases the new Code, which was not a type of rigid mathematical formula as previously, required the Commission to have the following considerations in mind:

(a) the need to recover costs incurred in efficiently supplying goods and services and in maintaining the value of the relevant businesses;
(b) the desirability of encouraging reductions in costs by improvements in the use of resources and of securing reductions in prices of goods and charges for services in consequence of such improvements;
(c) the need to earn, from selling goods and providing services in the United Kingdom, profits which provide a return on the capital employed in producing the profits which is sufficient, taking one year with another —
   (i) to defray the cost of the capital (including compensation for the risk involved in producing the profits), and
   (ii) to provide money for, and to encourage the promotion of, innovations and technical improvements in and the expansion in the United Kingdom of the enterprises which consist of or include the relevant businesses;
(d) the need to take account of changes in prices in determining the value of assets;
(e) the desirability of maintaining the quality of goods and services and satisfying the demands of users of goods and services;
(f) the need to safeguard the interests of users of goods and services by promoting competition between suppliers or, where competition must be restricted or cannot be promoted (either because certain suppliers control a substantial share of the relevant market or for any other reason), by restricting prices and charges;
(g) the desirability of establishing and maintaining a balance between the supply of goods and services and the demand for them; and
(h) the need to avoid detriment, from restraints on prices and charges, to the United Kingdom's balance of payments and the need to increase the share of United Kingdom enterprises in markets in the United Kingdom and elsewhere.

The detailed control over price increases by reference to allowable costs was dropped. Control over net and gross margins was continued for one more year.

In order to implement the Code large firms engaged in manufacturing and services are, as before, required to pre-notify their intention to raise prices. It is for the Price Commission to decide which notifications should be investigated. Increases can be frozen while the investigation proceeds.[34] The emphasis in the new policy is upon selectivity. If we ask what determines which notified increase is selected for investigation the answer seems to be that the absence of competition is high on the list. To quote the Commission:

> In every case . . . we have been concerned with the degree of competition in the market place for goods and services . . . if competition was absent or restricted we were aware that this reduced the pressure on suppliers to reduce costs . . . a second important factor was the need to discover whether restricted competition might be allowing an inefficient supplier to mask his own inefficiency and, not least, to avoid giving consumers the information that would allow them to form their own judgement.[35]

In short, where competition is intense problems are not likely to arise – in this the Price Commission has formed the same judgment as its predecessor the NBPI.

If an investigation suggests to the Commission that a price increase ought to be disallowed, reduced or delayed, attempts are made to reach a voluntary agreement. If this fails the SSPCP can make an Order. As in the previous phase, the Secretary of State may instruct the Commission to investigate the costs, margins, prices and profits of sectors of industry and commerce. Some of these may arise out of pre-notifications but investigations are not limited to these firms. The Code criteria, laid out above, apply in such cases. There is however one major change, namely that the Secretary of State has a specific order-making power in such cases – the object is not just publicity. J. D. Gribbin has also pointed out another significant aspect of this provision, namely that it enables the Commission to go beyond the behaviour and performance of a single firm when considering questions of competition. The Commission can indeed look at markets, as can the Monopolies and Mergers Commission, but the Price Commission studies will be more rapid.[36]

It is also worthy of note that the monitoring of undertakings and orders concerning prices, arising from Monopolies and Mergers Commission reports, has been passed over to the Price Commission.

The consumer has only a limited role to play in this policy. The Price Commission does provide a complaints mechanism and has received a large volume of complaints. These may prompt Commission officials in regional offices to investigate and seek direct redress. Apparently nothing is too small – in one case the price of bundles of firewood, sold mainly to pensioners, was reduced from 40p to 20p per bundle.[37] Occasionally consumer complaints may spark a full investigation. This was so in the case of the report on the margins of coal merchants in West Wales,[38] which incidentally uncovered an unregistered price agreement. Significantly, representatives of the consumer have been appointed to the Commission, including in 1978 at least one member of the National Consumer Council.

The consumer has been a beneficiary of the Commission's activities. Two cases will illustrate this point. In the report on tea prices[39] the Commission found that the auction price of tea in the London market rose from an average of 98p per kilogramme in the second quarter of 1976 to 270p in the first quarter of 1977. Thereafter it fell back to an average of 114p in December 1977. The Commission was anxious to find out why, after a period of stability, the price rose so markedly and why when it fell the fall was not reflected in the price to the consumer. The answer to the first question was straightforward – world demand exceeded world supply against a background of rising coffee prices which induced an expectation that consumers would switch to tea. The answer to the second was more interesting. When prices were going up the Price Code had allowed the tea blenders to price on a replacement cost basis – i.e. what it would cost to replace stocks that were getting dearer and dearer. Prior to this pricing had been on a historic cost basis. When the auction prices fell the blenders conveniently shifted to a historic cost basis so that prices to consumers reflected the prices that the blenders had paid for tea and not the price they were now paying. It was estimated that, if falling auction prices had been fully passed on to the consumer, the price in December 1977 would have been about 20 per cent lower. The upshot of this was that the Secretary of State took action and secured reductions of 8–10 per cent in the retail price.

In the report on Fison's agrochemical and horticultural products[40] the Commission took objection to a differential price increase. Although the company made higher profits on amateur products, it proposed to raise prices by 28–31 per cent whereas for the professional market it proposed only a 10 per cent increase. Apparently amateur gardeners are loyal to brands and somewhat insensitive to price. The Commission decided to act as their guardian and recommended that the amateur prices be increased by only 20 per cent.

Not all goods and services have been subject to the Price Codes. Certain exceptions have been provided for. These included fresh foods; exports and imports; goods subject to international agreement (this obviously covered the price of agricultural products under the EEC Common Agricultural Policy (CAP), and we shall have more to say about the consumer and the CAP in Chapter 11); commodity markets; auction sales; second-hand sales; international transport and communications (which are often subject to international agreement); goods sold by competitive tender; defence contracts and taxi-fares. The price of ethical pharmaceuticals sold to the National Health Service has for several years been controlled by the Voluntary (now Pharmaceutical) Price Regulation Scheme.[41] Insurance premiums were placed under the surveillance of the Department of Trade. Domestic (as opposed to business) rents have long been regulated; control legislation goes back to the Increase of Rent and Mortgage Interest (War Restrictions) Act 1915. A series of Rent Acts[42] has been passed that has created degrees of protected tenancy for unfurnished and furnished premises and either prescribes formulae for fixing rents or creates rent officers and rent tribunals who can fix rents.

GUARANTEEING STANDARDS AND PREVENTING INJURY

Standards

Some of the earliest consumer protection legislation was concerned with the protection of standards. This is true of the statutes passed in the period 1860–75,[43] which were essentially concerned with the problem of adulteration, a subject that attracted considerable publicity in the press and in journals such as *The Lancet*. The possibility of doing something about it was facilitated by the development of analytical chemistry. The Select Committee on Adulteration of Food 1855 paved the way for the Adulteration of Food and Drink Act 1860. This, as its title suggests, covered food and drink but not drugs. The Act made it an offence knowingly to sell food containing an injurious ingredient or which was adulterated. The Act empowered but did not require local authorities to appoint public analysts. Individuals could have samples analysed for a fee. Unfortunately, the Act was weak in several respects. Few analysts were appointed. Enforcement was in the hands of those private individuals who were prepared to take the trouble to have products analysed. No actual minimum standards were prescribed. There was one other flaw, which we shall deal with presently. The reform lobby succeeded in getting a further Act passed – the Adulteration of Food, Drink and Drugs Act 1872. It extended control to drugs, made the appointment of analysts obligatory and provided for local authority inspectors to procure samples for analysis. As a result of the latter, official enforcement then began to operate and has ever since been a prime feature of British food and drug legislation. Both Acts however contained one significant stumbling block. This was the *mens rea* provision; i.e., it required the enforcers to prove that the supplier *knowingly* supplied adulterated, etc., goods. This provided a stiff test which inhibited those concerned with enforcement. Significantly, it was the courts who next delivered a blow on behalf of the consumer by declaring in a series of key cases[44] that the proof of *mens rea* was unnecessary. This point was subsequently embodied in the Sale of Food and Drugs Act 1875. The Act declared: 'No person shall sell to the prejudice of the purchasers any article of food or any thing which is not of the nature, substance or quality demanded by such purchaser.' Heavy fines and imprisonment were specified in respect of proven offences.

The importance of these Acts lies in the fact that the state was accepting a duty to protect the consumer. The current Act – the Food and Drugs Act 1955 – is a direct descendant of the 1875 legislation.[45] We shall describe its main provisions at this point although some refer to the problem of hygiene and injury. Before we turn to the specific sections it is important to note that the drugs aspect is now covered by the Medicines Act 1968. As we noted earlier, there are parallel Acts for Scotland (1956) and Northern Ireland (1958) which have the same philosophy as the 1955 Act.

Section 1 of the Act makes it an offence to sell for human consumption food injurious to health. Such injury may arise from adding a substance, abstracting a substance or subjecting a food to any process or treatment. This obviously covers additives, and its practical consequences will be discussed below. Section 2 makes it an offence to sell food not of the nature, substance or quality demanded by the purchaser. This relates to adulteration and the incorporation of inadequate quantities of essential ingredients – it is therefore relevant to the immediate discussion. Section 4 allows ministers to make regulations relating to matters such as additives and standards. Section 8 makes it an offence to sell food unfit for human consumption. This deals with microbiological contamination – a problem not appreciated at the time of the early legislation. Section 13 enables regulations to be made concerning hygiene – again, the practical consequences fall due for consideration later.

The task of enforcement falls to local authorities (although the Ministry inspectors also play a role). Following local government reorganization the question of composition of foods (i.e. standards, additives) is a matter for county councils and specifically the Trading

Standards, or Consumer Protection, Officers. Hygiene is a matter for district councils and specifically Environmental Health, or Public Health, Officers. Powers are conferred upon authorized officers to enter premises, take samples, and have samples analysed. Relevant local authorities must appoint public analysts. Enforcement may require action before the courts – offences under the Act are punishable by fines, imprisonment or both.

In order to assist it in drawing up regulations on food consumption standards the Ministry of Agriculture, Fisheries and Food (MAFF), the Secretary of State for Social Services (SSSS), the Secretary of State for Northern Ireland and the Secretary of State for Scotland have as their advisor the Food Standards Committee (FSC).[46] The FSC, created in 1947, acts on references made by Ministers. It carries out reviews to see if regulations are needed and, if so, in what form. An independent committee, it has a chairman and nine members, three being appointed for their scientific expertise, three being from the food trades and three having special concern for consumer views. Its reports are submitted to the Minister who then publishes them, inviting comments. Only after this final consultation procedure has been carried out are detailed regulations drafted and submitted to Parliament. Regulations have, for example, been issued concerning the composition of ice cream, cheese, sausages, meat pies, sausage rolls, fish pastes and jams. Reports of particular interest include those on novel proteins (1975)[47] and date-marking (1971, 1972).[48] In the latter the committee distinguished between short-life and long-life foods. It was in respect of the former that there was most public concern, and these were defined as products that the manufacturers considered should be sold within three months, taking into account the time needed by the purchaser to keep them at home. It was recommended that, from 1975, such foods would be required to show a 'sell by' date conspicuously on the label where it could be seen by the purchaser and retailer. In respect of long-life foods, the committee recommended a system for showing the date of manufacture or pre-packing in a way that would facilitate stock rotation. Two points need to be made. The first is that, increasingly, open-dating has been introduced, although it is not illegal to sell goods after the 'sell by' date – unless the food is deteriorating, in which case Section 8 of the 1955 Act applies. Second, this open-dating recommendation did not initiate the phenomenon. Progressive firms had (under the pressure of press publicity) already embarked on this path and the recommendation was designed to make it more general. Open-dating is discussed further in Chapter 6 below.

There are other statutes that refer to standards. For example, the Seeds Act 1920 imposes standards for seeds including some used in the garden. The Rag, Flock and Other Filling Materials Act 1951 regulates the purity, and cleanliness, of fillings used in cushions, upholstery and mattresses. Minimum constructional standards (which admittedly also have a safety element) also arise in connection with building regulations enforced by local authorities — this activity derives from the Public Health Act 1936. Mention must also be made of the British Pharmacopoeic Commission, which sets standards for standard preparations (generic drugs) sold over the counter. Hence the terms BP (British Pharmacopoeia) and BPC (British Pharmaceutical Codex).[49] This Commission operates under the Medicines Act 1968 and more will be said on the topic of drugs later.

Services are another area where the protection of standards is evident. In a number of liberal professions restrictions on access to the market (on the part of the supplier) take the form of the imposition of qualifications as the condition of the performance of an activity by a person. Clearly, this kind of activity does provide some protection for the public, although of course the body granting the qualifications could abuse its power. If it raised standards unnecessarily and thereby deliberately restricted entry, those already in the profession would gain in terms of remuneration by virtue of the artificial scarcity but the consumer would clearly lose. Rules relating to entry into liberal professions are in many cases laid down in statutory form. Generally these statutes set up Registration Councils which require members to have passed certain examinations, had prescribed amounts of experience, etc. See, for example, the Architects (Registration) Acts 1931 and 1938; Dentists Act 1957; Medical Acts 1956 and 1969; Opticians Act 1958; Professions Supplementary to Medicine Act 1960 (this refers to chiropodists, dietitians, medical laboratory technicians, occupational therapists, physiotherapists, radiographers and remedial gymnasts); Solicitors (Scotland) Acts 1933, 1949 and 1958 and Solicitors Act 1974; Insurance Brokers (Registration) Act 1977. In these cases it is an offence for an unregistered person to use practitioner titles and/or to practise the particular profession. Technical competence is the objective of these regulations, although moral probity may enter in as, for example, in the case of Scottish solicitors who must by the statute satisfy the Council of the Law Society in Scotland that they are fit and proper persons.[50]

There are other occupations that require their members to have passed certain examinations before a person is recognized as a fully qualified member of a profession. A distinction has however got to be made between those professions in which the passing of the examination is necessary before a person can be recognized as fully qualified (e.g. chartered accountants or surveyors) and those where the matter at issue is one of promotion (e.g. banking). However, even in the former case, in the absence of statutory powers exclusion of unqualified persons from practice is not possible. There is however an exception to this rule in that the Bar has what can be termed a common-law monopoly of audience before the superior courts in the UK, and in neither the Scottish nor the English case is this based on statute.[51]

There is also a series of services of a financial kind where safeguarding restrictions, sometimes in the form of licensing, are imposed. The Prevention of Fraud (Investments) Act 1958 requires all dealers in securities to be licensed, although there are a number of important exceptions (recognized members of stock exchanges, recognized associations of dealers in securities, the Bank of England, a statutory or municipal corporation, any exempted dealer or any industrial provident or building society and officers of authorized unit trusts). Licences can be revoked where there is a conviction under the Act or if the Department of Industry, which is the licensor, thinks the person is not fit and proper.

Insurance is highly regulated, in this case by the Insurance Companies Act 1974. This control has followed in the wake of insurance company insolvencies. There was a series of failures in the sixties and this led to some rather hurried tightening of control via Part II of the Companies Act 1967. Then in 1971 and 1974 there were further failures involving respectively the Vehicle and General and the National Life. Under the 1974 Act insurance business is restricted to insurers authorized by the Secretary of State for Trade. No authorization will be forthcoming unless certain safeguards are satisfied. One relates to the margin of solvency, i.e. an excess of the value of assets over the value of liabilities. Another relates to the adequacy of reinsurance arrangements. The Act also lays down strict requirements in respect of rendition of accounts, periodic actuarial investigations and audits. Accounts and actuarial reports must be deposited with the Secretary of State. Most important of all, significant powers of intervention are provided which enable the Secretary of State to refuse to sanction the appointment of persons whom he deems to be unfit to be directors, controllers or managers. The Secretary of State can intervene in the running of the insurance company by, for example, restricting the taking on of new business, and controlling the investment of funds. Under the Policyholders Protection Act 1975 a scheme is imposed that is funded by a levy on authorized insurance companies. The aim of this arrangement is that, if an authorized insurance company becomes insolvent, individual policy-holders will nevertheless be protected. A Board is charged with this task and its protective activities may involve transferring the failed company's business to other firms or issuing substitute policies. If either of these fails the Board may pay consumers 90 per cent (in the case of compulsory insurance 100 per cent) of the value of policies.

The banking industry has been regulated by the Department of Trade under the provisions of the Protection of Depositors Act 1963. However this has been less than satisfactory, and following the 1976 White Paper, *Licensing and Supervision of Deposit Taking Institutions*,[52] itself a response to the crisis among fringe banks in 1973–74, the Banking Act 1979 was passed. This provides for a licensing system operated by the Bank of England. Only licensed bodies will be able to accept deposits from the public, and only bodies officially recognized as banks will be able to call themselves such. The proposal also envisages consumer cover through the establishment of a deposit protection fund, run by a Deposit Protection Board. Licensed institutions will have to contribute to the fund and depositors will be reimbursed with 75 per cent of the first £10,000 deposited.

Statutory control is also promised in respect of estate agents. In 1975 the Department of Prices and Consumer Protection issued a consultative document, *The Regulation of Estate Agency*, and the Estate Agents Act 1979 now embodies a scheme of control. The Director General of Fair Trading will be able to prohibit persons from practice if he finds them unfit to do so on certain clearly specified grounds. The SSPCP will also be empowered to ensure that persons engaged in the residential property aspect of estate agency work satisfy minimum standards of competence. The Act also establishes a system in which estate agents will have to maintain a client's account and will have to pay any deposits received into it. Such deposits will have to be covered by insurance or other indemnity arrangements.

Mention must also be made of the protection schemes that operate in respect of holidays abroad. A good deal of public concern has been expressed on the subject as a result of well publicized failures of package tour operators (e.g. Court Line). A number of safeguards now exist. First, British air travel organizers have to be licensed by the Civil Aviation Authority. It may refuse to license a firm unless it is made financially sound by the injection of additional funds. Second, licensees must take out a bond, related to turnover, or make arrangements giving equivalent security either with the Association of British Travel Agents or another approved body. The funds so made available enable deposits to be repaid or stranded passengers to be repatriated. Third, in order to deal with the more serious cases, the Air Travel Reserve Fund Act 1975 set up a Reserve Fund to which all licensed air travel organizers must contribute 2 per cent of their turnover. The Act also envisaged the possibility of loans of up to £15 million from the government.

There are other instances of licensing but in these cases protection of the consumer is not a major concern.[53]

Prevention of Injury

We have seen that the Food and Drugs Act 1955 explicitly addresses itself to hygiene — Section 13 allows regulations to be made on the subject. At this point we should note that normally before making such orders ministers consult the Food Hygiene Advisory Council (FHAC)[54] — a statutory committee created under Section 82 of the Act. General regulations, specifically the Food Hygiene (General) Regulations 1970, as amended, lay down general rules about hygiene in relation to food manufacturing, catering establishments, shops — indeed, anywhere where food is handled. The enforcement is as we have seen a local authority responsibility. Separate regulations have been made for places such as docks, warehouses, cold stores, carriers premises and markets — see Food Hygiene (Docks, Carriers, etc.) Regulations 1960, as amended, made under Section 13 and 123 and Food Hygiene (Markets, Stalls, and Delivery Vehicles) Regulations 1966, as amended, made under the same sections. There are also specific regulations relating to milk and dairies — see Milk and Dairies (General) Regulations 1959, as amended, made under Sections 29 (which specifically relates to milk and dairies), 30, 87 and 123 of the Act. Dairy farmers have to register with the MAFF. If the MAFF refuses to register a dairy then it cannot carry on business, and failure to meet hygiene requirements may be the grounds for such a refusal.

In Section 16 the Act provides for the special requirements of certain products — specifically mentioned are ice cream and sausages. Premises shall not be used for manufacture, storage, sale, etc., unless registered for this purpose by the local authority. Again registration can be refused if hygiene standards are not met. The Slaughterhouses Act 1974 requires that slaughterhouses and knackers' yards be licensed. Licenses can be refused if hygiene requirements are not complied with. Codes of practice relating to hygiene have been agreed in respect of the meat and fish trades, the transport and handling of fish, the dressing and packing of poultry, the bakery trade and vending machines. Mention must also be made of the Food and Drugs (Control of Food Premises) Act 1976. Under its provisions a local Environmental Health Officer can with court authority close dirty premises within three days if he thinks that there is an imminent risk to health.

We shall be discussing the regulation of medicines in due course. At this point it suffices to note that under the Medicines Act 1968 the licensing body (the Medicines Division of DHSS) licenses not only the production of specific products but also the manufacturers themselves. The latter are subject to inspection and a number of factors are taken into account including the adequacy of the provisions for guaranteeing hygiene and sterility.

This is also a suitable point to indicate that danger to health may proceed not from lack of hygiene but from diseased food, and obviously this is most likely to arise in connection with meat. Meat inspection is therefore an important function, and the Meat Inspection Regulations 1963, as amended, made under Sections 13 and 123 of the 1955 Act, lay a duty of inspection on local authorities. A list of diseases is specified and meat affected by any of them cannot be used for human consumption.

We have already recognized the danger inherent in food additives and contaminants. We have also noted that Section 1 of the Food and Drugs Act 1955 addresses itself directly to this problem. In order to advise themselves on this matter the MAFF, the SSSS, Secretary of State for Scotland and the Head of the Department of Health and Social Services in Northern Ireland have the benefit of advice from the Food Additives and Contaminants Committee (FACC). It became a separate committee in 1966, having previously been a subcommittee of the FSC. The Committee is concerned with additives and certain contaminants. The effects of pesticides and veterinary medical products, and for that matter foreign bodies in food, are not its concern. The committee, like the FSC, acts on ministerial references. Its specific role is to evaluate substances from the point of view of (a) need (Section 4 of the 1955 Act requires ministers to have regard to the desirability of restricting as far as possible the use of substances of no nutritional value) and (b) safety. In respect of the first aspect the committee has to be convinced that there is a definite technological need that could not be met by using an alternative substance or that the use of the substance could be obviated by using another technique. Like the FSC, its reports are published for comment although submissions may have been made by the trade while the report was being prepared. Only after the final consultation process is over are regulations produced. These take the form of lists of permitted additives for particular purposes. In addition standards have been laid down about the maximum amount of contaminants such as lead and mercury that can be allowed. Examples of additives that have been banned (e.g. cyclamate) have already been given.[55]

Unintentional contaminants arising from pesticides and veterinary activities are dealt with by separate machinery. With a few exceptions there is no statutory control over pesticides. Instead there is a voluntary notification scheme agreed between government departments and pesticides producers. Producers make submissions as to nature, usage and toxicity of pesticides. These are considered by a Scientific Sub-Committee which reports to the Advisory Committee on Pesticides and other Toxic Chemicals. The conditions for use are agreed with the industry and endorsed by the agricultural and health departments. Recommendations as to use are then issued which it is assumed users will abide by.

Veterinary medicines that may leave residues in meat are subject to statutory control. Such products are licensed under the Medicines Act 1968 and the licences prescribe the conditions of use. The questions of safety, and efficacy, are evaluated for the licensing body by a statutory body, the Veterinary Products Committee. The latter has a link with the MAFF.

In the case of drugs we have already mentioned that they are now controlled by the Medicines Act 1968. The important point here is that licences are required before products can be marketed.[56] The licensing body, to which we referred earlier, is the DHSS (Medicines Division). To help it in its task the Medicines Commission has been created. It in turn has a number of committees including the Committee on Safety of Medicines, the Committee for the Review of Medicines and the British Pharmacopoeia Commission which we referred to in connection with generic drug standards. On the question of safety it is the first of these bodies that is important. Its origins lie in the Thalidomide disaster, which led to the creation of the Committee on Safety of Drugs which was subsequently retitled Committee on Safety of Medicines. The earlier committee relied on voluntary collaboration with the drug industry but under the present regime pre-market testing of *new* drugs is obligatory and the committee's judgments have the sanction of a licensing law. In testing new drugs the committee has to be satisfied as to efficacy, quality and above all safety. Provision is also made for post-marketing surveillance.

When the Medicines Act came into existence those products already on the market before 1 September 1971 were given licences of right. However under a commitment to the EEC the Committee for the Review of Medicines is reviewing all medicinal products individually. They will have completed their work by 1990 and a significant reduction in the number of products on the market seems likely.

We come now to consumer goods including durables. The Molony Committee was concerned about the delay in dealing with these by statute. In order to speed matters up the Consumer Protection Act 1961 gave the SSPCP a power to regulate the sale of goods liable to cause death, injury or disease by Statutory Instrument. Under that more speedy process regulations were, for example, made about electrical wiring colour codes, carrycot stand safety, oil heaters, fireguards, paint on toys, flame resistance of children's nightwear and toys, and cooking utensils. Prosecution powers were tightened up under the amending Consumer Protection Act 1971. Once a safety standard had been laid down it was a criminal offence for a trader (but not a private individual) to sell an article that did not comply with it. Enforcement was however subject to one drawback, namely that local authorities were not under a positive obligation to enforce this legislation – unlike that concerned with food, weights and measures (see below). Nevertheless most of them did so. The protective work of the 1961 Act is now being superseded by the Consumer Safety Act 1978. Existing regulations under the 1961 Act will remain in force but will be replaced by regulations made under the new Act. The new Act widens the regulation-making powers conferred in 1961. It enables rapid action to be taken to ban the sale of dangerous goods. A power is provided to require distributors of dangerous goods to publish warnings about the hazards they present. The SSPCP can serve notices requiring information to be supplied to him in order that he can discharge his functions under the Act. A duty of enforcement is now laid on local authorities, and this has remedied the deficiency that we noted earlier.

The Road Traffic Act 1960 provides for regulations to be made concerning the construction, weight and equipment of motor vehicles. It requires that tests be carried out as to roadworthiness and that motorists should possess obligatory test certificates concerning their vehicles, and it prohibits the sale of vehicles that are not roadworthy. Criminal penalties are prescribed for breaches of these three requirements. Various regulations were subsequently made including the Motor Vehicles (Tests) Regulations 1968, as amended; the Motor Vehicles (Production of Test Certificates) Regulations 1969; the Motor Vehicles (Construction and Use) Regulations 1969. Under the Road Traffic Act 1972 it is an offence to sell or hire crash helmets for motorcyclists or rear lights or reflectors unless they comply with the appropriate British Standards specifications. The Gun Barrel Proof Acts 1868, 1950 require in the interests of public safety that all guns be examined by a proof house and bear a proof mark. Under Section 1 of the Fabrics (Misdescription) Act 1913 the Secretary of State for Industry may make regulations prescribing standards of non-inflammability to which textile fabrics represented to be non-inflammable shall conform.

Where the possibility of injury arises consumer protection sometimes takes the form of procedures that restrict the access of individuals to particular products. This is the case with drugs where some may be sold only upon prescription from a registered pharmacy (registered by the Pharmaceutical Society). On the other hand, drugs on the General Sales List can be sold without prescription and the government has accepted that there is no need to restrict their sale to pharmacies. The statutory order giving effect to these decisions derives from the powers provided under Part 3 of the Medicines Act 1968. In the case of dangerous drugs (cocaine, morphine, etc.), which following the Misuse of Drugs Act 1971 were redesignated as controlled drugs, particularly stringent controls exist as to storage, prescription and the recording of sale in a controlled drugs register. These controls are embodied in the Misuse of Drugs Regulations 1973.

Under the Medicines Act 1968 regulations have also been made that require drugs to be sold in safe containers. For example, both pharmacy and non-pharmacy outlets may not sell products containing aspirin or paracetamol (subject to a limited exception) other than in child-resistant containers.

Poisons are another area of control. The relevant legislation here is the Poisons Act 1972, a statute that retains the Poisons Board, an advisory committee, and the Poisons List, both of which were established by the Pharmacy and Poisons Act 1933. Unrestricted sale is not allowed. Some poisons can be sold only by registered pharmacists. Others may be obtained from other outlets licensed by local authorities. Poison Rules are also laid down that govern the mode of sale. These relate to labelling (e.g. cautioning the user as to the nature of the product and the need for care) and also stipulate that sales be recorded in a Poisons Book. It should be noted that some poisons are also controlled drugs and as such are also subject to the Misuse of Drugs Regulations.

We conclude this section by noting the existence of controls over the sale of fireworks. Reacting to public pressure, the Explosives (Age of Purchase, etc) Act 1976 increased to sixteen years the age of people to whom fireworks can legally be sold. It also raised the penalties for sale below that age and for letting off fireworks in a public place. A voluntary agreement has also been reached with manufacturers for the phasing out of the more dangerous type of firework and for restricting the period during which fireworks can be sold to the public.

THE EEC DIMENSION

We mentioned in Chapter 2 that the task of the EEC Commission is to dismantle the various non-tariff, as well as tariff, barriers to trade. There are several forms of non-tariff barrier,[57] but not all are directly relevant to consumers, as for example restrictions arising in connection with 'buy national' attitudes in public purchasing. The non-tariff barriers that are relevant to consumers (apart from those dealt with in Chapter 3) are those connected with the national standards, relating to food, drugs, consumer goods, etc., laid down by governments. The need to harmonize such standards was recognized by those who drafted the Rome Treaty and Articles 100–102 on the approximation of laws apply. Article 100 provides for the Council, on a proposal of the Commission, to issue unifying directives when laws, regulations and administrative actions of member states directly affect the setting up or operation of the Common Market.

The consumer has two possible sources of gain from such activities. First, the admission of foreign supplies intensifies domestic competition. Admittedly, foreign goods could enter in the absence of harmonization, but in such a case they would have to be modified to meet the standards laid down in each market. The economies of long runs of a standardized product would be lost. Second, the possibility exists that in the process of achieving a Community standard the best national practice will be adopted. For example, additives that may give rise to injury, or the possibility of injury, will be banned. It is perhaps worth noting that at the Paris Summit meeting of 1972 the heads of state and government emphasized the importance of developing a Community with a human face. This undoubtedly gave a fillip to the development of consumer protection policy at the Community level. In 1975 the Council adopted a Resolution on a preliminary programme for consumer protection and information policy. Significantly, under the Resolution the Community consumer's first right is the protection of health and safety. (The others are the right of protection of his economic interest, the right to redress, the right to information and education, and finally the right to be represented and consulted when decisions are made which affect him.)

The Community has in fact made slow progress in the area of harmonization. This has been partly due to the need to go through the lengthy Community decision-making process. The Community has also encountered the problem that directives have taken so long to thrash out that they have been in danger of becoming out of date before they were finally agreed. The Community has therefore had to produce a speedier process for modifying directives in order to keep pace with change.

In the early years harmonization directives were promulgated in the area of food, specifically colouring matters in 1962 and preserving agents in 1963. This was probably a spillover of political will from the CAP. Harmonization in respect of industrial products was slow in coming – the 1965 directive on pharmaceutical products was a very isolated achievement. During the seventies the process was speeded up and a variety of directives has been issued, ranging widely over the field of manufactured products. Various mechanical, electrical and safety features of motorcars, tractors and agricultural machinery have proportionately been a very significant part of harmonization activity. Particularly interesting was the 1977 directive harmonizing cosmetics. The directive bans the use of some substances and sets limits to the use of others. Notable in the latter category was hexachlorophane, the lethal effects of which we referred to earlier.

A variety of approaches to harmonization is adopted. Total harmonization implies that national standards have been relinquished and one Community standard has been adopted. This is highly appropriate in cases such as cosmetics. Alternatively, the system may be optional – national standards may exist alongside a Community one. Those who adopt the former can sell only in their own boundaries but those who adopt the latter have access to the whole EEC market. There have also been some institutional developments, notably in the field of food. In 1974 the Commission set up a Scientific Committee for Food to advise it on matters such as the composition of food, the use of additives, etc. In 1975 the Advisory Committee on Foodstuffs was set up in order to speed up the consultative process in relation to draft directives. The Committee includes among others consumer representatives.

6 Preparing to Buy – Acquiring Information

INTRODUCTION

Having considered the international and national forces that operate to provide the market in which the domestic consumer is dealing, we must now move on to look at the assistance that is given to a consumer faced with a range of goods from which he must make a selection. The provision of a wide range of goods by manufacturers competing for markets is one of the results of the policies that we have already discussed, and this diversity of choice will usually lead the consumer to seek that product which he thinks will give him the best 'value for money'. It is left ultimately to the consumer to weigh value against cost, to assess the worth of one product against another and to make a final choice.

It is in the nature of things that the choice made will differ from consumer to consumer because of the differing requirements and resources of individuals, but we need to be concerned less with the final choice than with the method by which it is made. It is currently assumed that a consumer faced with a choice may make a rational decision only if he has access to information about the products available, their composition, their performance and their price. That assumption can hardly be challenged, but legitimate differences may arise in settling the amount of assistance the consumer should be given in the acquisition and interpretation of information concerning products.

Economically, the provision of information about the available products is said to facilitate competition by allowing the consumer a discerning choice, and legally there have always been some controls over the supply of misinformation by individuals dealing together as well as by businesses.[1] The legal sanctions have been strengthened in recent years by the addition of criminal penalties,[2] and all the legal constraints on the provision of deceptive or misleading information will be discussed in the following chapter. Sanctions on the provision

PREPARING TO BUY — ACQUIRING INFORMATION

of misinformation do not, however, achieve the desired object of placing the consumer in such a position that he may make an informed choice, and the first part of this chapter is about the measures that *require* manufacturers and retailers to make information available to the consumers.

Additionally there is information that is regarded as helpful or desirable, and there are a number of agencies that exist to arm the consumer with facts and opinions about the range of products available in the market. These agencies assist the consumer materially but are the subject of argument about the degree of public funding that should be available to them and about the extent to which they are providing functions that ought properly to be the responsibility of the individual consumer. That responsibility may lead the consumer to seek out information for himself, and it is at this point that it is convenient to consider the role of advertising.

OBLIGATORY DISCLOSURE

At present the consumer is not on equal terms in his dealings with major manufacturers and retailers. Deceptive packaging is simply one of the difficulties, which the OFT drew attention to with an entertaining poster,[3] besetting the consumer in his quest for a comparison between rival products. There are many other advantages possessed by the business side.

As a possible counter to the prevailing inequality manufacturers may be required to provide basic facts and information concerning their product. We have already noted the controls on standards and quality imposed in the interests of consumers[4] and have contended that these represent market interventions that mitigate the potential dangers of unrestricted competition. The obligation to disclose should not be regarded in the same way as an intervention mechanism, since there is good authority for the proposition that an informed market assists competition rather than hinders it.

It is fairly clear that a policy combining the limited intervention of government with a strong line against restrictive practices, monopolies and mergers imposes an obligation on the government to ensure that the consumer is adequately prepared to exercise the choice thereby created. Because the consumer is required to choose he must be enabled to do so sensibly and rationally on the basis of readily available information.

Those who would agree that intervention in the market is necessary to ensure the health, safety or economic interests of consumers would not necessarily assent to further controls to protect the interests of consumers. Rather, the non-interventionists would argue that the provision of the required basic information is sufficient protection and will also provide the ammunition to exert pressure for change where that is desirable.

Obligatory information may be communicated in a number of ways, though the actual method of communication will normally be specified in the measure that makes it obligatory to disclose the information. Broadly speaking, a manufacturer may communicate information about his products (whether he is obliged to or not) by way of their presentation in the shop or by way of their advertisement at the point of sale or elsewhere. The retailer may display information relating to the terms of the contract of sale. The consumer may seek facts from other sources, but it is difficult to imagine other ways in which the manufacturer himself could communicate direct with the consumer. There are examples of all these methods in current use and they are discussed further below.

The tremendous range of consumer products makes it difficult to compile a complete list of qualities of which information should be given and which will be applicable to all products. However, apart from labelling, price information and dating, which are sufficiently important to be considered separately, it is possible to discover requirements of disclosure relating to quantity, quality, safety, place of origin, credit terms and usage of products. Armed with all this information, the onus is then on the consumer to make the sensible choice and the one that will offer him the greatest satisfaction and protection.

Labelling

There is a whole battery of legislation with the object of requiring the manufacturer of goods to give the consumer information about the composition, quality and safety of his goods. The Food and Drugs Act 1955 comes high on the list of statutes giving consumers valuable rights, and it is interesting that in relation to turnover relatively few complaints are received by the Office of Fair Trading each year concerning the operation of the Act.[5] We have already discussed the contribution of this line of legislation to the eradication of impure food,[6] but we are more particularly concerned here to note its effect on the information disclosed by the manufacturer. Under the Act, a Food Standards Committee is constituted[7] and this is the body charged with the consideration of regulations on labelling. The current regulations are the Labelling of Food Regulations 1970.

Quite apart from the criminal offences created by the statute in respect of misleading claims and mis-descriptions (considered in the next chapter), there are certain minimum standards laid down for the packaging of pre-packed food. Such food must have a label attached stating the ingredients, giving a description of the food and providing the name and address of the packer. The most useful provision for the consumer is that which requires the ingredients to be listed in descending order of quantity (excluding water content).

The Weights and Measures Act 1963 (as amended by the Weights and Measures Act 1976) also exhibits this dual approach of criminal offences of mis-statement of quantity and regulations requiring the disclosure of quantity in respect of certain specified foodstuffs, fuels and other miscellaneous goods. The statute further specifies the quantities in which certain goods *must* be sold. Schedule 4 of the 1963 Act, which can be varied from time to time by the Department of Prices and Consumer Protection, gives a detailed list of goods and the specified quantities for sale. An example familiar to very many readers will be the quantity in which alcohol is served in public houses – beer must be sold in quantities of $\frac{1}{3}$ pint, $\frac{1}{2}$ pint or multiples thereof, and gin, rum, whisky and vodka must be sold in multiples of $\frac{1}{4}$, $\frac{1}{5}$ or $\frac{1}{6}$ of a gill.[8] It is interesting to note that there is no prescribed measure for the sale of brandy, liqueurs or wine by the glass. Still in the bar, the compulsory display of prices of drinks has recently been introduced,[9] and there are new regulations on the way to ensure that a pint of beer is served in a glass that has the pint mark below the rim so as to allow for the froth, which will not in future form part of the pint for measuring purposes. The alert customer can find much to help him in the bar – perhaps the legislature is only too well aware of the weakness of the consumer's position!

Very little food escapes the quantity regulations, from chocolate bars to breakfast cereals, although the onset of metrication may make the provision of quantity information distinctly less useful until people are familiar with the new system.

Dangerous drugs have always been subject to more stringent labelling requirements, and in particular the Medicines Act 1968 deals with drugs and medicines. The safety aspect of this statute has been dealt with above in Chapter 5.

Unit Pricing and Price Display

Statements of quantity are all very well and serve to inform the consumer of what he is getting, but they are of relatively little value when they are not standardized. It is quite easy to make price comparisons between different packets of tea that are all presented in standard quantities, but it is much more difficult to compare 2.75 kilo of fillet steak for £12.92 with 2 lb 13 oz for £4.93. Unit pricing is the term applied to the disclosure of the price per pound or per kilogram. At the moment, some meats, some fish, hard cheeses, and fruit and vegetables must bear the unit price as well as the quantity and the selling price,[10] and it is the intention of the government to bring a wide range of goods under similar regulation. A number of shops already undertake unit pricing for a great many of their goods on a voluntary basis.

The discussion of unit pricing assumes that there is a selling price displayed. The Prices Act 1974 enabled orders to be made that would require the prices of specified goods to be displayed in a particular way, and it is these powers that have been exercised to achieve the unit pricing referred to above, and the display of prices in public houses. The most recent action has been taken against the display of prices at petrol stations, which were destined to mislead the motorist. Now, the prices displayed have to be clear and they must be in respect of at least two grades of petrol (one of which must be 4-star). The price for part gallons must be displayed if it is different to the ordinary price (Petrol Prices (Display) Order 1978).

Shelf-life

The Food and Drugs Act 1955 makes it a criminal offence to sell food that is unfit for human consumption,[11] but most consumers would prefer to have uncontaminated food rather than a prosecuted shopkeeper. The shopkeeper himself has an obvious interest in making sure that the food on his shelves is in good condition, and he finds life particularly difficult in relation to perishable foodstuffs. To help the shopkeeper many manufacturers have introduced an advisory date-marking system for their products and it is now common to see 'sell by' dates on many perishable goods. The system was not intended directly for the consumer, and a number of manufacturers adopt a secret code system which cannot be understood by the consumer. The consumer organizations regard this as a lost opportunity for consumers in assessing the freshness of the products on the shelves and are pressing for the codes to be revealed and the date-marking of particular goods to be made compulsory.

The 'sell by' date creates no legal obligations, and there is no penalty imposed on the shopkeeper who ignores the advice so long as the food is still in reasonable condition, but the EEC has issued a draft directive concerning the compulsory marking of a number of products,[12] and it may be that shelf-life dates will become mandatory before too long.

Miscellaneous Disclosure Requirements

One of the crucial factors for many consumers in the acquisition of large and expensive products is the credit available. Purchases on credit are commonplace and the various forms of credit vary considerably. An important requirement, which will eventually be introduced by regulations made under the Consumer Credit Act 1974, is that the true rate of interest on credit must be disclosed to the consumer. It had proved relatively easy for the providers of credit to disguise the true cost of the loan to the debtor and it was extremely difficult to weigh up the real cost. Tables have recently been published which can be relied on to provide the true rate of interest and the total charge for various forms of credit.[13]

It may also be appropriate here to note that certain chemicals are subject to rules about disclosure,[14] and that the cigarette manufacturers have been forced to display a warning on their packets. Whether the disclosure that cigarettes can damage your health is novel, startling or effective can be the subject of debate, but it was certainly intended as a consumer protection measure.[15]

A variety of other information for consumers must be provided and it is interesting to note the various pressures that combine to force the legislature into action. The European Economic Community is taking an increased interest in consumer affairs (the draft directive on date-marking has already been referred to) and the requirement that the fibre content be shown on textile products resulted from an EEC directive. A voluntary scheme for the labelling of consumer products containing asbestos came into operation in October 1976 after the fears of asbestos poisoning, and there it was obviously in the interests of the manufacturers to reassure the public by cautionary labelling.

SUPPLEMENTARY 'OFFICIAL' INFORMATION

We have argued earlier that there is some obligation on the government to ensure that the consumer has sufficient information to make a wise choice from the goods available. This view does not find favour with everyone, and it is strongly argued that consumer protection should be concerned solely with the preservation of the health and safety of the consumer and the prevention of actual deception and that it should be no part of the service to provide information that will help the consumer choose well – that is the sole responsibility of the consumer himself. It is this line of argument that led to the debate on the utility of the consumer advice centres established by a number of local authorities, and that also leads to close scrutiny of the amount of money spent on the official provision of supplementary information.

The Consumer Advice Centres

It is quite possible to identify different types of consumer information which move progressively further away from the simply informative to the critically evaluative and which are intended to be more or less directive of the choice made by the consumer. At the most basic level an advice centre can provide factual information about products that are the subject of inquiry. This information may be unavailable at the point of sale, or it may be easier for an advice centre to obtain it from a manufacturer, or the consumer may simply prefer to have it from an independent, uncommitted body. Whatever the reason, there can be no denying that the centres provide a good service. In addition, it is possible to gather information about a number of products under one roof without having to trail round to the various stockists in the locality.

 Most advice centres progressed beyond this informative role and began to offer the consumer factual comparisons between competing goods. These comparisons are not, in many cases, difficult to make

PREPARING TO BUY — ACQUIRING INFORMATION 139

and will often require only an analysis of the label on a tin. Again, this information is helpful because shoppers rarely have the time or the inclination to do their own comparisons and with the more expensive consumer durables there is not the same 'try it and see' possibility as with a tin of meat.

The comparison of factual statements of obligatory information about products can hardly be exceptionable unless it be argued that the consumer ought to be doing this work for himself, but many centres then progressed to the comparison of other information supplied by manufacturers.

The sheer volume of information put out by some manufacturers can pose almost as much of a problem for the average consumer as a lack of information, and it became tempting for the advice centres to offer an analysis of the information available. After analysis it becomes very hard not to begin to evaluate the merits of respective products, especially in the light of the pioneering work done by the Consumers' Association and others in the testing of goods. Comparisons of products became available and useful to the consumer.

From the comparison of products it was but a short step for one or two advice agencies to the comparison of professional services provided by some of the professions in their areas.[16] The inquiries made and the published results were not always welcomed by the professions involved and there was a powerful voice against the work of the centres.

At this point the centres had certainly gone beyond the simple provision of information and were doing, with public money, a job similar to that done by the Consumers' Association and financed by the subscriptions of its members. It is fair to say that there was certainly not the level of testing undertaken by the Consumers' Association, but the objects being served were much the same.

The supplementary information being provided by the advice centres was undoubtedly of use to the consumers in a particular locality but two major questions were raised about its efficacy. In the first place, there were some who doubted whether the information that was being dispensed was actually proving useful. While the supporters of the centres pointed to some remarkable statistics about the growth of consumer inquiries following on the establishment of the centres,[17] their detractors asserted that statistics could not themselves establish the real need for the service and claimed that a majority of those inquiring did so from convenience rather than need.

Second, even where it was conceded that the information was genuinely sought and genuinely useful, doubts were cast on whether the information was getting through to the right people. It was suggested that the people who were using the advice services were the same people who could afford to belong to the Consumers' Association or could manage to acquire the facts for themselves without the assistance of a publicly financed advice service. The less well off, it was claimed, did not use the facilities available. This conclusion was supported by some evidence from opinion polls and a survey conducted by the National Consumer Council.[18] The advice centres became the subject of political controversy in some areas of the country. This controversy grew when it became apparent that government funding for the centres would dry up by the end of the financial year 1978–79, and certain local authorities decided that the information which they had been happy to provide when the Government was paying did not seem quite so important when the ratepayers were having to foot the bill. Consumer advice centres in Nottinghamshire, Derbyshire and the West Midlands were closed down.

Quality Controls

We have discussed in an earlier part of the book the requirements as to the safety of certain products,[19] but the safety of the product may only be one factor in a consideration of that indefinable quality, 'quality'. Again, we have already mentioned the law relating to food additives and the regulations that prohibit the filling of sausage-skins with sawdust[20] with the object of showing that intervention in the market is sometimes necessary for the protection of the consumer. What we are concerned with here is protection in its widest sense of ensuring that the consumer has the information to make a sensible choice. The law says very little about identifying the quality of goods and most of the recognizable symbols of quality are awarded by independent, voluntary institutions. Not *all* symbols fall into this category and the law does take an interest in that well-known symbol of quality, the hallmark.

Gold and silver were (and still are) so important to the economy that special rules were formulated to protect those who bought the commodities from fraud and cheating. There is also the problem that gold and silver are often alloyed and the purchaser needs some indication of the quantity of precious metal in the article that he is buying.

Thus, hallmarking is an indication both of quantity and quality and is, perhaps, one of the oldest forms of product labelling. Articles containing gold and silver (and, now, platinum, which was included within the protective legislation in 1975) must be hallmarked by one of the Assay Offices if they are to be sold under the description of gold or silver. The offence, created by the Hallmarking Act 1973, is the application to an unhallmarked article of a description indicating that it contains one of the precious metals.

The other quality indications are much less precise and depend upon accepted British standards of design and manufacture. The British Standards Institution draws up standards for all kinds of products and allows the manufacturers of those products that meet the standards to attach the 'Kitemark' to them. This is an indication of quality, but it is salutary to note that the BSI, though subsidized by a government grant, is financed mainly from industrial sources and from selling the standards to manufacturers, and there are those who doubt its real interest in the field of consumer protection. It has been suggested that it is much more interested in defining standards for industry and that any consumer benefit is incidental.[21] The BSI also sets safety standards for products and those products that comply will normally display a separate label. Other bodies active in this field are the British Electrotechnical Approvals Board, which actually carries out tests on household electrical equipment to establish compliance with British Standards for safety. Their approval is usually marked by a tag, which is also the means of indicating that a product has been chosen by the Design Centre. The London-based Design Centre takes into account practicability in use and value for money as well as good design and safety when deciding which products to select for commendation. All these are quasi-official sources of information and opinion for the consumer and it would be interesting to see how much an individual is actually influenced by this type of information.

CONSUMER-COLLECTED INFORMATION

However much is done for the consumer in the way of provision of information, opinion and evaluation, it will still remain his ultimate responsibility to select the goods that he wishes to buy. Nothing can take away the privilege of being extravagant, reckless, gullible or just plain wrong, but the consumer will usually feel that he has to make some effort to discover the comparative qualities of the goods that he is contemplating buying. The *comparative* qualities – for the range of choice created by the market system leads to an inevitable comparison of one product with another. Price as an indicator of quality may have been accepted at one time as the most significant factor, but an increasingly aware public are becoming accustomed to acquiring information for themselves in the battle for the best buy. It was the quest for comparative evaluations of consumer products that led to the formation of the largest consumer interest group, the Consumers' Association.

Which? and the Consumers' Association

The organization, growth and objects of the Association have already been dealt with in Chapter 2,[22] and we are here primarily concerned with the Association's role as a disseminator of consumer information. The influence of the magazine, *Which?*, with its details of tests carried out on different makes of a single product, cannot be underestimated. The magazine has a subscription list of just under 600,000 and the number of readers must be considerably greater. Because the magazine does not limit itself to presenting factual information and the results of tests, but also recommends a 'best buy' or commends a product as 'value for money', the effects on sales of the various products must be significant.

It has been argued that the recipients of the advice offered by *Which?* are those who least need it, the intelligent, articulate middle-class people who would be able to gather most of the information for themselves without the assistance of the Association. The people who really need the strong advice on quality and value for money are not likely to see the magazine and will still battle on without help. These consumers cannot be expected to pay for the sort of information provided by *Which?* and ought to be given similar help through official channels. That may be so, but the benefits of the Association are not limited solely to its members. The members might argue that they should be, but it must be of benefit to the consumer body as a whole that an independent organization wields such significant influence as the Association. Manufacturers must obviously take note of faults exposed in their product and may rectify them to everyone's benefit, and those whose products are commended may take steps to

PREPARING TO BUY — ACQUIRING INFORMATION   143

publicize that fact in advertisements. The Consumers' Association seal of approval is a valuable thing. Finally, it may be said that the annual subscription to the magazine is not very high and cost should not deter many from making use of the facilities available. Those in most need of help may not read the magazine, but that highlights a defect in consumer education rather than a defect in the Consumers' Association — they can hardly be criticized for not being read widely enough!

Although *Which?* is the flagship of the Consumers' Association fleet, the success of that publication has permitted the Association to branch out into other activities which include the publication of other magazines and books on more specialized topics[23] as well as the operation of six advice centres. The crucial question for the Association over the coming years will be the extent to which it is prepared to become involved in the political arena as a consumer pressure group attempting to influence ever wider spheres of public life.[24]

Specialist Publications

The consumer may consider that when he is buying particular goods he can obtain assistance from a publication that deals exclusively with the field in which he wants to purchase. However, such magazines often appear to be of most assistance to the specialist, who may best be able to judge for himself the performance of specialist equipment. The layman may become even more confused by a perusal of a hi-fi magazine, which is written in a language that he doesn't understand and discusses at length refinements of which he was completely unaware. Obviously there are some publications that are written at a rather more general level, (for example *What Car?*, *What Hi-Fi?*), but the average reader may find that he is overwhelmed by the amount of detail presented by the specialist publications.

Manufacturers' Information

Information provided by the manufacturer will usually be available through the retail outlets, but where it is not there is nothing to prevent the zealous consumer from approaching the manufacturer direct. Normally information obtained in this way will not be of a comparative nature and will be restricted to the products of the manufacturer approached, but it can be quite useful to have the manufacturer's publicity material as well as any technical specifications that might be available – the publicity material may contain the terms of any guarantees or exclusions. The only drawback is that such acquisition may expose the consumer to the risk of doorstep selling once his name and address are in the files of the manufacturer.[25]

ADVERTISING

The information that the advertiser would like the consumer to rely on may be contained in the advertisement of the product. Of course, advertisements don't just contain information; they contain inducements, suggestions, blandishments, comparisons, extravagant claims – in fact, almost everything *but* information. It is, however, appropriate to deal with the form and content of advertising primarily in a section on the influence of information on the consumer, because advertising is really about the combination of factors that will be most likely to lead the consumer to exercise his choice in favour of the particular product advertised. Consumer choice is, after all, what all information is directed towards. At the moment there is relatively little formal control of the form and content of advertising and debate is just beginning over the effectiveness of the current system of voluntary control of any excesses perpetrated by over-enthusiastic manufacturers and advertising agencies. Advertising and the budget allotted to it by the manufacturer also have economic implications for the price of the product, and this aspect has been examined earlier.[26]

The Content of Advertisements

What goes into an advertisement is as indefinable as the limits of human imagination, but it is quite possible to identify the types of advertisement that are used as a means of selling. At one extreme, there are the classified adverts which appear in long columns in national and local newspapers and which are pored over by countless readers seeking that elusive bargain. They seek simply to communicate fact in an unspectacular, utilitarian way. Manufacturers and retailers may also advertise facts, such as the prices at which goods are being sold, without making any other claims. The form of the advert may be somewhat larger than the classified type, but they are essentially in the same mould; they are saying, 'These are our prices', or 'We have this range of goods in stock', or 'These are the specifications of our product'.

At the next stage of persuasion are the advertisements that seek to emphasize the qualities of the product in question by making claims on its behalf, such as, 'Persil washes whiter', 'The most advanced wristwatch in the world', or 'Wood roof trusses are versatile'. These statements are sometimes clearly statements of fact, sometimes are statements of opinion and sometimes are regarded as mere 'puffs' – sales talk.

An advertisement may make no claims of fact but seek to sell the product by comparison with some symbolic character, such as, 'Put a tiger in your tank', 'Fiat 132: A wolf in sheep's clothing', or 'Citroen CX Safari: A different kind of animal'. Alternatively, the quality of the product may be suggested indirectly by the surroundings in which it is placed, or by the way that people are represented as reacting to it, as 'I simply flew when he said Je Reviens'.

We could go on with many more examples of the way in which the agencies seek to influence the choice of the consumer, but the reader will have had the opportunity to discover that for himself. Indeed, it will be a fortunate or exceptionally sheltered reader who has not been bombarded with propaganda through television, the press, hoardings, sports sponsorship and in a host of other ways. The problem for the government, the consumer protector, is the extent to which the normal restrictions on the freedom of speech (defamation, obscenity, incitement to racial hatred, etc.) should be extended to ensure that unfair or improper pressure is not exerted on consumers by the advertising agencies. At what point does the harmful effect of advertising (whether through simple misinformation or through the suggestion of anti-social and undesirable habits as normal) outweigh the right of the manufacturer to sell his product in the way that he thinks fit? It must be noted that the interests to be protected in the regulation of advertising are not simply the consumer interests but also the general interests of society in the suppression of advertising material that is indecent, offensive, immoral or otherwise in bad taste.

Legal Controls on Advertising

The next chapter is devoted in its entirety to the ways in which the law protects the consumer from actual deception by the manufacturer, retailer or vendor; and any advertisements that can be brought within the terms of the various criminal offences or can be regarded as giving rights in contract or tort will be subject to the appropriate legal rules. It is much more difficult to pinpoint the role of the law in proscribing those advertisements that are simply offensive, or are couched in a way that does not actually tell a lie, or present a completely misleading impression of the product they are trying to sell.

It is fair to say that the object of the law at the present time is to prevent untruthfulness in advertising. The Trade Descriptions Act 1968, the Misrepresentation Act 1967 and the Theft Act 1968 are concerned mainly with *false* statements, and exercise only limited control over the ambiguous statement, the half-truth and the exaggeration. A different approach in the Advertising (Hire-Purchase) Act 1967 required specific disclosure and we consider the advertising of credit in Chapter 8. As a result of an EEC draft directive on misleading advertising,[27] we may have to move towards legal controls of these shady areas. It will be interesting to see how much the powers given to the Director-General of Fair Trading under the Fair Trading Act 1973 are used against advertising.

The provisions of the Fair Trading Act do represent a potential legal control depending upon the way in which the Director-General chooses to exercise his powers. You will recall from our discussion of the role of the Consumer Protection Advisory Committee in Chapter 2 that the Director-General may decide to refer matters impinging upon the general consideration of whether a consumer trade practice is adversely affecting the economic interests of consumers in the UK to the Committee for consideration. Advertising is within the definition of consumer trade practice adopted in the Act, at least as far as it is in connection with the supply of goods or services to consumers. A major report is being prepared by the Office of Fair Trading in conjunction with the Consumers' Association and the Advertising Association; but in advance of the publication of the report the then Prices Secretary, Mr. Hattersley, indicated that the Government were considering legislation against advertisers who fail to abide by the voluntary code of practice.[28] Naturally enough, this threat has been criticized by the Advertising Association, who claim that the extent of the problem of misleading advertising will not be known until the OFT makes its report. This will clearly be an important document, both for its analysis of the extent to which advertisements currently conform to the code of practice and for the possible action it may inspire in the government in going beyond the terms of the EEC draft directive. Although the signs are that advertising may come under stricter legal controls, we must still examine the basis of the present voluntary control of the industry.

Voluntary Regulation

The role of the Advertising Standards Authority and the alleged benefits and detriments of self-regulation have been discussed in Chapter 2, but we wish now to look at the way the Code of Practice applies to some of the forms of advertising that we noted above.

The advertising claim about the quality of a product should be governed by the paragraphs in the section of the Code headed 'General Principles', which provides that descriptions, claims and comparisons that relate to ascertainable fact should be capable of substantiation, and further that,

> Advertisements should not contain any statement or visual presentation which, directly or by implication, omission, ambiguity, or exaggerated claim, is likely to mislead the consumer about the product advertised, the advertiser, or about any other product or advertiser.

Particular mention is made of claims about value, terms of purchase, conditions of delivery, exchange, return, repair or maintenance, terms of guarantee, etc.

The other general principles prohibit advertisements that contain statements or visual presentations offensive to the standards of decency prevailing among those who are likely to be exposed to them, and those that play on fear, exploit the superstitious, support violence or support or condone criminal or illegal activities. Comparisons with other products are permitted provided they are fair and not calculated to mislead, and do not unfairly attack or discredit other products or advertisers. The rest of the general principles are intended to give protection to particular sections of the community – the young, those giving testimonials, those whose privacy might be invaded, etc.

From the general the Code proceeds to the specific and deals with the advertising of particular products including alcohol and tobacco. Although the advertising of cigarettes is forbidden on television, the other rules are not enormously restrictive, as one can observe by looking at the television advertisements for drink and posters advertising cigarettes. The special attention paid to the advertising of these products does not represent any altruistic concern on the part of the ASA for the consumer; it resulted from the pressure for control that was exerted by the public, mainly on behalf of young people.

The effectiveness of voluntary regulation will be assessed by the report of the OFT, and in the absence of other systematically gathered evidence it is difficult to comment upon the work of the ASA. Some of the drawbacks to self-regulation we have already noted and there are signs in the wind that the days of self-regulation may be numbered.

7 Preparing to Buy – Preventing Deception

INTRODUCTION

In the last chapter we examined the ways in which the consumer may gather the information necessary to enable him to make an informed choice from the goods available, and we concluded that, generally speaking, the persistent shopper could find out a good deal. However, there remains danger in permitting or even encouraging an uncontrolled supply of information, because skilful presentation of that information can be misleading and also because the omission of vital information is less easily noticed in a welter of the unnecessary and the irrelevant. The policy of encouraging manufacturers and retailers and others to publish material about products and prices imposes a corresponding obligation to ensure that the consumer is not deceived or misled by the information he has come to expect and to rely on. Information published about goods and services or statements made at, or before, the point of sale can range from the downright fraudulent through the careless to the completely innocent misrepresentation. The law must formulate a policy to deal with all these cases as well as those in which the advertising of products is overoptimistic. It is at this point that we make the fundamental distinction, which is central to the whole field of consumer law, between civil remedies, which the consumer must seek himself in the civil courts, and criminal sanctions, which are imposed by the state after a successful prosecution initiated on its behalf.

CIVIL AND CRIMINAL REMEDIES

It is difficult for the lawyer to produce a satisfactory definition that pinpoints the difference between the civil courts and the criminal courts; indeed, many of the courts in the structure of the English legal system exercise both civil and criminal jurisdiction, and it will be important to remember that fact in the remaining chapters when the courts are referred to by name.[1] Fortunately, however, there is less difficulty in distinguishing the form and function of proceedings.

Civil proceedings are the means by which the consumer may assert private rights conferred on him by statute or common law against any other private individual or business.[2] The consumer alone takes the decision on whether to initiate proceedings, how to carry on the action, what remedy to seek and when to terminate proceedings. He may give up at any point in the proceedings and, as we shall see later, the pressure upon him to do so may at times be considerable. Subject to the availability of legal aid the consumer is entirely responsible for financing the action. If he is successful he can expect to receive a proportion of his costs from the unsuccessful party, but this principle also requires him to run the risk of having to pay the other party's costs if he should lose the case, except where the claim is for less than £200, when no costs are awarded to either side.

Civil actions in consumer matters will be begun either in the County Court or the High Court unless some special provision has been made in the contract of sale[3] and many potential litigants are frightened of commencing proceedings on account of cost, complexity and delay. The current trend seems to be towards the encouragement of the individual to bring cases on his own in the County Court.[4] Views differ as to the necessity for a lawyer to be involved in consumer cases, and the extension of consumer protection by the strengthening of private law rights might be criticized on the grounds that too much is expected of the consumer. The procedural dice, it is said, are loaded so heavily in favour of the defendant in a civil action that only the most confident plaintiff will pursue his private law rights through the courts.

Criminal actions, on the other hand, are generally pursued through the courts by other agencies. Once a criminal charge has been brought against a defendant by the police or by public officials (in Scotland, the Procurator Fiscal), that charge must result in a court hearing unless there is intervention by the Director of Public Prosecutions or the Attorney-General or the court itself gives leave to withdraw the charge. The responsibility for the preparation, presentation and financing of the case rests with the prosecutor who is acting on behalf of the state. Therein lies the essential difference: the state itself has an interest in criminal proceedings, which are conducted on its behalf.

It would be wrong to suggest that the private individual has no opportunity to commence criminal proceedings, but the number of private prosecutions is now very limited.[5] In theory the private citizen may institute proceedings against anyone whom he considers to have infringed the criminal law, but that right is cut down by legal and practical considerations. Legally, an increasing number of crimes (and all the really serious ones) may be the subject of proceedings only if consent is given by the Director of Public Prosecutions or the Attorney-General, and those who prosecute the lesser offenders privately must be very sure of their evidence if they are not to risk a civil action for malicious prosecution at the suit of the defendant. Practically, the difficulties of acquiring evidence and the prohibitive cost of financing criminal proceedings deter all but the most incensed citizens.

The outcome and the object of civil and criminal proceedings are, from the point of view of the consumer, quite different. In the normal civil case the consumer will be seeking money compensation for the wrong that he is alleging was committed by the defendant. That compensation will be assessed, if he is successful, on the basis of putting him into the position he would have been in if the wrong had not occurred (in the case of a tort) or if the contract had been adhered to (in the case of contract). Damages are always expressed in money terms and the courts will not refuse an award of damages where a wrong has been established simply because there is some difficulty in assessment. On occasion, the consumer may be seeking a specific remedy (e.g. an injunction), but the normal award is one of damages. Such an award may be enforced by the plaintiff, but it is important to note that the decision in any particular case only binds the parties to that case and has no formal legal effect on the decision of other similar cases, save through the application of principles of law formulated by the judge in arriving at the decision. English law does not acknowledge the concept of a 'test case', although the practical effect of a successful action by one of a class of aggrieved consumers may be to induce the defendant to settle the claims of the other people in the class without undue delay.[6]

Compensation is not the usual object of criminal proceedings, and it is acknowledged that the outcome of successful prosecutions will be the punishment of the offender in the way provided for by the common law or statute. An absolute discharge, or even a conditional discharge, may not generally be regarded as punishment, but there will have been a conviction even in those cases, and the stigma of conviction of a criminal offence may be considerable. Punishment of the offender will not be of any direct benefit to the victim of the crime, except perhaps by gratifying his vengeful instincts, and the traditional solution had been to allow the victim his civil remedy against the offender. There is nothing at all to prevent the same set of circumstances giving rise to both civil and criminal responsibility. The duality of actions has been reinforced by the differing procedures adopted by the criminal and civil courts and the different levels of proof required.[7]

The futility of instituting separate proceedings to determine very similar issues, particularly where small sums of money were involved, became apparent, as did the unwillingness of the victims of criminal offences to resort to the civil courts.[8] The situation was partially remedied by the Powers of Criminal Courts Act 1973 as amended, which gave the court that had tried the defendant the power to order him to pay compensation to the victim of his crime. There is no limit to the amount that may be granted where the trial is in the Crown Court, but the Magistrates' Court is limited to £1,000. A compensation order is normally sought by the prosecution or by a representative of the victim at the time of sentence, although there is nothing to prevent the court making an order of its own volition. This part of the Act applies only to England and Wales.

Despite the criticism that compensation orders involve the criminal courts in deciding the extent of the loss or injury of the victim and in assessing that in money terms (a job to which they are not accustomed), the new powers have been welcomed as a cheaper and easier solution to the problem of compensating the victim than the commencement of a civil action. The existence of the orders also invests the decision of successive governments to create new criminal offences in the consumer field with added significance. The differing effects of the creation of private rights or the creation of criminal offences must be highly relevant in deciding on the most efficacious way of protecting the interests of the consumer. The recent tendency has been towards the creation of criminal offences, with the additional burden imposed upon the Consumer Protection Departments for policing and prosecuting when necessary.

DECEPTIVE STATEMENTS – CRIMINAL OFFENCES

It is convenient to treat the criminal offences that encompass deceptive statements in descending degrees of generality, for not all of the offences applicable have been created specifically to deal with consumer protection. After the general provisions, some of the more important statutes affecting the consumer are considered individually.

The Theft Acts 1968, 1978

These statutes contain the law relating to theft and related offences involving deception, and several of their provisions may be invoked to protect the interests of a consumer faced with a dishonest vendor. The most pertinent section in the present context is that which makes it an offence dishonestly to obtain property (including money) belonging to someone else by any deception.[9] The offence carries a maximum penalty of ten years' imprisonment and is treated seriously by the criminal courts. The Act contains a definition of deception that may be of interest in our later consideration of practices and statements that are alleged to be deceptive or misleading.

'Deception', for the purposes of the Theft Act, means any deception, whether deliberate or reckless, by words or by conduct, as to fact or as to law.[10] The definition includes any deception as to the present intentions of the person deceiving or any other person. The definition is widely drawn and includes many situations where consumers are misled into parting with money without receiving anything in return as well as those in which the qualities of the article sold are not as described by the vendor. (Note, however, that the deception must be deliberate or reckless and it must have induced the victim to part with his money in order to constitute the offence.[11])

The Trade Descriptions Acts 1968, 1972

The statutes on trade descriptions are probably the best-known consumer protection measures. Whether they are always fully understood is another matter. Football crowds on their way home from a particularly depressing match have been known to mutter darkly that describing 'that bunch' as a football team was 'a crime under the Trade Descriptions Act', although the Act is drawn more narrowly than is commonly supposed.

The predecessor to trade descriptions, the Merchandise Marks Acts 1887–1953, had proved ineffective in providing protection for consumers against mis-description and for traders against misuse of trade marks. These objectives were not happily contained within one statute and the difficulties were compounded by the reputed indifference of the Board of Trade towards prosecution and the trifling penalties imposed upon conviction. The Molony Committee[12] considered a great deal of evidence about the working of the Acts, and its recommendations led to the Trade Descriptions Act after a suitable period of discussion and consideration of the proposals.

The Molony Committee drew attention to five areas that merited attention in new legislation, and it is useful to rehearse their recommendations in order to set up standards by which to judge the efficacy of the statutory provisions. The Committee directed their proposals towards:

(i) the removal of defects in the existing Acts which made their meaning obscure, their application unfair, or their administration difficult;
(ii) the extension and amendment of the term 'trade description';
(iii) the incorporation of a statutory power to define imprecise or corrupt terms used in trade descriptions;
(iv) the extension and amendment of the term 'applying' a trade description;
(v) an improvement in the enforcement of the statute.[13]

The Trade Descriptions Act 1968 went a considerable way towards implementing those proposals, and although it has given rise to some difficult cases has been judged generally successful in its first ten years. The drafting was good and there has been little textual criticism; the enforcement of the statute through the local Consumer Protection/Trading Standards Officers has been effective and produced a measure of uniformity; the definitions adopted, while contested in particular cases, have been workable and easily understood. The working of the Act has been reviewed by an interdepartmental committee chaired by the Director-General of Fair Trading, and the criticisms that are made in their Report are directed as much towards the decisions of the judges interpreting the Act as towards the Act itself.

The scheme of the Act is to create criminal offences in respect of three major types of deceptive statement: false or misleading trade descriptions applied to goods; false statements as to price; false or

PREPARING TO BUY — PREVENTING DECEPTION

misleading statements about services, accommodation or facilities. These offences will normally be prosecuted by the local Consumer Protection Officers, but there is nothing to prevent an individual bringing a private prosecution if the local authority takes no action. Defences are provided in certain circumstances to mitigate the rigour of what would otherwise be largely strict liability.[14]

False trade descriptions Section 1 (1) of the Act creates the major offence in fairly simple terms, but the words of that subsection must be read in the light of Sections 2–6 which contain their definition. The subsection provides:

> Any person who, in the course of a trade or business, –
> (a) applies a false trade description to any goods; or
> (b) supplies or offers to supply any goods to which a false trade description is applied;
> shall, subject to the provisions of this Act, be guilty of an offence.

The Act is intended to catch the dishonest trader rather than the private individual, hence the restriction to a person applying a false trade description 'in the course of a trade or business'. This does not necessarily mean that the trade or business must be the main occupation of the person involved, but there must be evidence of something other than a purely private transaction.[15] The words 'any person' include a company or a partnership, and it is interesting to note that the description may, in unusual circumstances, be applied to the *buyer* of goods. Where a motor dealer told a customer that his car was irreparable and could only be scrapped, the Divisional Court held that those statements were capable of being false trade descriptions applied to goods. The buyer was the expert and making statements about the car in the course of his trade or business.[16]

Sections 2 and 3 of the Act contain substantial definitions of the central phrase, 'false trade description'. Section 2 provides that a trade description is any sort of indication about goods or parts of goods concerning (among other things) quantity, size, composition, fitness for purpose, testing, place of manufacture, previous ownership or use, and almost every other possible quality possessed by goods. Section 3 then provides that such a description is false if it is false 'to a material degree', or if it is misleading, and further provides that anything that is not a description within the meaning of Section 2 may be deemed to be a false trade description if it is likely that it would be taken for a trade description. This gives a very wide meaning to the phrase in question, so it is perhaps easier to note what falls outside the section than to note what is covered.

Statements of opinion will often be outside the definition of trade description unless they are demonstrably also statements of fact. 'This is a beautiful car', 'In exceptional condition throughout', 'Really exceptional condition throughout' and 'Immaculate condition' are all phrases with which the second-hand car buyer will be familiar, but they give rise to difficulty for the courts in deciding whether they are capable of amounting to false trade descriptions. The decisions have not always been consistent. The clearest exposition of the difficulty came in the case of *Cadbury Ltd*, v. *Halliday*,[17] where the defendants had put on their chocolate bars a 'flash' with the words 'Extra Value'. This had been done after the purchase tax on chocolate had been reduced in 1973 and bigger bars were being sold at the same price as smaller bars had been sold previously. The Divisional Court held that this was not a false trade description, even when new, cheaper bars of chocolate were produced. Value was a claim about which opinions could legitimately differ.

The description must be 'applied' to the goods. It is sufficient if the goods are marked with the description, or it is fixed to them, or to their packaging, or if the statement made is likely to be taken as referring to the goods. The innovation here, not entirely recommended by the Molony Committee, is to make a statement that was made at the time of the sale capable of being a trade description.[18] It is also useful to note that an alteration of goods, or the concealment of a structural weakness that causes the goods to 'tell a lie about themselves' without any description being applied by the retailer, will still be caught by the Act.[19]

One of the most fertile sources of prosecutions under the Act is the false odometer reading on used cars. It is apparent that there are used car dealers who are not averse to tampering with the odometer to show that the car in question has done fewer miles than is actually the case. There are some difficulties even for the honest trader, in that the odometer may have been altered before he bought the car. Many traders attempt to avoid liability by issuing a disclaimer to the effect that the odometer reading is not guaranteed, and thus try to ensure that the odometer reading is not a trade description 'applied' to the car. The Divisional Court has held that a disclaimer may be effective to neutralize a trade description so long as it is as bold, precise and compelling as the description itself. It must also be brought to the attention of the buyer.[20] This may be thought to negative part of the effect of creating the offence, but the rules laid down by the Divisional Court seem sufficiently stringent to safeguard the consumer in most situations. What he should be on his guard for is the total or blanket disclaimer which attempts to repudiate any description whatsoever.[21]

False statements as to price   Section 11 of the Act was the subject of some of the criticisms of the OFT review group,[22] and it may be because the concept of legislation controlling the display of prices is a new one that the section of the Act concerned has not received unanimous approval. Taking account of the comments of the Molony Committee,[23] Section 11 of the Act provides:

(1) If any person offering to supply goods of any description gives, by whatever means, any false indication to the effect that the price at which the goods are offered is equal to or less than –
(a) a recommended price; or
(b) the price at which the goods or goods of the same description were previously offered by him; or is less than such a price by a specified amount, he shall, subject to the provisions of this Act, be guilty of an offence.
(2) If any person offering to supply any goods gives, by whatever means, any indication likely to be taken as an indication that the goods are being offered at a price less than that at which they are in fact being offered he shall, subject to the provisions of this Act, be guilty of an offence.

The section was intended to deal with the very common practice of indicating that goods were being offered at bargain prices by comparing them with the recommended prices or with usual prices. In particular, department stores would buy in special stocks for sales, passing them off as astounding bargains. This practice is now made more difficult since the trader (and the Divisional Court has held that the section ought to be read as though it continued the words 'in the course of trade or business')[24] must not display a price at which the goods have previously been offered unless they have actually been on offer at that price for at least twenty-eight days during the preceding six months. However, the usefulness of this provision has been somewhat diminished by the decision in *House of Holland Ltd* v. *London Borough of Brent*,[25] where the Divisional Court held that the onus lay on the prosecution to show that the goods had *not* been offered at the displayed higher price for the twenty-eight-day period. Proving a negative is always difficult and this decision may well inhibit future prosecutions under the section.

The straightforward representation of goods as costing a lower price than they actually do is a criminal offence, but devices rather more subtle than the plain lie are also caught. An advertised price exclusive of VAT was held to be a false indication of price[26] (the advertisement said nothing about the tax), as was the display of a bottle of Ribena without adequate notice as to the deposit charged on the bottle.[27]

The OFT review group was not entirely happy at the working of Section 11 and suggested modifications without adopting the extreme solution of a widely worded general offence. The OFT have themselves published a report on bargain offer claims, and the Director-General is reported to be considering what proposals he should put forward in the light of the response to the original report.[28] The OFT has also reported on the practice of quoting prices that are exclusive of VAT, and the CPAC have made their report to the Minister.[29] After the particular difficulties with petrol retailers over price display resulting in the introduction of an order under the Prices Act 1974 making the display of prices compulsory, this is clearly an area in which we can expect further interest and action on behalf of the consumer. The Director-General himself has reported that the present difficult economic conditions are leading to greater use of 'bargain', 'value' and 'worth' offers, and the Secretary of State is likely to be taking action before long to regulate these practices.

False or misleading statements about services, accommodation or facilities The offences so far discussed have been offences of strict liability; that is to say, the prosecution does not need to prove that the false trade description or false description as to price was deliberate, or that the defendant knew, or even suspected, that the description was false. The new offence under Section 14 of the Act would appear to be different in that it requires *mens rea*, a mental element, on the part of the accused person.[30] The section provides:

(1) It shall be an offence for any person in the course of any trade or business –
(a) to make a statement which he knows to be false; or
(b) recklessly to make a statement which is false; as to any of the following matters, that is to say –
(i) the provision in the course of any trade or business of any services, accommodation or facilities;

(ii) the nature of any services, accommodation or facilities provided in the course of any trade or business;
(iii) the time at which, manner in which or persons by whom any services, accommodation or facilities are so provided;
(iv) the examination, approval, or evaluation by any person of any services, accommodation or facilities so provided;
(v) the location or amenities of any accommodation so provided.

The extension of the law to encompass false statements in relation to services as well as goods has given rise to difficulties for the courts in deciding when to impose liability for statements relating to the future. This difficulty has been most clearly illustrated in the numerous cases involving travel companies and their holiday brochures. The principle that seems to emerge from the decisions is that where the statement that is made relates solely to the future and does not contain within it a statement of existing facts, it cannot be brought within the terms of the Act. Forecasts or promises, however optimistic, cannot be caught by the Act unless they contain statements of present fact that are false. Consequently, it is no offence to promise in a holiday brochure that a swimming pool will be provided and that a hotel will provide good food with English dishes available, if those are promises or forecasts and do not contain false statements of existing fact.[31] However, if the brochure is false when it is published, e.g. by representing that there is a night club on the beach outside the hotel when there is not, an offence is committed if the statements have been made knowingly or recklessly.[32]

This distinction has been accepted by the House of Lords in *British Airways Board* v. *Taylor*,[33] where the policy of the former BOAC of 'overbooking' airline seats was called into question. A passenger had booked a seat on a flight to the West Indies and received written confirmation of his booking. Because the flight had been overbooked in the expectation of cancellations there was no seat for him when he arrived at the airport. The Airways Board, charged under Section 14, alleged that the booking was only a promise or a forecast and that no false statement of fact had been made. The House of Lords refused to accept this contention, holding that when the confirmation had been sent a false statement of fact was made to the effect that a seat was definitely available, although the policy of overbooking made it impossible to guarantee the truth of that statement.

The review group of the OFT has criticized this distinction and has proposed reforms that would make it clear that it is an offence to supply a service to which a false trade description has been applied. This aligns the offence with the application of a false trade description to goods and might make for a more consistent policy.

The courts may have been restrictive about the *actus reus* (the acts of the accused) of the offence under Section 14, but they have given a wide interpretation of the words that import the mental element necessary to ground liability. In most other circumstances in the criminal law the word 'reckless' is taken to connote a state of mind in which the accused has chosen to ignore a risk that he has actually contemplated – 'The statement I am about to make may or may not be true, I don't know and I don't care.' However, in relation to Section 14 the Divisional Court held in *MFI Warehouses* v. *Nattrass*[34] that recklessness did not involve dishonesty, and that a person could be reckless in the meaning of the section if he acted without having any regard to the truth or falsity of a statement. The court relied upon the definition in Section 14(2)(b), which provides that:

> (b) a statement made regardless of whether it is true or false shall be deemed to be made recklessly, whether or not the person making it had reasons for believing that it might be false.

It could have been argued that even that definition at least required the person making the statement to advert to the possibility of its falsity even though he might have no reason to believe it to be false, before he could be said to have made the statement recklessly. However, the Lord Chief Justice said:

> I think it suffices for present purposes if the prosecution can show that the advertiser did not have regard to the truth or falsity of his advertisement even though it cannot be shown that he was deliberately closing his eyes to the truth, or that he had any kind of dishonest mind.

That is a very wide formulation, and one that puts the innocent purveyor of services in as much peril as the dishonest. If this is the correct definition of recklessness it is difficult to see the real distinction between this offence and the strict liability offences discussed earlier.

Weights and Measures Act 1963/Food and Drugs Act 1955

These statutes have already been considered in the preceding chapter in respect of the obligatory disclosure of information to the consumer. It will also be necessary elsewhere to return to the stringent standards contained in the Food and Drugs Act which offer protection to the consumer at the point of sale. However, we must note briefly in this section on the prevention of deception of the consumer that both statutes have provided criminal offences in connection with the supply of false, deceptive information.

The Weights and Measures Act 1963 (WMA) makes it an offence to misrepresent the quantity of goods sold or purchased,[35] and it is equally an offence to overstate the quantity of goods that is pre-packed or in a container.[36] There are other similar offences in respect of goods made up for sale[37] and in respect of false statements in documents associated with goods.[38] These offences illustrate the difficulties that manufacturers find in utilizing modern methods of packing which can leave individual packets short of weight. Potato crisps are notoriously difficult to pack, but the consumer is entitled to expect that the weight that is represented on the packet will be the weight that is inside the packet. The present law requires a minimum weight to be stated with permitted deviations. Although the offences require no *mens rea* on the part of the retailer, the Act provides that a person shall not be convicted of a short-weight offence unless, if similar goods are on sale at the same premises, a reasonable number of articles was tested.[39] Further, if the prosecution is in respect of one package, the court are directed to, 'disregard any inconsiderable deficiency or excess'.[40]

The Weights and Measures Act 1979, which is not yet in force, has altered the minimum system in favour of the average system that is commended by the EEC. This change has been forced on the UK by directives,[41] and it will mean that the legal obligation is shifted primarily to the manufacturer to produce packets that are, on average, of the specified weight. There will be permitted tolerances varying according to the nature of the goods, and testing ought to be simplified since the enforcement agencies could test in bulk in the factory rather than at random in the shop. The protection afforded to the consumer ought not to be diminished, and the liability would still remain on the retailer to deliver the correct weight in relation to non-packaged goods and goods packed by the retailer.

The Food and Drugs Act 1955 makes it an offence to sell food or to expose it for sale with a label that bears a false description or that is calculated to mislead as to the nature, substance or quality of the food.[42] The regulations mentioned in the last chapter[43] reinforce this offence by prescribing a wide variety of foods to which labels must be attached, and the consumer's interest is protected still further by the decision that whether or not a label is misleading is a matter for the court acting as ordinary men rather than for expert evidence. Would the label mislead the ubiquitous reasonable man?[44]

Other Criminal Offences

The annual reports of the Director-General of Fair Trading provide lists of the criminal legislation that has given rise to complaints by consumers. Not all of these statutes concern mis-descriptions and deception, but there are a number of them that contain offences of that nature. For example, it is an offence to publish false and misleading advertisements in relation to medicines,[45] as it is also to represent that that material which is not in accordance with standards of non-inflammability prescribed by regulations is, in fact, non-inflammable.[46]

There are a number of other provisions that are tucked away in statutes relating to specialized areas, but there are no other major provisions with a wide, general application.

DECEPTIVE STATEMENTS – CIVIL RIGHTS

The civil law gives a mixture of rights to the individual who is the victim of a false statement and the precise nature of the right, and the remedy, will depend upon whether the statement was made innocently, negligently, recklessly or fraudulently and, where a contract is involved, whether the statement has become a term of the contract. It should be noted that the law to be discussed is not solely related to consumers; it applies to all deceptive statements, but the following discussion will be in the context of a consumer transaction.

Representations as Terms of a Contract

In the majority of consumer transactions a contract will be in contemplation when statements or promises are made by one contracting party to the other with a view to persuading him to buy the product. There may be cases in which a contract is not in contemplation or in which the person making the statement is neither the contracting party nor his agent; and, in either event, there will be no possibility of the statement forming part of a contract. However, in the normal case the first question to ask when considering action on a representation that turns out to be false is, 'Was the statement or promise intended by both parties to be part of the contract so that the person making it was undertaking to comply with what he was stating or promising?' If the answer to that question is in the affirmative and the statement or promise is unfulfilled, the victim will have an ordinary action for breach of a term of the contract.[47] How can one tell whether a representation becomes part of the contract?

There is no precise test, and the judges have tended to rely on the test of intention that governs so much of the law of contract – did the parties *intend* the representation to be a term? However, there are examples of factors that are considered important in settling that question and imputing intention to the parties. How important was the statement or promise? When was it made? Did it clinch the deal? Was the party making it an expert in the field? Was the victim invited to verify the statement by inspection of the goods? All these questions are directed towards an assessment of the *weight* of the statement, and the weightier the statement, the more likely it is to be construed as a term.[48] If it is not held to be a term of the contract, it is sometimes referred to as a 'mere' representation and the remedies available to the consumer will depend upon the nature of the misrepresentation.

Innocent Misrepresentation

The false statement that is made to the consumer might be made quite innocently with the maker of the statement believing implicitly in the truth of what he was saying. 'This fine car was once the property of the Maharajah of Bahpoor', says the car salesman, relying, quite reasonably, on the forged certificate of ownership that has been presented by the last vendor.

In these circumstances the Courts of Equity provided a discretionary remedy for the victim of the false statement, considering a petition for rescission (cancellation) of the contract on the grounds that it would be unconscionable to allow the enforcement of a contract based on a falsity. But the remedy of rescission is not always available, for it involves handing back the property in the same condition and restoring the parties to the position they were in before the contract was made. Difficulties also arose if third parties had acquired rights in the goods in question, for they could not be interfered with.[49]

Rescission, when available, is an awkward remedy, unattractive to most consumers. Assistance was given to the victims of innocent misrepresentation by the Misrepresentation Act 1967.

The Act took a rather odd course by providing that, where a person has entered into a contract[50] after a misrepresentation has been made to him, then if the person making the representation *would* have been liable if he had made the statement fraudulently, he will still be liable to compensate the victim's loss unless he can show that he believed the statement to be true and had reasonable grounds for doing so. This is a convoluted way of providing liability for misrepresentation by postulating a hypothetical liability for fraud, and appears to raise the question as to whether the damages should be assessed according to the contract rules or the tort rules.[51]

It will be observed that the Act does not impose liability for an innocent misrepresentation in the sense of one that was reasonably believed to be true, but the onus is on the maker of the statement to show the existence of his belief in the truth of the statement and the reasonableness of that belief. The makers of statements who give no thought to their veracity will not be able to escape liability under the Act.

Additional assistance that the Act gave to consumers was to provide that, in cases where the plaintiff would be entitled to the remedy of rescission (i.e. cases of completely 'honest and reasonable' misrepresentations), the court may award damages instead if it is of the opinion that it would be equitable to do so.[52] This will assist the consumer who does not want to go to the drastic lengths of returning the subject matter of the contract (e.g. his house) but wishes to be compensated for the loss that he has suffered as a result of the misrepresentation, i.e. the difference in money value between what he was promised and what he got. Liability for misrepresentation cannot be excluded except in so far as the exclusion is fair and reasonable (Misrepresentation Act 1967, Section 3, as amended by the Unfair Contract Terms Act 1977, Section 8).

Negligent Misrepresentation

In the sense discussed above the Misrepresentation Act deals primarily with negligent or careless false statements, but the phrase 'negligent misrepresentation' more often conjures up a historic decision of the House of Lords in *Hedley Byrne & Co.* v. *Heller & Partners.*[53] Prior to that decision there had been no remedy for the victim of a careless statement that caused economic loss, unless rescission was available. In some cases it wasn't, and in others no contract had been made so it was inappropriate anyway.

The House of Lords decided in *Hedley Byrne* that liability in the tort of negligence could be established in respect of a statement negligently made by a person who holds himself out as competent and willing to advise, if that statement causes loss. The original principle in *Hedley Byrne* has been subject to discussion in subsequent cases but it has not been substantially modified and represents an alternative for the consumer who finds himself without another cause of action.

Fraudulent Misrepresentation

There is nothing to prevent the victim of a fraudulent misrepresentation relying on the Misrepresentation Act as presenting an easier way of establishing liability than undertaking the onerous task of proving fraud on the part of the defendant. However, if it should be necessary to prove fraud the consumer must show that the statement of which he complains was false and that the defendant either knew that or was reckless about its truth, i.e. didn't care whether it was true or false.[54]

The action in this case will be in the tort of deceit, and the successful plaintiff may seek to have the contract rescinded, and will be entitled to damages. The proving of fraud is so difficult and the alternative of the action under the Misrepresentation Act so attractive that it is hard to conceive of circumstances in which the action in the tort of deceit will be appropriate.

DECEPTIVE STATEMENTS – ADVERTISING

Although we have already made mention of the problems of advertising in a number of places in the text, and particularly in the preceding chapter, we must none the less relate the civil and criminal law just discussed to the practice of advertisers. You will recall that we said that there was little legal control on the form and content of advertising and that reliance had to be placed on the voluntary code of practice to ensure that consumers were not deceived.[55] We must now say a little more about why the general law has such minimal control.

The criminal law is directed towards specific deception of an individual, and although it is possible to point to successful prosecutions under the Trade Descriptions Act where the advert in question has made a specific claim,[56] there is nothing that the Act can do about the many different kinds of non-specific advertising. It may no longer be possible to say of a product, 'Gubbins is good for you', but there is absolutely nothing to prevent the same message being put over by implication. It is true that there are a few statutes that have something specific to say about the advertising of particular products, but they are of relatively limited effect because of the special fields to which they relate.[57]

The civil law seems to accord to advertising claims a special niche all of their own and it is extremely difficult to establish liability for misrepresentation in respect of advertising. In the first place, the advertiser/manufacturer is unlikely to be a party to the contract with the consumer. Holiday contracts and mail order contracts represent exceptions to that rule, but if the contract is not made with the manufacturer/provider of services the consumer must try and show that the retailer by implication adopted the false claim, which is not an easy task. Second, the law seems to allow a great deal of freedom for advertisers (and retailers) to indulge in 'sales-talk'. For a misrepresentation to be actionable it must be shown that it induced the consumer to make the contract and that it was significant, not a 'mere puff'. Statements of unverifiable opinion cannot be misrepresentations. Only when something is done to make it clear that words contained in adverts are meant to be relied upon will the courts come to the assistance of the consumer.[58]

The result of all this freedom is the voluntary self-regulation of the advertising industry, but legal controls are looming, and they are much more likely to operate through statutory bodies with defined obligations than through the private law rights of individuals. It is unlikely that the civil rights of the consumer will be diminished by legislation, but in the future he may be more effectively protected by the Director-General of Fair Trading than by the exercise of his own personal rights.

DECEPTIVE PRACTICES – THE FAIR TRADING ACT 1973

We should look back at this point to the powers given to the Director-General by the Fair Trading Act 1973. Under that statute he is able to invite the Consumer Protection Advisory Committee to consider whether a particular trade practice adversely affects consumers' economic interests and has one of the effects specified in the Act. If the Committee agrees with the Director's proposals, or agrees to modified proposals, its report goes forward to the Secretary of State with a view to his exercising the power given him in the Act of making these practices unlawful.[59]

We have already mentioned the attention that is being paid to the effectiveness of the self-regulation of advertising, but it is also interesting to observe the use of these powers in curbing deceptive practices that might otherwise not be caught by the criminal law. For example, the Director-General made references to CPAC early in its career relating to the display of statements in shops and elsewhere which purported to exclude or limit the rights of consumers that could not, by law, be so excluded or limited, and relating to the practice of traders who would advertise articles for sale in the classified columns without disclosing that they were traders.

These were both practices that were misleading consumers – in one case as to their rights, in the other as to the person they were dealing with. They clearly fell within the statute, and the CPAC agreed with the Director when they reported that they were practices that should be prohibited.[60] Both of them were then the subject of Orders made by the Secretary of State which made it a criminal offence to do either of these things.[61]

The trade practices that the Director-General may consider are not limited to those that involve an element of deception, but he has shown a marked preference for the investigation of practices of this nature. References were made to the CPAC concerning the display of prices that do not include VAT, and direct to the Secretary of State concerning 'bargain offer' claims.[62]

These powers are an extremely useful supplement to the existing civil and criminal law and it is likely that we shall see an increased use of them to attack unfair and deceptive trading practices.

8 Preparing to Buy – Acquiring Finance

INTRODUCTION

By now we have permitted the individual consumer to select the product he wishes to buy from among those on offer in the market. He has acquired the information necessary to make an informed choice and he has been protected from the deceptive statements and practices that can accompany selection. For many consumers, however, a significant problem remains. How is the product to be paid for? This question may be significant where the individual concerned does not have the ready cash to pay on the nail, or where he wishes to arrange his cash-flow in such a way as to facilitate the purchase, or where he estimates that to purchase at advantageous rates of credit will be economical, or simply where it is more convenient not to pay cash. There are many ways in which a consumer transaction can be financed and the law is now concerned to regulate credit arrangements.

The provision of credit for the purchaser of goods goes back a number of centuries, as long as there have been purchasers who wished to enjoy the benefit of goods or services before they were actually able to put down the price. From the rudimentary arrangements of a periodical bill presented by the tradesman, through the pawnbrokers and moneylenders, to the finance houses and credit card companies of the present day, the availability of credit has increased, and with that increase has developed the necessity for imposing some sort of control on the granting of credit.

Economic arguments dictate that there should be a supply of credit available to the consumer, and the control of the credit available has been one of the tools used by successive governments in the manipulation of the economy. The amount of money tied up in the provision of credit is very significant for the economy, and we must note some of the economic aspects of the granting of credit before we move on to examine the legal controls.[1] We should make clear at this point that we are not going to discuss the provision of credit for the purchase of land or property; although this is likely to be a major expenditure, the problems raised are outside the scope of this work.

Types of Finance Available

Retailers, finance houses, the banks and, to a lesser extent, the credit card companies provide the majority of the finance for consumer transactions where credit is involved. The relative influence of each of these providers of finance has differed from time to time, and the advent of the credit card companies is a fairly recent phenomenon.

Retailers have always been in the front line for credit provision through informal arrangements like the rendering of monthly or quarterly accounts, 'putting it on the slate', deferring payment for a fixed period, or through more formal arrangements in credit sales and, a recent innovation, budget accounts funded by a monthly payment from the customer allowing a fixed amount of revolving credit.[2]

The form of credit that gained in popularity in this country after the turn of the century was the system of hire-purchase whereby a finance house purchased goods from the dealer and then hired them to the consumer, giving him an option to purchase the goods on completion of a stipulated number of payments. This scheme presented considerable advantages for the finance houses and the suppliers, and it became so popular that Parliament sought to exercise greater control over the formalities of the hire-purchase agreement and the remedies available to the finance house when the hirer defaulted on payment. The Hire-Purchase Act 1938 was the first attempt at statutory regulation of this form of credit, and since then the activities of the finance houses and the terms on which they do business have been regulated.[3]

The consumer might simply seek a loan to allow him to pay for the goods immediately and then repay the loan over a period of time. There has never been a shortage of people willing to provide loans for a variety of purposes but the terms and conditions upon which they are granted will vary enormously. A friend may be willing to provide a few pounds, but the major providers of loans are currently the banks and the finance houses. The banks have various schemes under which their customers may borrow money (although they are subject to legislative control like anyone else), but it is important to note that many banks will make loans only to their own customers. Those people who do not have bank accounts, and quite a lot who do, may approach the finance houses for a 'personal loan'. The finance houses discovered that if they made a loan to a consumer for the purchase of goods they were not subject to the restrictions imposed by hire-purchase legislation, and, in particular, they bore no responsibility to the consumer for the quality of the goods supplied by the dealer.

These personal loans were also clear of the restrictions on moneylending transactions after the decision in *U.D.T.* v. *Kirkwood*,[4] and they represented an attractive opportunity for the finance houses. In the late sixties and early seventies, secondary banks and finance houses flourished and 'money shops' appeared in our city streets. These activities have been significantly controlled by the Consumer Credit Act 1974.

The credit card companies hit directly at the desire for immediate acquisition[5] and their advertising found many consumers at their most vulnerable. The credit card operation adopts alternative forms of repayment, but whichever of these forms is adopted the nature of the transaction is the same and the supplier of goods looks to the credit card company for payment for goods supplied to the consumer. The company then sends the consumer an account. By virtue of the Consumer Credit Act 1974 some of the companies have responsibilities towards the consumer for the quality of the goods supplied in credit card transactions.[6]

Other forms of credit exist – almost as many as the wit of man can devise – but the most significant of those not already mentioned is the system of check trading.

The Regulation of Credit Provision

There are both economic and legal aspects to the regulation of credit provision. The economic aspect relates to the manipulation of available credit for the purpose of achieving macroeconomic objectives. In certain circumstances (e.g. unemployment or inflation) the amount of credit available is increased or decreased and/or the terms upon it which it may be offered are changed. Clearly, when availability and/or terms are altered the consumer interest is directly affected although the reasons for the alteration may be justified in national economic terms. These direct interferences with the supply of credit do not however affect the relationship between the consumer and the supplier of credit, and it is that relationship which has been the subject of legal regulation.

The Consumer Credit Act 1974 is a comprehensive piece of legislation which is designed partly to increase the protection given to consumers against unfair credit practices and partly to rationalize the existing common law and statutory principles into a more coherent whole. The objectives of the Consumer Credit Act, resulting as it did from the Crowther Committee on Consumer Credit,[7] may be stated as the regulation of consumer credit transactions according to their nature, their separation from commercial dealings and the assimilation of the rules relating to hire-purchase, instalment sale and loans for consumer transactions.

Although the Consumer Credit Act is concerned with the regulation of the relationship between the supplier of credit and the recipient, it also contains provisions creating criminal offences with the object of preventing certain unfair and undesirable trade practices in the credit business. Further, it imposes obligations on the Director-General of Fair Trading to monitor and keep under review the operation of the Act in particular and the consumer credit business in general, to administer the Act and enforce it, and to run the system of licensing introduced by the Act.[8] It will be observed that the Act combines all the elements of consumer protection that we noted in the chapter dealing with the prevention of deception. There are provisions that create civil rights and obligations, provisions that stipulate the content of agreements, provisions that give further powers and responsibilities to a public body, and criminal offences that are designed to underpin the system. The Consumer Credit Act 1974 may impart a new flavour to consumer protection, but it has been cooked up according to the classic recipe!

Protecting the Defaulter

Altering our title slightly, it is appropriate to ask at this point what protection is offered to the consumer who defaults on repayment of hire-purchase instalments or a loan. It might be argued that we should pay no attention to defaulters – that the law of consumer protection should apply only to those who have entered transactions that they have been able to carry out. Consumers need to be protected from unfair or oppressive bargains and from accepting credit on terms that are unreasonable, but once the transaction is complete and the law has been complied with, the consumer who does not meet his obligations should be left to the mercy of the creditor without further protection.

In our view these arguments ignore matters of fundamental importance. There is good evidence that the highest incidence of default is among the lower socioeconomic groups in our community.[9] Various reasons may be advanced to explain that phenomenon. Such people may take no precautions against the interruption of earnings because of sickness or unemployment; there may be a natural inclination to over-commit resources; there may be undue optimism about ability to meet repayments; more importantly, there may be a much lower resistance to the methods of salesmanship employed when the goods are originally sold. It is highly likely that the true significance of transactions is not fully appreciated, and that the poorer, less sophisticated consumer is more vulnerable to smooth talking and high-pressure salesmanship.

If this is indeed the case, as we would suggest it is, then it is quite legitimate to extend the concept of consumer protection to include those who are left to cope with their mistakes — mistakes that may have been induced by the very system that is condoned and encouraged by our society. Defaulters are as entitled to a fair deal as everyone else, and the restrictions on the remedies available to creditors in this situation need to be examined.

FINANCING A CONSUMER TRANSACTION

In order to appreciate the full implications of the Consumer Credit Act 1974, which we consider below, it is necessary to have a clear picture of the various forms of consumer credit that are available. The Act is concerned with consumer credit in all its forms, but it applies differently to different forms of credit and we need to be able to distinguish them for the purpose of analysis.

The Finance House – Hire-purchase; Loan for Sale

Although some dealers will still operate their own credit schemes for the benefit of customers, by far the majority use a finance house to make credit arrangements for customers. The utilization of the resources of finance houses did not make any difference to the legal characterization of the transaction, and the hire-purchase contract recognized in *Helby* v. *Matthews*[10] became the usual form of agreement between the finance house and the consumer.

The hire-purchase agreement involves the sale by the retailer of the goods to the finance company, which then hires them to the consumer in return for regular payments, giving him an option to purchase the goods on completion of the payments. The consumer does not become the owner of the goods until the option has been exercised, and it is this factor that distinguishes the hire-purchase agreement from the credit sale or conditional sale agreement. Under the latter two agreements the consumer is committed to purchase the goods, even though the price may be payable by instalments. With a conditional sale agreement, property in the goods will pass to the buyer on the fulfilment of an expressly stipulated condition (often the making of the final payment), whereas with a credit sale agreement ownership will usually pass immediately and the price will be paid subsequently.

The finance houses use all these types of agreement and are at liberty to stipulate the most advantageous bargain subject to the provisions of the Supply of Goods (Implied Terms) Act 1973 and the Consumer Credit Act 1974. The Hire-Purchase Act 1965 has been largely incorporated into the Consumer Credit Act 1974 since it represented a satisfactory regulation of hire-purchase, and it will remain in force until the appropriate provisions of the Consumer Credit Act have been brought into operation.

Particularly at the end of the last decade, the finance houses and the secondary banks began to move into an even more advantageous form of credit supply in the form of the personal loan. The drawback to the hire-purchase agreement was that the finance house was regarded as the supplier of the goods involved[11] (although there were some advantages in being able to repossess the goods if the consumer defaulted on payment) and the personal loan avoided this difficulty. Very high rates of interest were charged for these loans but they were attractive simply because of their availability. The Consumer Credit Act places certain restrictions on this form of credit, and the reputation of the secondary banks has suffered from the difficulties encountered by some of their number who were forced into liquidation after over-ambitious dealing.

Banks

The major banks provide extensive credit facilities which are normally restricted to customers of the bank involved. Some of these facilities may involve the provision of security by the debtor, but we are considering only those loans where security is not required. The personal loan, given for a specific purpose and repayable over a stipulated period with a fixed rate of interest, is a most popular form of credit for financing a consumer transaction. However, it is not the only possibility, and the customer may prefer simply to ask the bank to extend an overdraft facility, which will allow him to borrow up to a specified sum on his current account. Occasionally this sum is debited to a separate account (a loan account) and is repaid by agreed instalments from the current account, but more often it is debited to the current account and repaid as agreed. The agreement for the repayment of overdrafts is a matter for negotiation with the bank manager and may involve periodic repayment or total repayment by a specified date. The interest paid on overdrafts fluctuates with the movements of the minimum lending rate.[12]

An overdraft may provide a form of revolving credit in that a borrowing limit may be imposed without any stipulations as to repayment. In that case the customer may continue to borrow to the specified limit, having paid off part of the overdraft, without further reference to the manager. The clearing banks are also involved in the two major credit card companies, but this form of credit is considered below.

Credit Cards and Check Trading

Credit card companies differ in their methods of requiring repayment from the customer but they all extend credit for some period. Each of the companies operates by allowing their customers to use a card to pay for goods and services at specified outlets. The retailer then sends an account to the credit card company, which will pass the cost on to its customer. Some companies require immediate payment of the total debt by a single instalment (e.g. Diner's Club and American Express) and the customer only benefits for the period of time it takes for him to receive the bill from the company, while others (notably Barclaycard and Access) merely require monthly repayment of at least a stipulated minimum figure. In the latter case the customer may choose to pay off the entire debt, and he will then incur no additional expense, or he may pay the minimum amount or a sum less than the total debt, in which case he will pay interest on the debt outstanding.

The credit card gives considerable advantages to the discerning user. It allows a period of free credit so long as the total debt is settled at the end of the account period; it allows considerable flexibility in the amount of credit (usually up to a stipulated maximum); it obviates the need for carrying large amounts of cash; and it allows the debtor to vary the period of repayment to suit his commitments. Against those advantages are set the encouragement to spend more than can be afforded, not solely from the possession of the card but also from the advertisement of the facility.[13] The rate of interest charged on the debts outstanding is substantial when expressed in yearly rates.[14]

Check trading is a form of credit card trading although it is not done by means of a card. The customer acquires a check ('credit token', in the words of the Act) from the trading company for a specified sum which may be spent with any retailer prepared to accept it. The retailer will look to the trading check company for payment and the company will recover the money from the customer, usually by means of fixed instalments collected from door to door. The system is a rudimentary form of credit card trading although not as flexible and for smaller amounts. The trading check does not represent revolving credit since the total amount is fixed and once spent may not be used again.

Shops

Shops are perfectly free to arrange their own forms of credit as mentioned above, but one form of credit that can be extended only by shops has recently become popular. This is the revolving credit or budget account, whereby the shop agrees to allow the customer to purchase goods up to a certain specified amount in return for a regular monthly repayment. Interest is charged on the amount outstanding at the end of each month, and the customer is permitted to keep on spending so long as he has not reached his credit limit. As repayments are made, so the amount that the customer may spend on credit is increased.

Apart from any profit that the shop might make on the interest paid, the revolving credit is advantageous in building consumer loyalty to that shop in much the same way as the granting of account facilities did in the old days. There is nothing quite so conducive to purchasing goods as the knowledge that it can 'go on the slate', even though today the slate has been replaced by the computer.

Ancillary Businesses

As though enough people had not yet become involved in the provision of credit, there have been established ancillary businesses which derive their existence from the credit industry. They are mentioned here because they receive some coverage in the Consumer Credit Act.

Credit reference agencies collect, store and transmit information about the creditworthiness of individuals. They wield considerable power since a bad reference from such an agency will often be sufficient to ensure that the inquirer (a finance company or other creditor) does not give credit to the applicant. These agencies sometimes acquire their information from rather dubious sources, and the Consumer Credit Act gives the individual the right to discover and correct his credit record.

Debt collection agencies do not operate solely in the consumer credit field, but they exist to take over bad debts from creditors (including finance houses and other suppliers of credit) and recover them. They will purchase the debts from the creditors for far less than the face value and utilize all sorts of methods, from the subtle to the crudely persuasive, to induce payment. Ultimately they may take action in court against the debtors, the costs of the actions being minimized by the large scale on which they are undertaken.

Credit brokers exist to find credit for their customers (on payment of a fee or commissoin), and *debt counsellors* exist to offer advice to defaulters and negotiate on their behalf with creditors on payment of a fee or commission. The voluntary agencies operate as debt counsellors without making a charge, e.g. the CAB. One wonders whether some brokers and counsellors are really the same people with different signs on their windows? In any event the potential debtor can find someone to pay money to at every stage of the game.

THE CONSUMER CREDIT ACT 1974

The Consumer Credit Act 1974 (referred to hereafter in this section as the Act) is not a simple piece of legislation. That would hardly be possible in a statute that is seeking to implement most of the recommendations of the Crowther Committee[15] and provide a coherent and comprehensive statement of the law relating to consumer credit. However, the man mainly responsible for the drafting of the Act, Mr Bennion, has been an outspoken critic of obscurity and technicality in the law and the Act provided him with the opportunity to strike a blow for clarity. He accepted the challenge and readers should not be deterred from consulting the statute itself.

Reform of the law had been advocated by the Crowther Committee, which had undertaken a complete survey of the social, economic and legal aspects of consumer credit. Their report was not entirely accepted by the government[16] since it contained proposals not only concerning consumer credit but also concerning a restructuring of secured loans and the establishment of a register of securities. Few of the latter proposals have been implemented by the government, but the part of the report dealing with consumer credit was accepted and acted upon.

The Crowther Committee had concluded that, in relation to consumer credit, there were significant weaknesses in the law. In particular, the following three were noted.[17]

(a) *Transactions were regulated according to their form rather than their substance* A consumer might not perceive any important distinction between getting a bank loan to buy a car, getting a loan from a finance company, or getting the car on hire-purchase. In essence, the provision of money served the same function in each case – the immediate acquisition of the car – but different statutes applied different rules according to the type of transaction.

(b) *Consumer transactions were not distinguished from commerical transactions* Statutes that gave a measure of protection to the consumer interest were also relevant to commerical transactions, and it was argued that quite different considerations should apply to the regulation of the consumer interest and the commercial interest. One of the fundamental reasons for protecting the consumer in his dealings with business interests was his relatively weak bargaining position, and that argument could not be sustained in dealings between businesses.

(c) *Totally inadequate protection was being given to the consumer in consumer credit transactions* Following on from the second criticism, that no distinction was drawn between commercial and consumer transactions, the Committee reported that the safeguards for consumers in credit dealings were inadequate. They gave as examples the lack of any requirement that the true rate of borrowing be disclosed; the lack of central control over rates of credit; the lack of a requirement that a rebate be given for early settlement of the debt; and the lack of effective administrative machinery for the enforcement of the legislation that was supposed to be protecting the consumer interest at that time.

These basic criticisms led the Crowther Committee to the conclusion that amendment and piecemeal reform were unlikely to produce satisfactory results. They advocated new statutes to replace the entire range of the existing legislation, although much of the law of hire-purchase was retained. In the event, as mentioned earlier, part of the proposals were not implemented, but those relating to consumer credit became the Act. As a Bill the proposals gained support from both political parties, and although the original Bill fell with the Heath Government in February 1974, the Bill presented by the Labour Government in the next session of Parliament (in substantially the same terms) became law in July 1974. Parts of the Act still require implementation and the indications are that it might be some years before it is fully implemented. However, in the succeeding discussion we will proceed as though the Act were in force, with an indication of those sections that have yet to be implemented. To put the Act in its context it must be understood that many of the provisions to be found in it have their origin in the law of hire-purchase. The Hire-Purchase Act 1965 remains in force until the appropriate sections of the Consumer Credit Act are implemented. Reference will be made at points in the text to the hire-purchase background of some of the provisions.

The Scheme of Legislation

The reader will find it helpful to have some idea of the total effect of the Act before we begin discussing the individual provisions. The Act is in 12 parts and 193 sections, but the way in which we shall be presenting it is as follows.

Agreements within the scope of the Act   We shall mainly be dealing with those 'regulated agreements' that are caught by the provisions of the Act. A regulated agreement is defined as 'a consumer credit agreement or consumer hire agreement, other than an exempt agreement'. It is important to note also that the Act controls advertising and extortionate terms in *any* credit agreement.

The classification of the agreements
Licensing of those in the consumer credit business   The Act requires those in the business of providing consumer credit to be licensed by

the Director-General of Fair Trading. Enforcement machinery has been established under the auspices of the Office of Fair Trading.

Seeking business Restrictions have been placed on the manner and content of advertising of credit provision and on the canvassing of credit agreements off business premises – mainly on the consumer's doorstep.

Making a consumer credit agreement There are certain formalities provided by the Act and certain requirements as to disclosure of information. Further, there is a right in some circumstances to cancel an agreement before it comes into effect.

Incidents occurring during the currency of the agreement

Ending the agreement The Act provides for the debtor or the creditor to end the agreement, but places some restrictions on the remedies available to the creditor, particularly in respect of repossession of goods.

Credit inquiries and credit reference agencies The Act gives the consumer rights to acquire information about credit status inquiries and the nature of the information on file about him. Corrections may be required if the information is incorrect.

Fair trading The Director-General is given certain additional duties under the Act. Licensing has already been referred to, but it is important to note the new duties and the overlap with the other responsibilities of his office imposed by the Fair Trading Act 1973.

Discretionary judicial control The courts are given an assortment of discretionary powers to ensure the full operation of the protective provisions of the Act.

Agreements within the scope of the Act

Most of the provisions of the Act only apply to 'regulated agreements', i.e. agreements that are brought within the Act. The definition of a 'regulated agreement' is contained in Section 189(1): 'a consumer credit agreement, or consumer hire agreement, other than an exempt agreement'. The only important provisions of the Act that apply to agreements other than regulated agreements are those concerning advertising[18] and extortionate credit bargains.[19] This makes it vital not only to know what is meant by a consumer credit agreement and a consumer hire agreement, but always to ask whether any particular agreement under scrutiny can be brought within that meaning. If not, it is not subject to the Act.

A 'consumer credit agreement' is defined partly in relation to a personal credit agreement, so that we find in subsections (1) and (2) of Section 8,

(1) A personal credit agreement is an agreement between an individual ('the debtor') and any other person ('the creditor') by which the creditor provides the debtor with credit of any amount.
(2) A consumer credit agreement is a personal credit agreement by which the creditor provides the debtor with credit not exceeding £5,000.

The definition of personal credit agreement provided in the subsection is sufficiently wide to include simple loans, hire-purchase agreements, credit sale agreements, conditional sale agreements, credit card and check trading agreements.[20] Hardly anything is excluded other than a pure rental transaction, which we shall come to later. The wide definition is then cut down somewhat by the provisions of the second subsection, the most important qualification being that of the maximum credit figure. That figure needs more explanation, as does the word 'individual' in the definition.

When the Crowther Committee originally reported (in 1971) they recommended a figure of £2,000, and it is an interesting reflection on the decline in the real value of money that by the time that the Act was passed the government had seen fit to raise that figure to £5,000. No credit transaction will fall within the definition of a consumer credit agreement unless it falls within the £5,000 limit. This limit is calculated by reference to the *amount of the credit provided*, not by reference to the total repayments to be made. The Act provides that the 'total charge for credit' (i.e. the amount of interest to be paid, a procuration fee and any other item prescribed by regulation by the Secretary of State) shall not be treated as credit – the figure for credit is calculated without reference to it.[21]

It may not always be easy to unravel the various costs involved in a credit transaction, particularly in hire-purchase agreements, and some examples may help.

Joe agrees to purchase a car from Crippto Cars Ltd for £7,500. He provides a deposit of £3,000 and borrows from the Company £4,500 to be repaid in twenty-four monthly instalments of £250. The repayments total £6,000 but the interest will be ignored for the purpose of calculating how much credit has been extended, and the sum involved (£4,500) is within the limit. The loan agreement is a regulated agreement.

Bill agrees to enter a hire-purchase agreement by which an antique Persian carpet is sold to a finance company who, in turn, hire it to him for monthly payments of £150. Bill is given an option to purchase the carpet for £10 after due payment of forty monthly instalments. In order to establish the credit extended the amount of interest included in the monthly payments must be calculated, together with any other charges prescribed and deducted from the total price. If the final result is £5,000 or less the agreement will come within the Act.

The further difficulty that arises in relation to the £5,000 limit is the result of the distinction taken between fixed-sum credit and revolving or running-account credits. In the case of a credit card, a budget account at a shop or an overdraft facility, the amount of credit may be subject to an overall limit though the credit actually taken up may be less. In order to establish whether a revolving credit agreement comes within the definition of a consumer credit agreement, the following test can be applied. If any *one* of the following questions can be answered in the affirmative, it is a consumer credit agreement and subject to the provisions of the Act.

   (i) Is there any one occasion on which the amount of credit is limited to £5,000 or less?
   (ii) It is unlikely that the debt will rise above £5,000?
   (iii) Do the terms of the agreement become more onerous (e.g. the interest goes up) once the debt exceeds a stated figure of less than £5,000?[22]

Because these tests are rather strict it is likely that most revolving credit agreements will in fact fall within the Act as regulated agreements. A revolving credit agreement where the credit limit is below £5,000 presents no problems – it is within the Act. The other point to note in the definition of a consumer credit agreement is that it is restricted to agreements between 'an individual' and any other person.[23] This cuts out agreements between companies (since a company is not regarded as an individual for the purposes of the Act), but it does include agreements between a partnership and another person providing credit, even where the partnership is borrowing the money for business purposes.

The second part of the definition of a regulated agreement refers to a 'consumer hire agreement', which receives its definition in Section 15:

> (1) A consumer hire agreement is an agreement made by a person with an individual ('the hirer') for the bailment or (in Scotland) the hiring of goods to the hirer, being an agreement which –
> (a) is not a hire-purchase agreement, and
> (b) is capable for subsisting for more than three months, and
> (c) does not require the hirer to make payments exceeding £5,000.

The inclusion of this type of agreement takes account of the Crowther Committee's observation that rental agreements were totally free from legislative control. Rental agreements for cars that last longer than three months, for televisions and for other consumer durables will now fall within the purview of the Act. (Gas, water and electricity meters are specifically excluded from the operation of this section, as are the Post Office and the Kingston upon Hull City Council, which runs its own telephone service cheaply and most efficiently.[24])

Many general legal principles have exceptions attached to them and the definition of regulated agreement has its own exceptions. The final part of the definition excludes from the category of regulated agreements those that are to be known as exempt and that are listed in Section 16. The more important exempt agreements are those where the creditor is a building society or local authority and the credit is extended for the purchase of land or improvements to land or is secured on land. Other exempt agreements include those where there are no more than four instalments and which are not hire-purchase or conditional sale agreements, and those where a repayment is due from the debtor for credit extended during a regular period (e.g. American Express and Diners Club).

Finally, it should be noted that the Act applies only to regulated agreements made on or after 1 April 1977.

The Classification of Agreements

The Act, having defined regulated agreements, established a classification of agreements with precise definitions attached which is based very largely on the categorization suggested by the Crowther Committee. It is necessary to include these types of agreement because many other parts of the Act use the definitions to be discussed now. It may help to note that these transactions have been classified according to their nature and functions and not according to their form. The draftsman has thought about the ways in which credit is extended and has attempted to provide a coherent structure which adequately reflects the distinctions to be found in practice.

Restricted-use/Unrestricted-use credit is dealt with by Section 11, which draws the distinction between credit that is extended to allow a particular transaction to be financed, whether that transaction takes place between the creditor and the debtor or the debtor and another person, or is a refinancing of an existing debt owed by the debtor to the creditor or someone else, and credit that is extended without any strings attached. In practical terms the distinction may be taken between a personal loan from a finance company for the purchase of a specific car and an agreed overdraft from the bank for an unspecified purpose. Any credit agreement that is not restricted-use, as defined, is unrestricted-use. There are certain differences in the rules relating to the advertising of these different types of credit and also in relation to the disclosure of information.

A credit-token agreement as defined by Section 14(2) is a regulated agreement for providing credit by the use of a credit token, i.e. a credit card, check, voucher, stamp, etc., which can be produced to a supplier to pay for goods or services, or to procure cash in circumstances in which the person issuing the token will undertake to pay the supplier. The person issuing will then recoup the money from the individual. The credit tokens mentioned above are examples of those provided under an agreement defined in Section 14(2). The section does not extend to the ordinary bank card since the bank there is not paying the supplier for the goods or services provided to its customer but merely undertaking to honour the cheque given in payment when it is presented.

Debtor–creditor–supplier agreement is the awkward name given to a most important type of agreement covered by the Act. The Crowther Committee termed the situation a 'connected loan',[25] but it was quite clear that a distinction ought to be made between the situation in which the creditor advances money for the purchase of goods or services that he is himself supplying or that are to be supplied by someone with whom he has a close connection, and the situation in which the advance is made to purchase goods or services from any supplier or from an unconnected supplier. In the former situation the

Committee thought that there was such a community of interest between the creditor and the supplier that their interests ought not to be treated separately. Into this category of agreements would fall hire-purchase, credit sale, conditional sale, credit card, check trading, budget account transactions and deals in which the vendor of goods introduces the customer to a finance company by virtue of an agreement with the company. There are many examples of provisions of the Act that apply to this type of agreement only, but it will suffice at this stage to refer just to one. In a debtor–creditor–supplier agreement the debtor may pursue a claim in misrepresentation or a breach of contract against the *creditor*, if such a claim would lie against the supplier.[26] This gives the consumer a most useful weapon.

Debtor–creditor agreement is the term given to the second situation outlined above where the creditor advances money for the purchase of goods or services from any supplier (not himself) who is not connected with him under pre-existing arrangements. The normal bank loan, bank overdraft, loan from a moneylender or personal loan not geared to specific suppliers are examples of debtor–creditor agreements.

Licensing

It is important, when creating new safeguards for consumers, to make provisions for some effective supervision and enforcement machinery. One of the criticisms of the old legislation voiced by the Crowther Committee was directed at the lack of effective enforcement, and the Act accordingly assigns specific responsibilities for enforcement, coupled with a licensing system that is designed to allow close supervision of the operation of the credit business. The onus of ensuring compliance with the law has been removed from the individual consumer and placed on the Director-General of Fair Trading[27] working in conjunction with the local Consumer Protection/Trading Standards Officers and, for informational purposes, the voluntary agencies.

The selection of a licensing system to assist in the control of the credit business is a significant decision because of the implications for an individual or business of the loss of a licence. The refusal of a licence, its withdrawal during its currency or a failure to renew it at the end of the period of grant will have the most serious repercussions for the business. It will not be able to carry on trading. This is a far different consequence for a business than the loss of an occasional civil action brought by a disgruntled (and determined) consumer.

PREPARING TO BUY — ACQUIRING FINANCE

There are other advantages to a licensing system that are less easy to quantify but are none the less real. Consistent standards may be achieved by centralization along with the central gathering of information about the activities of those engaged in the credit business. Information that is gathered, sometimes informally, can be put to use in the grant or refusal of licences when it might be difficult or even impossible to introduce the information in a court of law. There are, however, safeguards in the elaborate procedure which have to be followed if licences are refused or withdrawn.

It is the fact that a system of licensing exists that is the greatest protection to the consumer rather than its requirements, so long as a certain standard is required, and we will not concern ourselves unduly with the detailed administration of a licence system. It is sufficient for our purposes to note briefly the people who need a licence, the types of licence issued and the grounds on which they are issued and withdrawn.

A licence is required by anyone who regularly (i.e. not occasionally) carries on a consumer credit or consumer hire business (Section 21(1)). That means any business that comprises the provision of credit under regulated credit agreements, or relates to such business, or any business that comprises or relates to the bailment of goods under consumer hire agreements. Some emphasis seems to be put on the regularity with which this sort of business is conducted so that a tradesman who sometimes makes a loan to enable a customer to purchase on credit would not, solely on account of those few transactions, be held to need a licence, unless he was holding himself out as a provider of credit. A licence will also be required by anyone who carries on any of the businesses ancillary to the provision of consumer credit, e.g. debt-collecting, debt-adjusting or the operation of a credit reference agency (Section 145(1)).

Two types of licence exist: the standard licence addressed to the person named in it, allowing him to carry on business under the name specified in the licence, and the group licence, which covers all the persons described in the licence (e.g. solicitors; the National Association of Citizens Advice Bureaux in respect of registered bureaux). In each type of licence the nature of the permitted activities must be specified. The standard licence is granted for a period of three years and the group licence for such period as the Director-General thinks fit.[28]

Application for a licence is made in the way that has been prescribed by the Director-General and he is directed by the Act as to the factors to be taken into account in deciding whether the applicant is a fit person to hold a licence. Section 25(2) provides:

> In determining whether an applicant for a standard licence is a fit person to engage in any activities, the Director shall have regard to any circumstances appearing to him to be relevant, and in particular any evidence tending to show that the applicant, or any of the applicant's employees, agents or associates (whether past or present) or, where the applicant is a body corporate, any person appearing to the Director to be a controller of the body corporate or an associate of any such person, has
> (a) committed any offence involving fraud or other dishonesty, or violence,
> (b) contravened any provision made by or under this Act, or by or under any other enactment regulating the provision of credit to individuals or other transactions with individuals,
> (c) practised discrimination on grounds of sex, colour, race or ethnic or national origins in, or in connection with, the carrying on of any business, or
> (d) engaged in business practices appearing to the Director to be deceitful or oppressive, or otherwise unfair or improper (whether unlawful or not).

That subsection appears to give the Director the widest powers in granting licences. He may consider any circumstances that he considers relevant and there are no provisions as to the nature of the evidence upon which the Director may act. That is a matter for him. The same factors are relevant on an application for a renewal as they are on a first application.

The Director may suspend or revoke a licence that he has granted if he, 'is of the opinion that if the licence had expired at that time he would have been minded not to renew it' (Section 32(1)). Certain safeguards are built in for suspension and revocation, as they are for refusal of an application or refusal to renew, in the form of an opportunity for the person involved to submit representations to the Director and then to invoke an appeal procedure involving the Secretary of State (Sections 34 (and 41)).

Carrying on a business that should be licensed without a licence is a criminal offence, and regulated agreements made while unlicensed may not be enforced against the debtor or hirer unless the unlicensed trader persuades the Director to grant an order that will allow enforcement (Sections 39, 40, 149).

Seeking Business

The doorstep has probably been the site of more consumer disasters than any other venue. The techniques of the doorstep salesmen are legion, even legendary. A smooth tongue, a ready story, a flustered, pressurized customer more often than not led to a sale that entailed commission for the salesman and hardship for the consumer. But it was not just on the doorstep that the consumer was vulnerable. The controls over advertising and the presentation of information were, before the Act, at best rather limited.[29] The Act provides new standards for advertising, canvassing and the display of information but these apply only to consumer credit or consumer hire business. It is not the selling that has come under regulation, but the selling of credit.[30]

Part IV of the Act controls any advertisement, published for the purposes of a business carried on by an advertiser, indicating that he is willing to provide credit or to enter into an agreement for the bailment of goods by him (Section 43(1)). Further provisions limit the scope of the controls to persons carrying on a consumer credit or consumer hire business or those who make agreements to provide credit to individuals secured on land (i.e. by mortgage), unless the advertiser can bring himself within the specific exceptions contained in Section 43(3) relating to the provision of credit over £5,000, or to companies.

The controls that have been imposed are awaiting regulations to be made by the Secretary of State as to the form and content of permitted advertising. When those regulations are made it will be possible to assess whether they achieve the statutory objective of requiring, 'a fair and reasonably comprehensive indication of the nature of the credit or hire facilities offered by the advertiser and of their true cost to the persons using them' (Section 44(1)).

The contravention of regulations made by the Secretary of State will be a criminal offence, and two further specific offences are created. In relation to advertisements covered by Part IV of the Act it is an offence to indicate that a person is willing to provide credit under a restricted-use agreement, when the goods in question are not available for cash from the advertiser or another supplier (Section 45), and it is also an offence to convey information in an advertisement that is false in a material respect or misleading (Section 46).

Each of the offences in the paragraph above can be committed not only by the advertiser himself but also by another person who is knowingly involved in the publication of the advertisement (Section 47).

Canvassing for business by way of regulated agreements off trade premises without a request from the consumer is an offence, as is the canvassing of debtor–creditor agreements off trade premises without a written request signed by the person making the request (Sections 48, 49). These provisions are designed to protect the consumer from doorstep pressure although there are possible difficulties in proving the offences.

The circulation of minors with invitations to take up credit or to apply for information about credit is an offence unless it was not known or suspected that the individual in question was a minor (Section 50); and finally, it is an offence to give credit tokens (e.g. credit cards) to those who have not made a written request for them (Section 51).

This battery of criminal offences may serve to deter the doorstep canvasser, but it will be interesting to see in future years how many charges are brought and convictions obtained under these sections of the Act.

Making the Agreement

The Act makes a number of provisions for the disclosure of information prior to the signing of the agreement and for the formalities that are to be observed on signing.

Section 55(1) provides a regulation-making power specifying information that must be disclosed in the prescribed manner to the debtor or hirer before the making of a regulated agreement. To date, no regulations have been made but the power is an important one since a failure to comply with regulations will make the contract unenforceable without the leave of the court. No doubt the information required will be such as to put the debtor/hirer into a position from which he can properly evaluate the terms of the agreement, particularly its cost.

The five sections under the subheading 'Making the agreement', Sections 60–64, give the regulation-making power to prescribe the form and content of the documents to be used in a regulated agreement, provide that the specified documents must be signed and legible, and impose a duty to supply a copy of an unexecuted agreement and an executed agreement and to give notice of the right of the hirer/debtor to cancel the agreement.

All these sections await the making of regulations for their detailed implementation, but they all have the common feature that if the requirements of the section are not observed the agreement is regarded as an 'improperly-executed' agreement and may be enforced later only by an order of the court.[31] The powers of the court on an application for an enforcement order are considerable, and account may be taken of all the circumstances of the transaction and the amount by which the debtor/hirer has been prejudiced by the impropriety.[32]

Incidents Occurring during the Currency of the Agreement

Part VI of the Act deals with certain incidents that may occur while the agreement is in force. Perhaps the most significant of these is the claim by a consumer against a supplier of goods or services in respect of misrepresentation or breach of contract. The consumer will now, by virtue of Section 75, have an additional claim against the creditor in these circumstances which may be very useful to him if the supplier is unwilling or unable to satisfy a claim. In hire-purchase, conditional sale and credit sale agreements, where the creditor is also the supplier, the agreeement can stipulate the terms of any liability and Section 75 does not apply. It is similarly inapplicable where the cash price is less than £30 or more than £10,000. This section has been in force for some little time in relation to debtor-creditor-supplier agreements entered into after 30 June 1977, and the credit card companies who are particularly affected have voluntarily assumed liability to people who become cardholders before that date.[33] The statutory liability extends to damages for loss and any personal injury resulting from the breach.

The further provisions of Part VI give the debtor the right to acquire certain information from the creditor concerning the amount of the debt outstanding, the amount paid and the amount required to settle the debt immediately (Sections 77, 78 and 97). Additionally the creditor must give the debtor seven days' notice of his intention to take certain action under the agreement, e.g. demanding earlier repayment (Section 76). The seven days' notice provision is also applied to any exercise of a right to vary the agreement between creditor and debtor (Section 82). These are all relatively minor provisions, but they increase the safeguards for a debtor and they will become of particular interest when we discuss, in the next part of this chapter, the protection given by the law to debtor-defaulters.

Ending the Agreement

The Act makes provision for the agreement to be cancellable by the debtor in certain circumstances, which is not strictly speaking a termination since the agreement will never have come into being; but it also provides for the circumstances in which the debtor or the creditor may bring to an end an agreement that is in force and is quite valid.

The cancellation provisions are directed specifically at the technique of doorstep selling. They are intended to allow a cooling-off period for debtors who have been the subject of high-pressure selling techniques, and they set up an exception to the general rule that a contract once made cannot be avoided. Section 67 of the Act provides protection where two conditions are fulfilled: first, that the negotiations prior to the agreement included oral representations by the creditor, or the owner of the goods, or the dealer; second, that the agreement was signed elsewhere than on business premises. Certain regulated agreements are excluded from the provisions of Section 67, but the majority of transactions will be caught.

The consumer who is a party to a transaction covered by Section 67 may give notice to the creditor or owner of the goods within five days of receiving the statutory second copy of the agreement that he intends to withdraw from the transaction (Sections 68, 69). On cancellation a debtor is entitled to recover any money that he has already paid and he can hang on to any goods that he has got until he actually gets any money due to him. Apart from this right, the debtor must return any goods that he has got under the agreement and, until return is effected, he must keep them in good condition.

At this point we are going to discuss only the termination provisions relating to the ending of the agreement by the debtor; we shall deal with the provisions relating to termination by the creditor in the next part of the chapter. The debtor may terminate a regulated hire-purchase or regulated conditional sale agreement at any time before the final payment becomes due (Section 99) as was the case under hire-purchase law. However, there are certain liabilities that he must discharge:

(i) He must pay all money owing at the date of termination.
(ii) Unless the agreement provides for a smaller payment or makes no provision at all, he must pay at least half of the total price of the goods, i.e. the difference between that figure and the amount he has already paid, if any.

(iii) He must pay for any failure to take reasonable care of the goods.
(iv) He must deliver up the goods to the creditor unless the court thinks that would be unjust.

The Court may vary the amount to be paid under (ii) above, if it is satisfied that the creditor will be adequately compensated by a sum less than half the total price of the goods. These provisions are contained in Sections 99 and 100.

Credit Inquiries and Credit Reference Agencies

The activities of credit reference agencies have given consumers cause for considerable disquiet and the Act has provisions that are designed to ensure that such information as is collected by these agencies can be made available to a consumer and can be corrected if it is inaccurate.

The first weapon for the consumer is provided by Section 157, which imposes a duty on a creditor, owner or negotiator to disclose to the debtor, after a written request made within twenty-eight days of the termination of negotiations for credit, the name and address of any credit reference agency from which he has sought information about the debtor. Failure to comply with such a request is a criminal offence.

Having obtained the name and address of the credit reference agency in this way the consumer may make a written request, accompanied by such information as would be necessary to allow the agency to identify his file plus the sum of 25p for a copy of the file. The agency must comply with this request by informing the consumer that it has no file, or by sending him a copy of it containing all the information held by the agency reduced into plain English if necessary (Section 158). Again, this requirement is supported by a criminal sanction. Together with the information supplied to the consumer must come a statement of his rights under Section 159 of the Act which allows the consumer to give notice to the agency to remove or amend any entry he considers to be incorrect. If the agency do not accept the correction for any reason, they must apply to the Director-General of Fair Trading who may then make such order as he thinks fit (Section 159).

Fair Trading

The Director-General of Fair Trading has just been referred to in the context of credit inquiries and he is given sundry other duties under the Act to add to his other duties in respect of fair trading and competition policy. The Director-General is responsible for the administration of the Act and is concerned with the interests both of traders and consumers. The DPCP is responsible for making the regulations that are required to implement various parts of the Act and the OFT has produced a whole range of well illustrated leaflets detailing the effects of the Act on the consumer and the trader.

Discretionary Judicial Control

Finally, there are provisions of the Act that give the courts powers to intervene in agreements made by debtors and creditors where there is evidence of unfairness or oppression on the part of the creditor or the debtor. Naturally the courts will have powers under many of the sections of the Act discussed earlier in this section of the chapter, but the following powers are a miscellaneous collection of varying importance.

Undoubtedly the most significant power is that given by Sections 137-9 to reopen a concluded credit agreement if, on application, the court finds a credit bargain to be extortionate. This provision does not relate solely to regulated agreements, and 'bargain' can include any associated transactions. The court is given power to reopen the agreement to 'do justice between the parties', but some restriction is placed on the power by Section 138(1), which defines an extortionate credit bargain as one that:

(a) requires the debtor or a relative of his to make payments (whether unconditionally, or on certain contingencies) which are grossly exorbitant, or
(b) otherwise grossly contravenes ordinary principles of fair dealing.

Some of the factors that the court might take into account are listed in Section 138 (2), (3), (4), and (5). They include the interest rates agreed, the age, experience, business capacity and state of health of the debtor, together with any financial pressure that he might have been under at the time of the transaction, and any other factors thought relevant. It should be noted that the payments must be grossly exorbitant, or the agreement must grossly contravene the principles of fair dealing, so that the court may not be very quick to grant relief under what might otherwise be a very wide section indeed.

If the court does find that the bargain was extortionate it has wide powers to set aside or amend the terms of the agreement (Section 139).[34]

In the light of these powers the other provisions may appear less significant, but they allow the court to adjust the rate and time of payments of instalments under an agreement (Section 127), to order the protection of goods in the possession of the debtor while proceedings under the Act are in progress (Section 131), and to vary the terms of any agreement or security (Section 136).

Protecting the Defaulter

One of the less savoury aspects of the former law of hire-purchase was the ability of the creditor to repossess the goods that were the subject of the agreement when the debtor was in default. This power was normally conferred in the hire-purchase agreement and it meant that the debtor had little or no security until every instalment had been paid, and that he might lose the goods, however much he had paid up to that point, if he got behind with repayment.

There are those who would argue that nothing ought to be done to help someone who has broken an agreement that he has signed and who is suffering the consequences specified by the agreement, but the better view is that consumer protection extends even to those who may not be entirely without fault. That view is exemplified by the Consumer Credit Act which places certain restrictions on the right of a creditor to terminate a regulated agreement. It should be noted that the common law still applies to all agreements that do not fall within the ambit of the Consumer Credit Act, but in respect of those agreements (as well as regulated agreements) the provisions of the Act relating to extortionate credit bargains may be invoked if the terms of the agreement seem totally unjust.[35] We are now to concern ourselves with the situations in which the creditor may terminate a regulated agreement on the default of the debtor.

The protection that had been given to debtors who defaulted in repayment has been extended by the Consumer Credit Act and the most important provision of the new statute is the requirement that the creditor serve a default notice on the debtor if he is contemplating the termination of the agreement as a result of the debtor's default.[36]

The service of such a notice is a precondition of termination, and the notice must contain prescribed information.[37] The nature of the breach alleged must be specified, and any action required to remedy the breach must be set out and the time limit for rectification (not less than seven days) given. Alternatively, the creditor may specify the amount of compensation required for the breach. If the breach is remedied before the expiry of the time limit the breach is to be treated as though it never occurred.[38] In practice, this means that a defaulter must be given the opportunity to pay the instalments that are due before the creditor has the right to terminate the contract. It may be said that the minimum period prescribed will not give the debtor a great deal of breathing space, but at least he need not fear that the goods are to be snatched back immediately.

Repossession of the goods is also limited by the Act in a way consistent with some of the former hire-purchase legislation, but once again giving extended protection to the debtor. The Act returns to the concept of 'protected goods' which can be repossessed by the creditor only by virtue of a court order. Goods that are the subject of a regulated hire-purchase agreement or a conditional sale agreement may not be repossessed without a court order where the debtor has already paid to the creditor one-third or more of the total price of the goods.[39] If the creditor is in breach of this provision the agreement will terminate and the debtor will be entitled to recover from the creditor all sums already paid under the agreement.[40]

A further safeguard is provided by Section 92 of the Act which prohibits the entry by a creditor into a defendant's premises with the object of repossessing goods unless he has the consent of the debtor or an order of the court. This protects the debtor from unlawful repossession, but it also requires the creditor to seek a court order in all cases in which he wishes to repossess goods against the will of the debtor. The section applies to regulated hire agreements, or conditional sale agreements.

In these various ways the lot of the debtor is improved by the Consumer Credit Act. Statistics seem to show that there are relatively few defaulting debtors and these provisions would seem to alleviate any hardships that would be caused by over-enthusiastic repossession without substantially worsening the position of creditors.

9   Protection at the Point of Sale

INTRODUCTION

We have now reached the point at which the consumer has been presented with a range of goods, with the information to make a choice and the means to do so. When that choice is made the consumer will enter into a contract for the sale of goods or the supply of services and will thereby acquire a substantial array of rights which will serve to protect him if the goods turn out to be defective, unsafe, unsuitable or not in accord with their description. Many of the rights arise out of the contract that has been made, but others arise through the imposition of liability upon manufacturers and others to ensure the safety of their products. This latter liability is founded in the tort of negligence and may result in obligations towards ultimate consumers of goods and services who have made no contract with the retailer or manufacturer. Finally, pressure from the Office of Fair Trading is leading to the adoption of codes of practice by various trade and professional associations. These codes rarely give the consumer any rights in excess of those that he possesses at law, but they do set out a formula that members of the trade or profession are expected to follow in the event of a complaint. Although voluntary, the codes are widely observed by those who are members of the association.

Contractual Rights

Before distinguishing the respective features of the contract for the sale of goods and that for the supply of services, we must say something of the types of obligation commonly found within a contract. Each contract, whether written or oral, is composed of a number of terms that prescribe the respective obligations of the parties to the contract. These terms may be either express, where the parties have specifically agreed to them in writing or orally, or implied into the contract by virtue of custom, statutory provision or the need to make the contract work.[1] (This latter possibility is difficult to pin down, but the courts have been prepared to imply terms into contracts where the parties have not actually agreed on an important point but where some agreement is necessary to allow the contract to operate.)

The express agreement between the parties, together with any terms that are implied, will represent the bargain that has been struck; but it is vital to know what rights accrue to the innocent party when the contract is broken by the other. Accepting the proposition that not all terms of the contract will be of equal importance to the parties, the courts decided that different consequences should attach to the breach of different terms. Some distinction had to be drawn between the more and less important terms, and at first the courts called the more important ones 'conditions', and permitted the innocent party to terminate the contract and claim damages on their breach. The less important were called 'warranties', and their breach only entitled the innocent party to claim damages.[2] That distinction was made in respect of both express and implied terms.

This twofold distinction was based primarily on the importance that was attached to the terms of the contract by the parties at the time that it was made, but it became apparent that the nature of the breach of contract could have important effects. It is possible to have a breach of warranty with very serious consequences for the innocent party or a breach of condition with relatively trivial consequences. The concept of the 'innominate term' was advanced in the *Hong Kong Fir Shipping*[3] case where the Court of Appeal decided that it was permissible to look to the consequences of the breach in order to establish the entitlement of the innocent party to his remedies. This introduces an element of uncertainty into the proceedings, for it might never be possible to know what remedies the breach will give rise to if the term that is broken is one that might be treated by the court as an innominate term. However, this difficulty can sometimes be overcome by the clear expression in the contract of the nature of the terms therein,[4] and the third category of terms is now well accepted.

The distinction between condition and warranty is still crucial and will have a direct effect on the utility of the consumer's rights on a breach of contract. In particular, the terms implied into contracts for the sale of goods by the Sale of Goods Act 1893 as amended are expressed to be either conditions or warranties according to their seriousness.

The usual ability of the parties to stipulate the remedies available on a breach reflects the wide measure of flexibility given to contracting parties under the traditional philosophy of the law of contract. The bargain struck between the parties is essentially a matter for negotiation and the law was reluctant to interfere with the terms of contracts even where it was quite apparent that there was a vast discrepancy in the bargaining power of the two parties. Modern developments have cut down the rights of the parties to conclude a bargain unfettered. The rights of the consumer have been increased by the implication of terms into contracts,[5] the restriction of rights to limit or exclude liability,[6] and the willingness of the courts, in some circumstances, to relieve one party of his obligations under a contract that has been forced on him by the superior strength of the other party.[7] All these developments represent a move away from the *laissez-faire* attitudes of the nineteenth century towards a recognition that individual consumers need considerable assistance in striking a fair bargain with retailers and manufacturers who are in a position of legal and economic superiority. Whether the consumers' rights to be discussed below have pushed the balance too far in the other direction is a matter of controversy.

The Sale of Goods

In contracts for the sale of goods the most important terms,[8] from the consumer's point of view, are the implied terms. The particular monographs dealing with the sale of goods[9] must look also at the terms relating to price, delivery, time, quantity and the like, but for our purposes we are concerned with a much narrower compass. What matters to the consumer, normally, is the quality of the goods, their fitness for the purpose for which they were bought, the rights of the seller to sell them, and their safety in use. Before the Sale of Goods Act 1893 these matters (apart from safety) were dealt with by the common law. That statute put the common law into a codified form and provided that certain terms should be implied into all contracts for the sale of goods (unless limited or excluded by the contract), and subsequent statutory innovations have seen strict rules about the ways in which retailers can limit or exclude their liability brought into force. The current rules about exclusion clauses are dealt with below, but we are first concerned to set out the normal obligations implied into a contract for the sale of goods.

Sections 12, 13 and 14 of the 1893 Act are the basis of the contractual protection for the consumer. They have been made more effective by their amendment in the Supply of Goods (Implied Terms)

Act 1973, and reference will be made later to the restrictions on the ability of the retailer to exclude liability.

Section 12 was amended by Section 1 of the 1973 Act so that Section 12(1) now reads:

> In every contract of sale, other than one to which subsection (2) of this section applies, there is —
> (a) an implied condition on the part of the seller that in the case of a sale, he has the right to sell the goods, and in the case of an agreement to sell, he will have a right to sell the goods at the time when the property is to pass; and
> (b) an implied warranty that the goods are free and will remain free until the time when the property is to pass, from any charge or encumbrance not disclosed or known to the buyer before the contract is made and that the buyer will enjoy quiet possession of the goods except so far as it may be disturbed by the owner or other person entitled to the benefit of any charge or encumbrance so disclosed or known.

(Subsection (2) of the section permits a seller to transfer to a buyer a limited title, i.e. whatever title he has to the goods, so long as he makes known all the limitations known to him and promises that he will not himself disturb the buyer's possession of the goods.)

This section demonstrates the distinction between the condition and the warranty which we discussed earlier, and the more important term for the buyer is the condition that the seller has the right to sell the goods in question.[10] In most circumstances this is the same thing as saying that the seller is promising that he is the owner of the goods, and if that turns out to be untrue the disappointed buyer can terminate the contract, claiming damages and/or the return of the purchase price. It is important to note that this section applies to private sales as well as to sales in the course of a business.[11]

Section 13, which also applies both to private sales and business sales, begins the implied stipulations about the quality of the goods involved. As a result of a recent decision of the House of Lords we have to point out that the quality in issue here is the identification of the goods — where the goods are identified and sold by a particular description, do they match up to that description? The section, as amended by Section 2 of the 1973 Act, now reads:

> (1) Where there is a contract for the sale of goods by description, there is an implied condition that the goods shall correspond with the description; and if the sale be by sample, as well as by description, it is not sufficient that the bulk of the goods

corresponds with the sample if the goods do not also correspond with the description.

(2) A sale of goods shall not be prevented from being a sale by description by reason only that, being exposed for sale or hire, they are selected by the buyer.

The significance of the section lies in the wide interpretation that has been given to the meaning of 'sale by description'. On first impression, one might think that a sale by description must be a very restricted type of contract resting on a close representation of the nature of the goods by seller to buyer. However, the Privy Council, in dealing with an irritating pair of woollen underpants, held that the purchaser of the underpants was entitled to claim that the sale of the pants was a sale by description provided that he could show that he was relying on the fact that the goods were corresponding to a description that was attached to them.[12] Even though the purchase is made of a specific article there will be the condition under Section 13 implied if the goods are sold as corresponding to a description. The purchaser of a car that had been advertised as a 'Herald, convertible, white, 1961' was buying by description despite the fact that he examined the car himself. His disappointment lay in the fact that only the back half of the car was of 1961 vintage – the front half was older.[13] Subsection (2), which was the part of the section inserted by the 1973 Act, now puts the question beyond any doubt.

The other matter that the courts have had to deal with under this section relates to the decision whether goods do comply with a particular description and, in deciding that, what is the exact meaning of the description. It is interesting to note that the fact that goods are defective in quality does not necessarily mean that they do not correspond with their description. Defect in quality may be considered under the next section of the Act, but we are mainly concerned here with the identification of the goods. This was illustrated by the case of *Ashington Piggeries Ltd* v. *Christopher Hill Ltd*,[14] which did not concern a consumer sale but which would apply equally to sales of that nature. In that case the House of Lords held that the sellers of 'herring meal' were not in breach of the condition as to description when they supplied a product in which the meal and the preservative had reacted together to produce a substance poisonous to mink. The meal was fed to mink. Because the goods supplied were those that had been described, with no additions or substitutions, the buyer had no remedy under Section 13. The goods may be absolutely useless for any purpose whatsoever, but so long as they are as described the seller has discharged his obligation under this section.

Section 14, however, deals directly with the quality of the goods being sold *in the course of a business*. That phrase is crucial because it takes private sales out of the scope of this section. As amended by Section 3 of the 1973 Act and the Consumer Credit Act 1974, Section 14 now reads:

(1) Except as provided by this section, and section 15 of this Act and subject to the provisions of any other enactment, there is no implied condition or warranty as to the quality or fitness for any particular purpose of goods supplied under a contract of sale.
(2) Where the seller sells goods in the course of a business, there is an implied condition that the goods supplied under the contract are of merchantable quality, except that there is no such condition –
  (a) as regards defects specifically drawn to the buyer's attention before the contract is made; or
  (b) if the buyer examines the goods before the contract is made, as regards defects which that examination ought to reveal.
(3) Where the seller sells goods in the course of a business and the buyer, expressly or by implication, makes known –
  (a) to the seller, or,
  (b) where the purchase price or part of it is payable by instalments and the goods were previously sold by a credit-broker to the seller, to that credit-broker, any particular purpose for which the goods are being bought there is an implied condition that the goods supplied under the contract are reasonably fit for that purpose, whether or not that is a purpose for which such goods are commonly supplied, except where the circumstances show that the buyer does not rely, or that it is unreasonable for him to rely, on the skill or judgment of the seller or the credit-broker.

  In this subsection 'credit-broker' means a person acting in the course of a business of credit brokerage carried on by him, that is a business of effecting introductions of individuals desiring to obtain credit –
    (i) to persons carrying on any business so far as it relates to the provision of credit, or,
    (ii) to other persons engaged in credit brokerage.

'Merchantable quality' did not receive any statutory definition until 1973, when Section 7(2) of the Supply of Goods (Implied Terms) Act added a new Section 62(1A) to the 1893 Act. That definition now provides that:

> Goods of any kind are of merchantable quality within the meaning of this Act if they are as fit for the purpose or purposes for which goods of that kind are commonly bought as it is reasonable to expect having regard to any description applied to them, the price (if relevant) and all the other relevant circumstances; and any reference in this Act to unmerchantable goods shall be construed accordingly.

This definition at least spells out some of the factors to be taken into account[15] – the price is relevant (presumably one is entitled to expect a better quality finish and durability from expensive paint than cheap stuff) as is the description (boots described as 'country footwear' may not need to live up to the same high standards as those described as 'Everest quality; suitable for experienced mountaineers in rough terrain'). The element of reasonableness has been introduced into the definition and the court may take into account all relevant circumstances.

The definition may help the consumer a little but he is still subject to the two traditional exceptions in the section. He may not allege a breach of condition if defects had been pointed out to him or if an examination that he undertakes ought to have revealed the defects.

Two other provisions of the 1973 Act are worth noting. The phrase 'in the course of a business' is used for the first time and denotes the types of sale to which the section applies. Sale in the course of *any* business is covered, whether or not selling is the object of the business. The phrase receives no definition but ought not to cause undue problems. Second, the protection of the section is extended to goods 'supplied under' a contract of sale as well as those sold. This clears up an old chestnut concerning goods that were rendered defective by the presence of other materials, although they were not, in themselves, defective. The English courts had been prepared to allow an action by a plaintiff in respect of extraneous objects,[16] but the Court of Session had not.[17] Now it is clear that the bottle in which the lemonade is supplied and the piece of explosive in the otherwise perfect load of coal can give rise to an action if they are not themselves 'merchantable', or render the goods unmerchantable.

The other limb of Section 14 deals with the fitness of the goods for the purpose for which they were bought. The buyer must make known to the seller (or credit-broker[18]) the purpose for which he is buying the goods, but since this may be done by implication there will not normally be any difficulty in establishing this point. The mere purchase of most goods will indicate the purpose for which they are intended.

As with the section dealing with sale by description, the courts might have taken a narrow view of the meaning of the words that exclude the implied condition where the buyer has not relied on the skill and judgment of the seller. It appears that only in the situation where the buyer asks for a particular brand of goods by name, demonstrating that he is not relying in any measure upon the seller, will he lose the protection of the section. That interpretation was put forward again in the *Australian Knitting Mills*[19] case by Lord Wright, who said that in purchasing from a retailer the buyer is relying on the skill and judgment of the seller in selecting his stock.

This section is extremely useful to the consumer, who should not be put off by the first subsection which harks back to the days of *caveat emptor*. It may be true that no terms are to be implied but for those in the section, but they are sufficient in themselves to give very useful protection to the consumer. Its utility is subject only to the general observation that the obligation will be on the consumer to pursue a civil action, which is sometimes difficult and hardly ever less than frustrating.

We have discussed so far under this heading the implied terms in the Sale of Goods Act 1893. As already noted, there are many other facets to the sale of goods which would take us far beyond the scope of this book. We should, however, end by noting that there is nothing to prevent any party to a contract trying to secure express conditions and warranties from the other. The consumer may attempt to get concrete promises from the other party and this is often of vital importance in the private sale where the important terms as to quality are not implied. Equally important are the attempts that may be made to exclude the liability that is imposed on sellers by the Sale of Goods Act 1893. We deal with that below.

Supply of Services

The implied terms that relate to the sale of goods are hardly appropriate where the commodity in question is not a bag of coal but the advice of a solicitor or an accountant. However, the common law developed implied terms relating solely to services. The usual remedies in contract are available subject to the terms of the contract that has been made, and there may be liability in tort if the advice that is given is negligent. We shall be considering the codes of practice relating to certain of the trade associations later in this chapter, but in respect of professional services the 'codes' of the respective professions and the discipline exercised by domestic tribunals might be much more useful to the consumer than a civil action or claim.

The major professions all have their own disciplinary system and, at least in the case of the National Health Service, there is a specially constituted independent tribunal to hear and consider complaints and grievances against a family practitioner.[20] The Law Society will review a solicitor's bill if the client requests it and maintains a fund to compensate those who are the unfortunate victims of malpractice among the profession.[21] Barristers have had a traditional immunity, even from actions in negligence, in respect of their appearances in court, although this protection has recently been reduced when the House of Lords decided that the protection did not extend to the preparation of papers except where they were intimately connected with court proceedings.[22] However, the Senate of the Inns of Court and the Bar exercises disciplinary powers over barristers in respect of professional misconduct, and it may disbar a barrister found guilty of misconduct.

The consumer may not feel that it is satisfactory to have complaints about professional services decided by other members of the profession, but they will often be a swifter and surer way of having grievances redressed than recourse to law.

NEGLIGENCE AND PRODUCTS LIABILITY

The classic case of *Donoghue* v. *Stevenson*[23] which has given rise to much of the modern law of negligence was, in essence, all about consumer protection. The poor lady who observed the decomposing remnants of a snail sliding into her glass from the bottle of ginger beer of which she had already consumed half could hardly have known that her nervous shock and gastroenteritis would prove to be the forerunner of a multitude of claims against allegedly negligent manufacturers. This lady also exposed the loophole in the framework of contractual rights that had been set up to protect the consumer – it only protected a party to the contract, i.e. the purchaser of goods, and gave no assistance to someone to whom goods had been given or lent. The judgment of the House of Lords on the preliminary point of liability, in which they decided that a manufacturer could be liable for damage caused by his negligent acts to one whom he could reasonably foresee might be damaged by them, gave the consumer an important new weapon in his armoury. The weapon, as we shall see, is not always very sharp and can be quite difficult to use, but it is a weapon none the less. At last, a person who suffered injury as a result of the negligent preparation of a product was entitled to recover damages even though there was no direct contractual link between him and the retailer or the manufacturer.[24]

The modern law has progressed to the extent that proposals are being considered that would impose strict liability on the producers of products for injuries caused as a result of their defects irrespective of the fault of the manufacturer.[25] We have moved a long way from *Donoghue* v. *Stevenson*, but, since strict liability remains a proposal and not an actuality, we should set out the basic rules of law which offer protection, through the tort of negligence, to the ultimate consumer who is injured by products negligently manufactured.

The Essentials of Negligence

The textbooks on tort[26] all recite the time-honoured formula that in order to establish liability in negligence the plaintiff must show that the defendant owed him a duty of care, that the duty was broken and that damage resulted. The first question for the consumer, 'Was a duty of care owed by the defendant, and if so, to whom?', can be answered partly by quoting the well-known dictum of Lord Atkin in *Donoghue's* case.

> A manufacturer of products which he sells in such a form as to show that he intends them to reach the ultimate consumer in the form in which they left him with no reasonable possibility of intermediate examination, and with the knowledge that the absence of reasonable care in the preparation or putting up of the products will result in an injury to the consumer's life or property, owes a duty to the consumer to take reasonable care.[27]

If a consumer has been injured by a manufacturer's products and they have reached him in the form in which they were manufactured, the manufacturer[28] will be liable if negligence can be proved. The meaning of consumer goes much wider than purchaser, and it is clear that someone to whom the product is lent or given[29] may have a cause of action, as would someone who uses the product in the course of his work,[30] or even someone who merely happens to be in the vicinity of the product if it can be foreseen that such a person would be injured.[31]

The difficulty for the plaintiff lies in establishing the negligence of the manufacturer. Although the law is prepared to assist the plaintiff in some situations where it appears obvious that the injury could not have happened were it not for the negligence of the defendant,[32] it can be a very difficult and costly exercise to prove negligence in the manufacturing process. The example of the *Thalidomide* case demonstrates the enormous problems that a plaintiff might face in proving negligence in a complex field like pharmaceuticals; but in a much humbler example, imagine the sort of investigation that might be needed to establish that a manufacturer of cosmetics had failed to take reasonable care to ensure that irritant dust had not got into a jar of hand cream during the manufacturing process. His whole system of work, previous record, quality control procedures and safety checks would have to be investigated and assessed. The liability is not strict. The manufacturer's duty is to take *reasonable* care, and the court is entitled to take into account the degree of risk involved in the activity, the likelihood of injury and the cost of taking foolproof precautions in assessing whether the manufacturer has behaved carelessly or negligently.[33]

The establishing of damage suffered will usually be the least difficult part for the plaintiff, but even then he must show not merely that he has suffered damage, but also that it is of a type that the law will permit him to recover. He is not permitted to recover pure economic loss, save in exceptional circumstances.[34] The plaintiff consumer must show that he has suffered physical damage to person or property. Economic loss may be attached to his physical damage, but it is not enough on its own. Further, physical damage will be recoverable only to the extent that it is reasonably foreseeable – the defendant is protected by the rules of remoteness of damage from being liable for *all* the consequences of his negligent act.[35]

Litigation can be expensive and hazardous for the consumer and this is nowhere more true than in the action for negligence. The plaintiff consumer may have difficulties of law to contend with, as well as the problems of proving negligence on the part of the defendant and showing recoverable damage. It is only when there is no possibility of relying on an action in breach of contract that an action in tort should be contemplated. No contractual action is open to the consumer who has not purchased the goods and he may have no choice other than to bear the costs of his injury himself. In all other circumstances the strict liability, no-fault approach of the law of contract is much more favourable to the plaintiff. In the field of what is now called 'products liability' that approach may be coming to the law of tort.

Products Liability and the Move to Strict Liability

Despite the reform in the law represented by *Donoghue* v. *Stevenson*[36] it is still the case that a person who is injured by a defective product and who does not stand in any contractual relationship with manufacturer or retailer must bear any loss that he suffers unless he can show negligence on the part of the manufacturer. This is regarded by many commentators as an unsatisfactory state of affairs and it is pleasing to be able to report progress on three fronts towards reform of this aspect of tortious liability. The Council of Europe, the EEC and the two Law Commissions[37] have all considered the problems of strict liability for injuries caused by defective products and it remains for the government to indicate its attitude in the light of these developments.

The Council of Europe began work on the problems of strict liability in 1970 with the appointment of a Committee of Experts whose task was to harmonize the laws of the member states of the Council of Europe in respect of the liability of 'producers'. After the Committee had considered the laws of the various countries involved, a draft convention on strict liability was produced and an explanatory report attached. The draft has now been adopted in its final form by the Committee of Ministers of the Council of Europe and it is open for adoption by the member states.[38] To date, only Belgium, France and Luxembourg have adopted the convention.

The convention provides for the strict liability of producers for defective products that cause injury to consumers. This liability is in the nature of tortious liability, and that allows some of the other features of actions in tort to be included, particularly the reduction of damages on account of the contributory negligence of the victim and the right of the producer to recover damages from others who might share his liability. Certain types of non-producers also have to put up with strict liability where they market goods produced by others under their own name, or sell imported or anonymous goods. The provisions of the convention are wide-ranging and provided a good model for the

Law Commissions to consider when they were in the process of issuing a consultative document and then a final report on the same subject.[39]

The Law Commissions examined the reasons of policy that are said to lie behind the imposition of strict liability on producers. In paragraph 23 of their final report they identify nine policy considerations which must have guided them in their conclusions and recommendations. Summarized, the considerations are as follows:

(i) losses arising from injuries caused by defective products should be borne by the risk creator, not the victim;
(ii) manufacturers are better able to control the safety of products;
(iii) manufacturers can most easily insure against the risks of injury by defective products;
(iv) public expectations of products, aroused by manufacturer's publicity material, are directed towards the manufacturer;
(v) procedural or evidentiary difficulties should be removed, where possible;
(vi) unnecessary litigation should be discouraged;
(vii) first-party insurance (i.e. arrangements made by the consumer) should not be discouraged;
(viii) the number of persons liable as 'producers' should be as few as possible, consistent with securing adequate rights for consumers;
(ix) the laws of the UK should not be so onerous as to put our own manufacturers at a disadvantage compared with overseas competitors.

This is an enormous list of considerations and the significance of all of them does not become apparent until the Law Commissions proceed to discuss the alleged defects of the present law and present their recommendations for the future. The Commissions reported that at present the difficulties in the way of a plaintiff were considerable and that the retailer was bearing a liability that he neither merited nor wanted. The ability of each supplier of goods to sue his supplier until the manufacturer was eventually reached led to a multiplicity of actions and was unhelpful.[40] These findings, together with the policy considerations, led the Commissions to recommend the imposition of strict liability for injuries resulting from defects in products that are put into circulation in the course of a business, and that the liability should rest primarily on the producer.[41]

Naturally, the report supports its detailed conclusions with close argument and illustration, and we must limit ourselves to its recommendations on the issues that are somewhat contentious and, in the light of the differing approach of an EEC draft directive,[42] might give rise to problems for the government. There are four areas in which the Law Commissions take issue with the EEC draft and they concern the commercial nature of production which would give rise to liability; liability for non-pecuniary losses; financial limits to liability; and liability for damage to property.

The Law Commissions recommend that only products that are manufactured in the course of a business should give rise to the strict liability envisaged.[43] We are familiar with that phrase in respect of the implied terms as to quality in contracts for the sale of goods and it may well be that the thinking that restricted liability in those circumstances is behind the restriction in this instance to commercial production. The EEC draft does not contain any such restriction and would, presumably, apply the principles of strict liability to the lady who manufactures soft toys for a stall at the local church's Christmas Fair. The Law Commissions think that this would be 'regrettable'.[44]

The English law of tort has always recognized the right to receive some compensation for non-pecuniary loss resulting from an injury. 'Pain and suffering' are normally compensated by a monetary award, and the Law Commission recommended that this head of compensation be retained in the new scheme (although they would not allow recovery of purely economic loss[45]). The EEC draft directive, while allowing recovery of damages for 'personal injuries', does not recognize that phrase as comprehending compensation for pain and suffering. Because this would represent a diminution of the rights of the UK consumer, the Commissions are opposed to it.

The EEC draft provides for a 'global' limit to the liability of the producer for 'personal injuries caused by identical articles having the same defect'.[46] The Commissions reject this approach as unworkable on the grounds that the difficulties of dividing a global sum over a number of years among an unascertained number of claimants with unquantified claims would be insuperable. The Council of Europe convention provided for optional global and individual limits and, even though they were very high limits, the Commissions disagreed with the principle.[47]

The strict liability of producers for damage to property arising from defective products was not fully considered by the Council of Europe

Committee of Experts, and it is quite likely that it will be the subject of a separate convention at a later date. The Law Commissions did consider the problem and came to the conclusion that the present law should continue to govern damage to property, partly because such liability would be very expensive and the costs would be passed on, and partly because people should not be discouraged from carrying their own insurance against such damage and bearing the cost of that insurance.[48] The EEC draft imposes liability for certain kinds of property damage with limits of 50,000 European Units of Account for immovable property and 15,000 European Units of Account for movables. This provision was criticized by the Law Commissions as 'unsound' and it was recommended that objection should be made.[49]

Article 1 of the Draft EEC Directive provides for the liability of the producer even if the product could not have been regarded as defective in the light of the scientific and technological development at the time that it was put into circulation. This is also likely to present problems in this country.

It can be seen from these limited observations that there are serious areas of disagreement about how any scheme of strict liability should work, and it seems likely that we are due for a substantial bargaining period with the EEC. The position in this country is further complicated by the recommendations of the Pearson Commission[50] about the establishment of a system of no-fault accident compensation in certain fields, and we are undoubtedly going to hear much more about products liability over the next few years.

EXCLUSION CLAUSES

The philosophy of freedom of contract permitted the parties to a contract to make as good a bargain as they could within very wide limits, and they were certainly permitted to do what they could to limit or exclude their liability for breach of contract. It was also possible by means of a contract to limit or exclude liability for negligence, thereby minimizing or avoiding the risk of an action in tort. The courts did little to protect the weak party to a contract who, with the advent of the standard form contract and the increasing power of the large-scale retailers and manufacturers, found himself forced to sign away his contractual rights in order to obtain the goods or services that he needed.

Gradually the realization dawned that the individual was not getting a very good deal out of the freedom of contract ideal and the courts began to take action to limit reliance on exclusion clauses. This was achieved in a number of ways – by construing the clause very strictly;[51] by giving the benefit of any doubt about the wording to the innocent party;[52] by requiring that clear notice of the existence of the clause be given;[53] by evolving a concept that came to be known as 'fundamental breach'.[54] These measures all helped the individual generally (and continue to do so)[55] but the consumer has been particularly assisted by statutory intervention and the consequent regulation of the availability and effect of exclusion clauses in consumer contracts.

The provision of the implied terms in the Sale of Goods Act 1893 was made less significant by Section 55 of the same Act which provided that:

> Where any right, duty or liability would arise under a contract of sale of goods by implication of law, it may be negatived or varied by express agreement, or by the course of dealing between the parties, or by usage if the usage is such as to bind both parties to the contract. . . .

The Unfair Contract Terms Act 1977 has added significant words to that section, and it now concludes, 'but the foregoing provision shall have effect subject to section 6 of the Unfair Contract Terms Act 1977'. You will gather from that that the 1977 Act has severely limited the rights of the seller to contract out of his liability under the Sale of Goods Act, and has also made other provisions to protect the consumer who finds himself on the wrong end of unfair clauses purporting to exclude or limit the liability of the other party in other ways.

There is a distinction made in the Unfair Contract Terms Act between consumer dealings and other dealings and, in the context of this book, we will confine ourselves to those provisions that are directed specifically towards the protection of the consumer. The phrase 'dealing as consumer' receives definition in the Act and we will end with a consideration of that definition; but we can first identify the three types of exclusion clause to which the Act applies. Separate provision is made in respect of exclusion of liabilities under the Sale of Goods Act 1893; exclusion of other contractual liability; and exclusion of liability for negligence.

Section 6 of the 1977 Act employs the tactic of rendering useless any attempt to exclude the liability for breach of obligations under Sections 12–15 of the Sale of Goods Act, but you will notice from the statutory wording that protection against exclusion clauses relating to Sections 13–15 is given only to a person dealing as a consumer. Section 6 provides:

(1) Liability for breach of the obligations arising from –
    (a) Section 12 of the Sale of Goods Act 1893 (seller's implied undertakings as to title etc.);
    (b) Section 8 of the Supply of Goods (Implied Terms) Act 1973 (the corresponding thing in relation to hire-purchase),
cannot be excluded or restricted by reference to any contract term.

(2) As against a person dealing as consumer, liability for breach of the obligations arising from –
    (a) Section 13, 14 or 15 of the 1893 Act (seller's implied undertakings as to conformity of goods with description or sample, or as to their quality or fitness for a particular purpose);
    (b) Section 9, 10 or 11 of the 1973 Act (the corresponding things in relation to hire-purchase),
cannot be excluded or restricted by reference to any contract term.

The provisions mean that a person making a private sale cannot contract out of liability to give good title to the buyer, and it will also be noted that they apply equally to hire-purchase and to the sale of goods.

In respect of other contractual liability an exclusion clause will in future be subject to the test of reasonableness. Section 3 of the 1977 Act provides:

(1) This section applies as between contracting parties where one of them deals as consumer or on the other's written standard terms of business.
(2) As against that party, the other cannot by reference to any contract term –
    (a) when himself in breach of contract, exclude or restrict any liability of his in respect of the breach; or
    (b) claim to be entitled –
        (i) to render a contractual performance substantially different from that which was reasonably expected of him, or
        (ii) in respect of the whole or any part of his contractual obligation, to render no performance at all,

except in so far as (in any of the cases mentioned above in this subsection) the contract term satisfies the requirement of reasonableness.

This section will be most useful in any consumer dealings for it will permit the consumer to challenge almost any type of clause that is designed to exclude liability or purports to relieve the other contracting party of all or any of his obligations under the contract.[56] Any consumer contract is affected by this provision and it should always be considered when a supplier or manufacturer tries to rely on an exclusion or limitation clause.

Finally, a similar approach is taken to attempts to exclude liability for negligence. However, this time the protection is not restricted to consumers, or even to exclusions contained in contracts, but is couched in general terms. Any sort of notice is covered. Section 2 of the 1977 Act provides:

(1) A person cannot by reference to any contract term or to a notice given to persons generally or to particular persons exclude or restrict his liability for death or personal injury resulting from negligence.
(2) In the case of other loss or damage, a person cannot so exclude or restrict his liability for negligence except in so far as the term or notice satisfies the requirement of reasonableness.
(3) Where a contract term or notice purports to exclude or restrict liability for negligence a person's agreement to or awareness of it is not of itself to be taken as indicating his voluntary acceptance of any risk.

The drafting of all three sections is very straightforward and comprehensible, but we need to consider two points: what is the requirement of reasonableness, and when will a person be dealing as consumer?

The test of reasonableness is explained in Section 11 of the Act and by reference to Schedule 2. To satisfy the test of reasonableness where it is required (i.e. in relation to exclusion clauses in any consumer contract and in relation to the purported exclusion for loss and damage other than personal injury or death arising from negligence) the term must be a fair and reasonable one to have been included in the contract having regard to the circumstances that were, or ought reasonably to have been, known to or in the contemplation of the parties when the contract was made.

Schedule 2 then provides 'guidelines' for the application of the test, although it is expressly provided that a court or arbitrator is not precluded from holding that an exclusion clause is not a term of the contract so as to avoid bringing into play the reasonableness requirement at all.[57] The guidelines direct the court towards the relative bargaining power of the parties; inducements offered to enter the contract with the term included; knowledge of the term on the part of the consumer; whether the exclusion was dependent upon the non-compliance with a condition; whether it was reasonable to expect compliance; and any other considerations that the court thinks relevant. The responsibility of showing that the exclusion clause is reasonable rests with the trader.

This gives the court wide powers to weigh up all the circumstances of the case and it must decide essentially on the 'fairness' of the clause complained of.[58] The message for the consumer is clear. There has never been fuller protection against the exclusion of liability, and if there is any doubt about an exclusion clause it should be tested.

That leads us to the final point in respect of this topic and we must note the definition of 'dealing as consumer' in the 1977 Act. This definition is important in relation to the purported exclusion of liability under Sections 13–15 of the Sale of Goods Act 1893, and the purported exclusion of other contractual liability. Section 12 of the 1977 Act provides that to bring himself within the protection of the appropriate sections a person must not be making the contract in the course of a business[59] (nor hold himself out as doing so) but the other contracting party must be making the contract in the course of business. Additionally, if the contract is one that is governed by the law of sale of goods or hire-purchase, the goods passing under the contract must be of a type ordinarily supplied for private use or consumption. If these conditions are satisfied the person involved is dealing as consumer, except where the sale is by auction or by competitive tender.[60] It is worth noting that the onus of proof will lie on the party attempting to show that the other is *not* dealing as consumer.[61]

The new statutory provisions, which apply to all contracts made after 1 February 1978, are of considerable advantage to the consumer and represent a long journey indeed from the 1893 Act. How the Act will work in practice and what the courts will accept as satisfying the requirement of reasonableness where that is necessary remains to be seen, but the benefits look substantial and will reinforce the other measures that have been discussed elsewhere in the book.

MANUFACTURERS' AND RETAILERS' 'GUARANTEES'

The practice of manufacturers and retailers giving guarantees with their products was quite often an attempt on their part to get the consumer to accept a limitation of his common law rights under the contract he had made. It is important to note that these 'guarantees' could operate only where there was a contract in existence. It was necessary to show a contractual relationship between the manufacturer and the consumer that depended on the device of a collateral contract[62] or on the sending in by the consumer of some form of card to secure the terms of the offer.[63] These guarantees have also come under the regulation of the Unfair Contract Terms Act 1977, which limits their ability to contain clauses that exclude or restrict the liability of the manufacturer or the retailer.

(1) In the case of goods of a type ordinarily supplied for private use or consumption, where loss or damage –
   (a) arises from the goods proving defective while in consumer use; and
   (b) results from the negligence of a person concerned in the manufacture or distribution of the goods,
liability for the loss or damage cannot be excluded or restricted by reference to any contract term or notice contained in or operating by reference to a guarantee of the goods.

(2) For these purposes –
   (a) goods are to be regarded as 'in consumer use' when a person is using them, or has them in his possession for use, otherwise than exclusively for the purposes of a business; and
   (b) anything in writing is a guarantee if it contains or purports to contain some promise or assurance (however worded or presented) that defects will be made good by complete or partial replacement, or by repair, monetary compensation or otherwise.

These provisions mean that a guarantee now can be only an addition to the common law rights of a consumer and, as such, can sometimes be worthwhile. A consumer has nothing to lose by accepting the terms of a guarantee and it may be that, where the trade or professional association involved is one that is party to a code of practice, the guarantee will contain additional rights. Consumers should not be misled by a guarantee that purports to exclude liability that is not properly the liability of the manufacturers at all. Some manufacturer's guarantees try to exclude the liability of the retailer!

CODES OF PRACTICE

As noted earlier,[64] the Director-General of Fair Trading is put under a duty by Section 124(3) of the Fair Trading Act 1973 to 'encourage relevant associations to prepare, and to disseminate to their members, codes of practice for guidance in safeguarding and promoting the interests of consumers of the United Kingdom'. Relevant associations for this purpose are those whose membership consists wholly or mainly of persons engaged in the production or supply of goods or services, and the Director has not been slow to encourage such associations to adopt standard codes for their members.[65]

There have been a number of codes adopted, and among the industries represented are the electrical goods industry, car dealers, shoe manufacturers and sellers, package tour operators, launderers and dry cleaners, and furniture manufacturers and retailers.[66] The codes are entirely voluntary and confer no legal rights, but they give the consumer the advantage of being able to enlist the help of the trade association in any dispute and also the reassurance that certain basic safeguards are being observed. It is, of course, true that not all suppliers and manufacturers in a particular industry belong to the appropriate trade association, and if not they will not be party to the code, but that drawback is inevitable in a voluntary scheme. It is hoped that membership of an association that operates a respected and fair code of practice will become an inducement to deal with that particular retailer or manufacturer. To that extent the whole operation may be considered a public relations or advertising exercise, but even so it has advantages for the consumer.

Inevitably the codes relating to the different industries have different features, but to take the furniture trade code as an example, it contains provisions about advertising and price markings, informative labelling, competent sales staff, delivery and price, repairs and complaints.[67] Nothing in the code can detract from the consumer's legal rights and, like guarantees, any protection that is given may be additional to those rights. The codes are drawn up in consultation with the Office of Fair Trading who can be expected to watch the consumer's interests.

OBJECTIONABLE SELLING TECHNIQUES

The Director-General has wide powers to act to curb unfair trading practices, and it is likely that attention will be directed towards selling techniques. For the sake of completeness we should record that among all the other protection offered to the consumer at the point of sale including the prevention of deception etc., two particular types of selling are prohibited or discouraged.

Pryamid selling is prohibited by Sections 118–23 of the Fair Trading Act 1973 and the regulations made thereunder. Pyramid selling involves the sale of goods through a network of agents who are encouraged to recruit sub-agents, who also recruit others and receive very little financial reward. Abuses in 1972 and 1973 led to the legislation, and this form of trading is now criminal.

Inertia selling is a technique that involves a demand for payment for goods that have not been requested by the consumer but have been supplied. These unsolicited goods can cause major problems and the demanding of payment for such goods was made a criminal offence by the Unsolicited Goods and Services Act 1971. The Act also provides that the recipient is under no obligation to pay for such goods, which become his after six months if he takes no action, or after twenty-eight days if a request to the supplier to collect the goods is not complied with.

10 Redress and the Enforcement of Rights

INTRODUCTION

Protection for the consumer depends almost as much on the range of remedies available and the means of their enforcement as it does on the existence of rights that are given to him by legislation and the common law. Some of the protection measures that we have discussed in the preceding pages have not required enforcement by the individual because that responsibility has been placed upon an institution, either national or local. However, many of the rights conferred on a consumer at the point of sale and before do need to be asserted by the individual and we ought to be aware of the way in which those rights may be enforced and the remedies that are available from the courts.

We discussed at the beginning of Chapter 7 the distinction between the creation of civil law rights and the imposition of criminal sanctions, and you would expect that distinction to pertain also for the method of trial and the resolution of the issue. The court primarily responsible for the resolution of civil law disputes concerning consumers is the County Court.[1] This is not because of any restriction on the type of case that may be brought in the High Court, but because the County Court has a limit to its jurisdiction in this area of £2,000, and consumer claims in the sense in which we have been considering them will rarely exceed that amount. Certain pressures are applied to ensure that cases that involve sums below £2,000 are started in the County Court.[2]

Criticisms have recently been made of the adequacy of the County Court as a consumer forum. It is alleged that the procedure is too difficult for a layman to master; that the costs of a solicitor are too high to make it worthwhile to acquire professional help; that the atmosphere is too formal; and that the whole system leans towards the businessman, prejudicing the consumer. We shall examine these criticisms later.

The County Court has available to it the full range of remedies that have been developed over the years by the superior courts. It is as a result of the historical separation of the English courts into two distinct jurisdictions – common law and equity – that the remedies given by the different courts are directed towards different ends and are based on different principles. Until the middle of the last century a plaintiff who wanted both a common law remedy and an equitable remedy had to begin two separate actions in two separate courts.

The primary common law remedy is damages. This remedy requires the payment of money to the successful plaintiff by the defendant with the intention of putting the plaintiff in the position that he would have been in if the wrong had not occurred. The wrong may be a breach of contract or the commission of a tort, and the calculation of the damages may differ according to the nature of the wrong alleged, but the basic principle remains the same. The courts will not allow the difficulty of calculating a money figure to deter them from giving damages where the plaintiff has proved the commission of a wrong.[3] Indeed, it is a feature of the common law remedies that they are available as of right – once the plaintiff has proved his case he is *entitled* to an award of damages even though his actual loss may be slight or non-existent.

It is the discretionary nature of the equitable remedies that marks them out from the common law remedies. The courts of Equity were originally under the guidance of the Lord Chancellor of the day and in their formative years the Lord Chancellor was usually a cleric. Clerical principles provided a basis for the grant of equitable remedies and it became the practice to scrutinize the dealings of both plaintiff and defendant before a remedy would be granted. Equity relied on concepts of justice, fair dealing, good conscience and the inadequacy of the common law remedy. This meant that petitions for the remedies were examined carefully with all the circumstances of the case taken into account – discretion was exercised.

Equity developed very useful remedies which were directed towards securing compliance with specific instructions – do this, do not do that – and that type of remedy found considerable favour with the plaintiff who wanted to have a contract enforced rather than to receive a money payment for its breach. Equally, the injunction was a remedy that prevented the infringement of rights by another by issuing specific prohibitions or requirements. The effectiveness of all the equitable remedies was ensured by the simple expedient of imprisoning anyone who failed to comply with the instructions. Such a failure was regarded as a contempt of court and the contemnor was imprisoned until he had purged his contempt by agreeing to do what was required by the court. Imprisonment concentrates the mind wonderfully and equitable remedies were, and are, very popular with plaintiffs.

There are many aggrieved consumers who may not want to pursue their remedies through the courts, or who may not be able to afford to, and there is considerable scope for individual action on a grievance that falls short of the court. It is, in fact, only a very small proportion of the disputes that arise that are eventually decided by a court, and we shall have something to say about the other steps that may be taken by a consumer on his own behalf.

Finally, the consumer must be aware of his rights when the trader has committed a criminal offence. Obtaining compensation in the court where the trader is convicted of an offence is not only possible but is often the simplest and quickest way of extracting compensation from an unwilling wrongdoer. Certain important decisions have established that some offences may be committed over and over again,[4] notably those connected with the dissemination of inaccurate information in a brochure or prospectus, and consequently the individual aggrieved may wish to institute a prosecution in order to pressure the company involved into settling his claim.

The importance of the system of remedies and enforcement cannot be overemphasized. It can be argued that rights are redundant unless the machinery is effective in allowing their enforcement and the appropriate remedy exists to compensate the victim of a tort or breach of contract. The efficacy of our whole system of consumer protection ought to be judged as much by the availability of remedies as by the existence of rights.

THE COUNTY COURT

It is tempting, but probably inaccurate, to point to the establishment of the County Court by the County Courts Act 1846 as one of the first consumer protection measures. However, it is fair to say that the major arguments for the establishment of a new court at that time were based on the inadequacy of the existing court structure when faced with claims for relatively small amounts of money. There was real concern for the plaintiff who was effectively barred from the courts because his claim did not make it worthwhile to undertake the expense of an action, and that concern was nowhere better expressed than in the speech of Henry Brougham to the House of Commons in 1826. That six-hour peroration sparked off a campaign lasting twenty years which ultimately resulted in the passing of the County Courts Act 1846.

The preamble to that Act will raise some echoes of the arguments now being put forward for the creation of another new court to deal with small claims. The pertinent part recites the object of the County Court, 'whereas the county court is a court of ancient jurisdiction ... and the proceedings are dilatory and expensive ... it is expedient to alter and regulate the manner of proceedings ... for the recovery of small debts and demands'. It is ironic that those objects were frustrated within a very short space of time. The statistics show that within five years of its establishment the County Court had become a great blessing for traders who were presented with an easy, quick and cheap way of recovering debts, and that a relatively small number of the actions begun were begun by 'consumers' alleging defective goods or inadequate services.

The County Court proved to be an extremely convenient forum for all sorts of cases and its jurisdiction was steadily increased both in type and in value. Its convenience lay partly in the fact that it was a local court with relatively easy access for members of the community, and partly in the fact that its procedure and style were less ponderous and complicated than the High Court. Statute added more and more to the County Court, and its jurisdiction at the present time is considerable.

At the outset in 1846 the County Court's jurisdiction in contract and tort was limited to claims not exceeding £20, but that figure has now increased to £2,000.[5] It is claims in contract and tort that will be of primary interest to those concerned with consumer protection, but it is worth noting that the County Court also has jurisdiction in bankruptcy, in actions for the recovery of land, in matrimonial matters, and in many specific areas assigned by statute. Consumer claims are but one of the County Court's responsibilities.

The financial limit is not the only limit on the County Court's jurisdiction – it must also confine itself to the geographical area in which it operates. There are detailed rules that provide for the circumstances in which claims may be linked with the appropriate

County Court, but it is always important for the consumer who wishes to begin an action to remember that he must identify the right court in which to start.

The court is staffed by circuit judges and the administration is supervised by registrars who also have certain judicial functions.

The financial limit of £2,000 can hardly be regarded as confining the County Court to small claims – the ordinary consumer, even in the purchase of major items of electrical equipment, would probably regard £2,000 as a very considerable claim. The importance of the actions heard in the County Court where sums close to £2,000 may be in issue (actions between businesses, for example) has led to a greater concern with formal procedures than might have been the case if the limit had been much lower. The formality of the court and its detailed procedure are part of the reason for the recent introduction of new measures designed to help the individual plaintiff present his own case.

THE COUNTY COURT ACTION

We have left out of account so far the High Court and the High Court action. That is deliberate since, although its jurisdiction is unlimited both geographically and financially, the High Court will rarely be the appropriate forum for the type of consumer dispute that we have been discussing in the preceding chapters. It may be useful for the individual consumer to consider whether there are any tactical advantages to be gained in choosing the High Court rather than the County Court if his claim is within the County Court limit, but in the vast majority of cases the cost of a High Court action would be out of all proportion to the amount of money at stake.

From the point of view of the consumer even the County Court procedure can provide difficulty.[6] The action is begun by a 'request', a form available from any office of the County Court, which is intended to provide the court with all the information it needs to serve a summons on the defendant. The court will normally serve the summons itself, although it is possible for the plaintiff to do it if he wishes to. The summons itself will depend upon the nature of the allegation that the plaintiff is making against the defendant. If it is alleged that some specific sum of money is owed, whether a debt or some precise claim, then it is appropriate to serve a 'default summons'; in all other cases the 'ordinary summons' is used.

It is advantageous to use the default summons if possible since the procedure is somewhat quicker. After a default summons has been served on the defendant the onus is upon him to make some sort of reply or risk judgment being given to the plaintiff automatically. Within fourteen days the defendant must admit the claim and make some offer of payment, or dispute the claim as to liability or amount, or admit or deny the claim and then make a counterclaim against the plaintiff. Unless the court receives one or other of these responses within fourteen days, the plaintiff is entitled to ask for judgment immediately on a simple form, again obtainable from the County Court office. If the defendant disputes liability or makes a counter-claim the Registrar will either fix a date for trial immediately or call the parties together for a pre-trial review, just as though the action had been begun by ordinary summons. From that point the procedure follows that for the ordinary summons.

The ordinary summons is also served on the defendant and contains a fixed date for a preliminary hearing before the Registrar called the pre-trial review. This hearing is something that is peculiar to the County Court and it was introduced to meet some of the criticisms of County Court procedure. The object of the review is to discuss how the action is to be dealt with, to make arrangements for the trial, to ensure that both sides will be prepared, and to fix a date for the hearing. Officially it does not have as its object the encouragement of a settlement between the parties in dispute but it would seem inevitable that when the parties finally meet in a court-like atmosphere with the prospect of a trial only a few weeks away they may be more disposed to accept a compromise than they had been previously. How much the Registrar uses his influence to effect a settlement is a matter for him but it will be much cheaper and simpler for the parties to agree at this stage.

If the action goes forward from the review it will be tried by the judge or, where the amount involved is very small, by the registrar. The trial will follow formal lines with the judge as an umpire who has no obligation to discover the facts. The adversarial procedure adopted in English courts imposes upon the two sides to the dispute the obligation of placing all the relevant issues and evidence before the court. This presents relatively little problem for the lawyer advocate, but there are considerable difficulties for the layman in knowing what to say, what evidence to produce, what law to argue, when to stand up and when to sit down. The examination and cross-examination of witnesses is a skilled job and the judge must not be seen to be interfering in the presentation of the case too much lest it be thought that he was favouring the one side or the other. The difficulties for the unrepresented plaintiff or defendant are considerable, but the costs for the represented are likely to be prohibitive – a very unsatisfactory position.

This has been a very compressed version of the County Court action and there are procedures omitted that may serve to confuse and intimidate the individual even further. However, one possibility of simplifying the procedure has been omitted and must now be considered.

ARBITRATION IN THE COUNTY COURT

Arbitration is a form of dispute resolution that is well known in English law but is primarily used in connection with large commercial contracts in which expert help would be required to resolve the difficulties caused by breach. It is also used by a number of trade associations in conjunction with traders to attempt to resolve consumer disputes. However, in this context we must consider its adoption by the County Court as a means of settling claims for small amounts in a more relaxed, informal atmosphere that would exist at trial.

In County Court actions where the amount of money in dispute is less than £100 the Registrar may refer the matter to arbitration at the request of one of the parties notwithstanding that the other party objects. On the agreement of the parties any other action may be referred to arbitration.

Why is this better? Arbitration is intended to be quicker, cheaper and less formal than proceeding to trial. The Registrar frequently appoints himself as the arbitrator[7] and he may choose to relax the rules of evidence, call his own evidence where necessary, conduct the hearing in his own way, and hold the hearing in private at a time convenient to the parties. In this way the unrepresented plaintiff or defendant is likely to have a much easier job in presenting his case and may receive considerable help from the arbitrator who is concerned to get at the facts in dispute. The arbitrator can quite properly adopt the sort of inquisitorial role that would be improper for a judge. The only drawback is that there are more limited rights of appeal from an arbitrator than there are from a judge.

Registrars have been particularly encouraged to use the arbitration procedure in relation to small claims and its significance will be further considered below.

SMALL CLAIMS

What can properly be termed a 'small claim' will often depend rather more on the income and resources of the plaintiff than upon any objective consideration of the amount at stake. We have already noted that the poorer sections of the community may well be at a disadvantage in making informed and rational consumer choices and in selecting the appropriate method of financing their purchases,[8] but it is also clear that, in so far as the procedures established for the pursuit of civil claims make it uneconomic to attempt to recover small amounts of money, these groups are again at a disadvantage. However, it is not just the poorer consumers who feel this injustice since the relationship between the amount of money involved and the costs that may be incurred in recovering it are the same for everyone. What is different is the ability of the more affluent consumer to pursue his case whatever the cost involved to vindicate a principle as much as to recover the money at stake.

It is not without irony that exactly the same arguments are now being used to advocate the establishment of a new court for the resolution of small debts and claims as were used in the last century to persuade the government of the day to establish the County Courts. The first evidence to support the contention that the County Court was not catering adequately for small claims came with the publication of a pamphlet entitled, *Justice Out of Reach*. This pamphlet, published by HMSO in 1970, was the work of the now defunct Consumer Council and demonstrated that the numbers of individual plaintiffs in the County Court was pitifully small. The vast majority of actions were begun by firms, corporations or the public utilities and it appeared that the court was actually being used as a most convenient debt-collecting agency.[9]

The response to the criticisms that were being made were disappointing to those who advocated the establishment of a new court. The Conservative Government made it clear in 1973, through Sir Geoffrey Howe and through the Lord Chancellor, that it would have nothing to do with the establishment of a new court system, and the following Labour Government gave no indication that it disagreed with the policy of the previous administration. Despite the unwillingness of the government to commit itself to new courts, there have been developments both inside and outside the existing system that have ameliorated the position of the plaintiff with a small claim. How far these developments have met the criticisms of cost, complexity and delay remains to be judged.

Reforms in County Court Procedure

The Conservative Government's justification for refusing to consider the establishment of a new system of courts lay in the three reforms of the existing County Court procedure designed to assist the person pursuing a small claim. Reference has already been made to two of these measures in our discussion of the current claim procedure, and the importance of the pre-trial review and arbitration cannot be overestimated.

The pre-trial review was introduced into the County Court procedure in March 1972,[10] and it is clear that it is of considerable help to the unrepresented litigant in preparing his case for trial. It is similar to the Summons for Directions in the High Court and is intended to ensure that all the administrative details are completed and that the parties are prepared for trial. Defects in the knowledge and preparation of an unrepresented litigant may be remedied at this stage and the knowledge acquired may lead either of the parties to take a different view of the strength of the case. Although the proceduce is not formally intended to put pressure on the parties to arrive at a settlement of their dispute, it is almost inevitable that a review of the law and evidence at the pre-trial stage will at least give the parties a clearer view of the merits. Settlements are fairly common and may even be encouraged by the Registrar.

Arbitration has been discussed above and its advantages are apparent. For the unrepresented litigant arbitration is a much more congenial forum for the resolution of the dispute, not least because the arbitrator may quite properly offer assistance to either of the parties in fulfilling his objective of conducting a full investigation of the case. The available evidence seems to indicate that the arbitration procedure works fairly well and is popular with litigants, particularly where a small claim is involved.[11]

The third procedural reform was also introduced in March 1972 and prevented any costs being awarded for legal representation where the amount of money involved was less than £20. This was intended to discourage the use of lawyers in small claims cases, both for the plaintiff and for the defendant. It was argued at the time that a person would be more willing to defend a small claim if he knew that he would not be saddled with legal costs even if he lost. This original figure of £20 has been raised successively to £75, £100 and £200.

It cannot seriously be disputed that these procedural reforms have had the effect of making the County Court both more available and more attractive to the plaintiff and the defendant in small claims. That was not really a tremendous achievement since the system was so heavily loaded against the small claim. The question ought not to be, 'Is the system better?' but rather, 'Is the system satisfactory?'

Research has recently been completed on the new procedures, and more is to be done, but the available evidence seems to indicate qualified approval. It is still significant that the majority of users of the arbitration procedure are firms and traders (acting as plaintiffs) and that the no-costs rule has not been successful in eliminating legal representation in cases involving less than £200. The Consumers' Association, in a fairly limited survey,[12] reported that their members were broadly satisfied with the more open, straightforward procedures and that the problems now being experienced related to the enforcement of a judgment once it had been obtained.

Innovations outside the County Court Structure

Impatient with the government's refusal to contemplate new courts for small claims, various groups have established their own 'courts' for the resolution of small claims arising in a particular geographical area. The most notable of these schemes are to be found in Manchester and London where, with financial assistance from the Nuffield Foundation, competent and effective courts have been set up.

Given the improvements made to the County Court by the reforms discussed in the last few pages, it may well be that the voluntary schemes will find their value as pointers to the future development of the County Court rather than as institutions that deserve support from public funds for their continuance.

A New Small Claims Court?[13]

Any treatment of this question at the moment must inevitably be speculative in the light of the firm expression of confidence by the successive governments in the ability of the County Court to cope adequately with small claims. The central features of a new court, according to its protagonists, would be informality, simplicity, speed and cheapness. These are the qualities that are always claimed for the tribunal system of adjudication which has been increasingly adopted. It is clearly desirable that the administration of justice should be characterized by all these qualities so long as their adoption does not prejudice the litigant. The point at issue with regard to a small claims court would be the extent to which standards might be compromised by abandoning formality, rules of evidence, careful preparation and attempting to over-simplify the legal problems involved.

Arbitration seems to be the key to small claims. It works relatively well in the County Court at the present time, though its effectiveness may be reduced by the fact that it is only compulsory where less than £100 is at stake and by the fact that it must be approached through the normal County Court procedure which some people find difficult to cope with. It also appears to work well in the voluntary schemes where there is a voluntary submission. Arbitral principles should obviously be at the root of any new small claims system.

The adoption of arbitration as the means of resolving small claims leaves other important questions to be solved. What is a small claim? What is the appropriate financial limit? Are debts regarded as small claims? Should the procedure be open to traders and businessmen as plaintiffs? Should legal representation be discouraged or prohibited? What relationship should a small claims court bear to the present court structure? What rights of appeal should exist? It is not within our brief to attempt an exhaustive analysis of the various possible schemes, but the problems raised would all be central to any scheme for a new court and would need to be resolved satisfactorily.

REMEDIES

Before any action is started in the County Court or the High Court the consumer will have to have decided what remedy he is seeking. Does he require money compensation for the wrong done? Would he prefer to have the contract performed so that he actually receives what the other party promised? Does he want to ensure that there are no further breaches of contract or torts committed? Having answered these questions the claim will be framed in the appropriate way, but it is important to note that there are distinct principles governing the recovery of damages or the award of one of the equitable remedies which may prevent the consumer recovering all that he thinks he is entitled to.

In the introduction we distinguished the common law remedies from the equitable ones and stressed the essential difference in their availability. Common law remedies are a right – once the plaintiff has proved his case he is entitled to damages – whereas the equitable remedies are discretionary and the court may take into account all the circumstances in deciding whether to exercise its discretion in favour of the plaintiff. However, even the common law remedies are restricted in certain ways by rules which affect the extent of the damages that may be recovered in any one case.

Damages

It is likely that a consumer who suffers loss by virtue of a broken contract or the commission of a tort will normally be thinking of money compensation to make up for the loss. In both cases the object of the law of damages is to put the victim into the position that he would have been in if the wrong had not been committed. In the law of contract this involves examining the rights that the plaintiff acquired under the contract and considering his position if the contract had been fulfilled as the parties intended, whereas in the law of tort the court will examine the position the plaintiff was in before the tort was committtted and try to restore him to that position. In either case we must enter the proviso that this object is achieved by the payment of money and it is sometimes very difficult to calculate the appropriate amount of money.

The general principle of compensation for loss suffered must be subject to restrictions, for the defendant might otherwise find himself liable for all sorts of loss that *had* actually happened as a result of the wrong but which he had never contemplated and which it would be unfair to impose upon him. In this brief account it is not possible to consider all the ramifications of the law of damages, but we can identify three constraints upon the principle that the victim is entitled to compensation for all his loss. First, the plaintiff must show that his loss was *caused* by the alleged wrong; second, the plaintiff must show that the law does not regard the loss as too remote from the wrongful act; third, the loss must not be of a type that for reasons of policy the law prevents a plaintiff from recovering.

Did the loss occur because of the wrongdoing by the defendant? The question of causation is one that has provided much material for debate by lawyers and philosophers alike and the law has never evolved a completely satisfactory test for determining whether one incident has caused particular loss. The most commonly referred to is the 'but-for' test: 'Would the loss have occurred but for the wrong?'[14] In consumer matters the questions are likely to be more prosaic – did the heel come off the shoe because of faulty manufacture or because the wearer of the shoe caught it in a grating? Whatever the question arising, the principle remains the same and the loss must have been caused by the alleged wrong if it is to be recoverable.

The second principle is much more significant and answers the question, 'How much of the loss caused by the wrongdoing is recoverable?' The law will not hold the defendant liable for *all* the loss resulting from a breach of contract or the commission of a tort if some of it is too far removed from the original wrong. The rules are referred to as the rules of 'remoteness of damage' and they are slightly different according to whether the claim is in contract or in tort. Losses arising from a breach of contract may be recovered only if they are such that they were within the reasonable contemplation of the parties at the time the contract was made.[15] The sort of loss that the court will accept as having been within the reasonable contemplation of the parties has given rise to difficulty, particularly in the definition of the degree of likelihood that is necessary and the state of knowledge of the parties. It is accepted that all losses that arise naturally from the breach would have been within the contemplation of the parties, but all the cases have concerned losses that were special in the sense of resulting from some particular circumstances unknown to the defendant. In the latest decision of the House of Lords[16] it was held that the loss would be recoverable only if there was a serious possibility that it would occur, or that there was a substantial probability. It is also clear that the test in the law of tort requires a lesser degree of probability and is usually expressed in terms of the reasonable foreseeability of loss occurring.[17] This distinction has been criticized but it remains part of the law until statute or the judges provide otherwise.

Even where the loss has clearly been caused by the wrongdoing of the defendant and it is not too remote, the plaintiff may still not be able to recover if it is the type of loss which the courts have decided is not recoverable. The most significant exclusion is that of 'pure economic loss' in the law of negligence. For reasons of policy the courts have decided that a plaintiff will not be able to recover economic loss caused by a negligent act unless that loss results from some physical damage. This may be illustrated by the case of *Spartan Steel and Alloys Ltd* v. *Martin (Contractors) Ltd*,[18] where the defendants negligently severed a cable carrying electric current to the plaintiff's factory. The loss of power in the foundry caused the 'melts' in the furnaces to deteriorate and damage the furnaces, and it prevented further melts from being processed until the power was returned. The Court of Appeal permitted the plaintiffs to recover damages for the lost material, for the damage to the furnace and for the loss of profit on the melt which was damaged, but they refused the largest part of the claim, which was for the loss of profits on melts that could have been processed while the electricity had been cut off. The court held that this was pure economic loss unconnected with any physical injury and was not recoverable.

In recent years the courts have relaxed the rule that in the law of contract no damages are recoverable for loss of enjoyment or disappointment caused by the breach of contract. In the case of *Jarvis* v. *Swan's Tours*[19] the plaintiff had been extremely disappointed by the failure of his skiing holiday to live up to the glowing descriptions in the tour company's brochure. On his return he sought damages not only for the reduced value of the holiday he actually received, but also for the disappointment he suffered because of the anticlimactic nature of his only holiday of the year. The Court of Appeal held that, where the contract is of the sort that provides for enjoyment and recreation, the failure to provide a satisfacory opportunity for the plaintiff to enjoy himself could be a breach of contract leading to damages for the plaintiff's disappointment. This interesting decision received favourable comment at the time but there have not been many other reported decisions in which its principles have been applied.

Specific Performance and the Injunction

There must be many people who have suffered a breach of contract and who would rather have the contract performed than receive money compensation for its breach. They want the court to require the defendant to honour the promises he made in the contract. However, for historical reasons the common law was never happy about enforcing specific obligations and it was left to the courts of Equity to supplement the common law by providing specific remedies. The key word in the last sentence is 'supplement', since the courts of Equity took the view that their remedies should be available only where the common law remedy was inadequate or unjust. This means that the equitable remedies have become the exception rather than the rule and the plaintiff who seeks them must be prepared to show why damages will not adequately satisfy his claim against the defendant. The two most important specific remedies are those that are indicated in the subheading and they will be considered briefly.

Specific performance is the requirement that a defaulting party complies with his contractual obligations. It is most often used to secure compliance with a contract for the sale of unique goods where the mere payment of compensation will not permit the plaintiff to purchase the same goods on the open market. Almost all contracts for the sale of land could be the subject of specific performance since no two pieces of land are identical, and contracts for the sale of any rare or unique article might also be enforced in this way. It will be rare for the payment of money to be enforced in this way,[20] or the performance of personal obligations. It is vital to remember that this remedy is unusual; it is only exceptional contracts that may be enforced in this way and the victim of a breach of contract will normally have to be content with damages.

In deciding whether to grant specific performance in the appropriate case the court may take into account all sorts of circumstances, including the behaviour of the plaintiff, that would not be considered in an action for damages. Various 'defences' are available to a defendant who is resisting an application for this remedy, notably delay in bringing the case, severe hardship or impossibility; and the court must also consider the position of any third parties who may have become involved with the property that is the subject of the application. Above all these considerations is the discretionary nature of the remedy – the court must weigh up the justice of the case.

The injunction is available to prevent threatened or continuing breaches of contract or torts. It may be more advantageous to a plaintiff to prevent the commission of a wrong than to wait until the damage has been done and claim compensation. This may be less applicable to consumer matters than to other areas of the law, but there may be situations where it is appropriate to try to restrain the commission of wrongs by traders and others.

The injunction operates as an instruction to the defendant to refrain from a particular course of action which, it is alleged, is infringing the rights of the plaintiff. It used to be the case that in deciding whether to grant an injunction the court would weigh up the relative strength of the plaintiff's case and decide whether there was a *prima facie* case, but after the decision in *American Cyanamid Co. v. Ethicon Ltd* [21] the court need only decide whether there is a 'serious issue to be tried'. Although this increases the possibility of obtaining an injunction for the plaintiff who will have less to prove, it renders the injunction less useful in the final resolution of the case. Previously, the parties would often take the court's determination of the *prima facie* case as a good indication of the likely result of the trial of the action, but now there is no such indication and the parties will be left in uncertainty. The object of the injunction is to preserve the *status quo* until the issue can be tried, and consequently it can be granted at very short notice and for a period fixed by the court which will usually be related to the date of trial.

The same considerations that will weigh with the court in deciding whether to grant specific performance will also be taken into account in granting an injunction. The means of enforcing the specific remedies is exceptionally effective. Any failure to carry out the instructions of the court is regarded as a contempt of court and is punished with imprisonment. The imprisonment lasts until the contempt is purged, i.e. until the prisoner promises to comply with the order of the court in future.

COMPENSATION IN CRIMINAL CASES

We have referred earlier to the procedure for making compensation orders. That procedure is however subject to certain restrictions. In the first place, a successful prosecution must be brought. A glance at the statistics will show that, of the numerous complaints received by the OFT and other agencies, relatively few result in prosecution and conviction.[22] Second, the aggrieved consumer must take steps to ensure that the court is asked to consider making a compensation order. Although the statute permits the court to act on its own initiative, or at the instance of someone other than the aggrieved person (e.g. the police or the Consumer Protection Officer prosecuting the case), the only sure way of having the matter considered is for the consumer to appear or be represented. Third, the higher courts have imposed some restrictions on the making of orders where the trial court would have to carry out a complicated review of the issues involved, perhaps even taking further evidence after the criminal case had been concluded. The criminal courts are not well equipped to investigate awkward questions of whether the loss resulted from the offence, and it has been suggested that the court should only make an order in the simpler cases.[23] Finally, in criminal cases the guilt of the defendant must be proved beyond reasonable doubt, whereas in civil cases proof is on a balance of probabilities. Thus it is obviously harder to prove a case in a criminal court.

Despite these restrictions the compensation is still a significant remedy for the consumer, the more so since the decision in *R* v. *Thomson Holidays Ltd*[24] permitted prosecution in respect of the same statement at the suit of individual complainants. The Divisional Court held in that case that a second prosecution in respect of the same false statement in a holiday brochure was neither improper nor oppressive, nor should it result in a purely nominal penalty. In each case the holidaymaker would have been entitled to ask for compensation for his own loss.

SELF-HELP AND EXTRA-LEGAL REMEDIES

Chapter 2 set out all the agencies that have some responsibility for protecting the interests of the consumer, and it would be idle to suggest that in every case the consumer must look to the civil or criminal courts for his remedy. He can get a lot of help from elsewhere, and he can take significant action himself to redress his grievances without darkening the doors of the courtroom. The procedures we have described in this chapter will often represent the last resort for the consumer, to be employed only when all else has failed. However, since this book is intended to be about the law and its enforcement we make no apology for treating the legal remedies first and spending only a few words in reminding you of a few of the multitude of ways in which the aggrieved individual consumer may choose to press his case without invoking the courts.

Many complaints are dealt with and settled at the level of discussion and negotiation with the trader or manufacturer involved. There is much to be gained by establishing a happy and contented clientele, and almost all the larger organizations have a 'consumer relations' department or something similar. Bad publicity will be persuasive in procuring satisfaction from recalcitrant traders and this is evidenced by the success of the consumer complaints service run by some national and provincial newspapers. The car owner who was dissatisfied with the service given under warranty by the garage from whom he purchased his car received very prompt and efficient attention after he had parked his car outside the garage with a large notice saying, 'This car was purchased from this garage — it has 35 faults and they won't put it right'. The more imaginative consumer can do a lot to help himself!

Apart from the normal consumer agencies, an aggrieved individual may seek help from the trade association involved, or from any group to which he belongs who may give specialist assistance, e.g. the Automobile Association. Even if he is driven to take legal advice there is often considerable scope for negotiation and settlement without commencing an action or, at least, without arriving in court.

11 Conclusion – The Way Forward

INTRODUCTION

The UK has over the years adopted an impressive array of measures to protect the consumer. We do not pretend that in the foregoing account we have dealt with them all but we hope that we have identified the more important ones.

Can we expect yet more protection of the consumer interest, or is the protection boom coming to an end? *Ought* it to come to an end? As a matter of pure common sense there must be a limit to the amount of help that can be dispensed. The individual must be expected to rely on his own intelligence and experience – in any event the government and business machines can hardly cope with much more legislation. There is no doubt that greater regulation would mean more administrative expense, which everyone would have to bear either through taxation or through the higher costs borne by enterprises, which would then feed through in the form of higher prices. Legislative activity may slacken off (without any diminution of the level of protection already achieved) and such a slackening would, in our view, be appropriate so long as some remaining issues are dealt with.

Before we deal with these issues we feel it is important to stress that consumers should be given the fullest opportunity to influence a wide range of policy issues. In this respect the activities of the National Consumer Council are highly beneficial, and we cannot emphasize too much the need for a period of stability during which the Council can develop its potential free from political interference. In Chapter 2 we noted that there might be some internal resistance to the idea that the Consumers' Association should go beyond product testing and should campaign actively on behalf of consumers in general. In practice recent evidence indicates that the CA may see such a role for itself. This was apparent in 1978 when it produced a joint response (in conjunction with the National Consumer Council and the National Federation of Consumer Groups) to a consultative document on monopolies and mergers policy.[1] We feel that the consumer should have a voice on all the main agencies that deal with matters of concern to the consuming public and in particular should be represented on some institutions concerned with pay and prices which we suggest below. We would also argue that if workers are to be placed on company boards then so should consumers. We also support the National Consumer Council proposal that the chairmen of consumer consultative councils should be members of the nationalized industry boards.

THE EEC DIMENSION

There are a number of developments that we believe ought to be introduced into EEC policy. The first is that, although antitrust policy has been quite successful, certainly more successful than forecasted by some early commentators, it does need to be strengthened in respect of mergers. Until this happens the EC Commission will have to rely on Article 86 of the Rome Treaty, which is a highly imperfect instrument of merger control. We would argue that the draft proposal for providing such a power needs modifying in that, although it enables consideration to be given to the benefits arising from mergers, the specific provision is unduly narrow.

The other main need for change lies in the area of agricultural policy. The Common Agricultural Policy (CAP) has a bad reputation in the UK although the criticism has been somewhat overdone. Space precludes a discussion of the details of how the CAP works.[2] What we should note is that Article 39 of the Rome Treaty, which outlines the aims of the CAP, lays down a number of objectives. These are: (a) increased efficiency; (b) a fair standard of living for the agricultural community; (c) market stability; (d) certainty of supplies; (e) reasonable prices for consumers. Efficiency has been steadily increasing although much still remains to be achieved. How much of that increase has been due to the CAP is difficult to say; the answer is probably not a great deal. The policy does seem to have contributed towards price *stability*, and there is no doubt that it has increasingly provided certainty of supply – indeed, over-supply! The main problem arises as between (b) and (e), which are likely to conflict in the absence of dramatic developments under (a). The policy has in the main been based on high prices, which have been necessary to cover the costs of the less efficient (although they have not been sufficient to eradicate the low-income problem). The high prices have of

CONCLUSION – THE WAY FORWARD   237

course put gold plate on the Mercedes of the efficient producers. The consumer has been doubly penalized. He has paid a high price for what he has consumed, but has also had to foot the bill for dealing with surpluses, which have in some cases been sold off on the world market at knock-down prices. Various solutions have been proposed.[3] Some have been concerned with structural change. The industry should be slimmed down and farms reorganized into more efficient units. More recently attention has switched to the support system itself. One suggestion is that, particularly in the case of surplus products, swingeing cuts should be made in real terms in the level of support prices. Other proposals include a modification of the open-ended nature of price guarantees. Full support prices should be paid only if the output of a product is kept within a specified global limit. If production exceeds that limit support prices should be appropriately reduced. These policies could of course produce considerable social and regional problems as well as political tensions.

A good deal of concern has also been expressed about the weak position of the consumer as compared with the farmers. There is a case for creating at the Community level machinery for representing the interests of food consumers when prices are determined by the Council of Ministers. In practice this means the Ministers of Agriculture who in the main see their prime task as looking after farmers. Only the UK minister is by title designated as being a Minister of Food, i.e. responsible for the consumer interest in food and food prices.

The National Consumer Council has recently drawn attention to the fact that, as a result of changes stemming from the CAP, marketing boards for milk and potatoes are no longer going to be under the specific control of the UK government.[4] They will become producer-controlled marketing organizations. The NCC points out that consumers will be in a weak position and that the appropriate remedy is that they be represented on the policy-making authority of the new boards.

A few words now need to be added on the subject of the harmonization of standards in the EEC. This has been greatly misrepresented in the UK. It may be that there have been instances of excess of zeal. However, the evidence suggests that where there has been strong opposition proposals have been dropped. Moreover, the idea that all national differences will be removed is nonsense. The object is, for example, merely to require certain standards to be adhered to in respect of those particular features of design or composition that may give rise to threats to life or limb. In the case of labelling the nature of the product is not indeed at issue. We should also note that in some cases harmonization may be optional. Products conforming to a Community standard can sell over the whole territory of the EEC; those not conforming can still be sold in the domestic market. There are of course potential consumer gains. Standardization can, by opening up a wider market, give rise to economies of large-scale production. If differences in national standards keep imports out then harmonization may pave the way for intensified competition. Harmonization may also lead to the general introduction of the best national practices available.

THE DOMESTIC DIMENSION

Antitrust Policy

It is fairly generally agreed that changes are needed in antitrust policy; the prime areas of concern are restrictive practices and mergers.

One line of development would be to tighten up on the attitude adopted towards restrictions of competition in the Restrictive Trade Practices Act. It would be possible to adopt the American *per se* approach, where agreements would be automatically banned with no possibility of mitigating arguments being brought in defence. Undoubtedly the great majority of agreements are designed to restrict competition rather than increase efficiency, etc. However, there are some instances where benefits are identifiable and this suggests that prohibition, or contrariness to the public interest, accompanied by the possibility of exemption, has something to be said in its favour. But there is no reason why the existing gateways should remain undisturbed. It can be argued that the gateways are in some cases too wide and in others are concerned with matters best dealt with by other policies (i.e. the gateways dealing with regional unemployment and exports). The more selective and rigorous approach adopted in Article 85 of the Rome Treaty has much to be said for it.

We have however posed a false distinction. There is no reason why the choice should lie between *per se* approach and the possibility of exemption approach. It would be possible to declare some categories of agreement to be *per se* illegal while the rest could continue to enjoy the possibility of exemption. Price-fixing agreements could be sub-

CONCLUSION – THE WAY FORWARD

jected to the more rigorous approach since they rarely produce any identifiable public benefit. The NCC has not gone as far as this but has suggested that collusive tendering should be prohibited *per se*.[5] It takes the view that collusive tendering, through its inherent secrecy, strikes at the heart of the tendering process itself. The NCC does however recognize that there might be a case for widening the attack so as to take in all forms of price-fixing.

The other main need for change lies in the area of enforcement. Quite simply, as we noted in Chapter 4, there is evidence that in a number of industries firms have deliberately chosen not to register their agreements. Added to that we must note that the powers conferred upon the Director-General of Fair Trading for the purpose of uncovering agreements are inadequate. Furthermore, the provisions for deterring concealment appear to need tightening up. This may all seem a little odd when we recollect that the Restrictive Trade Practices Act 1968 was partly designed to deal with the problem of non-registration. One of the reasons for the continued difficulty is that the Director-General has been hampered in his attempts to root out unregistered agreements. Under present restrictive practices legislation if the Director-General 'has reasonable cause to believe' that an agreement exists he can serve a notice on the persons concerned requiring them (a) to state whether they are parties to an agreement and (if they are) (b) to give particulars. Such notice having been served, the Director-General can also approach the Restrictive Practices Court asking it to make an Order requiring the parties to attend the Court and be examined under oath. Unfortunately in 1969 in the case of the *Registrar v. W. H. Smith*[6] the Court made it clear that in initiating this type of action a strong suspicion on the part of the Registrar was not enough. This means that the Director-General must have very firm evidence indeed before he has any real prospects of persuading the Court to make an Order, and of course the evidence may not match up to that standard. There is undoubtedly need for a change here and the government has recently announced that it intends to legislate on the matter. One possibility would be to change the wording of Section 36 of the 1976 Act so that it reads 'If the Director believes . . .'.[7]

Other changes have also been suggested. Although the Director-General has the power to require parties to an agreement to furnish relevant documents or information, he does *not* have power to enter premises and seize documents. Such powers have been conferred in other areas of consumer protection – see Section 28 of the Trade Descriptions Act 1968. British businesses are in any case now subject to such powers in connection with the implementation of Articles 85 and 86 of the Rome Treaty. A power to enter and seize, subject to safeguards, is desirable.

It appears that an agreement that has originally been concealed but is finally registered may still be heard before the Court under the normal processes and may be upheld. This seems to be carrying things too far. There is a case for following EEC practice of declaring that agreements that are not registered in due time cannot be considered for exemption.

In Chapter 4 we noted that the 1968 Act provided for individuals to claim civil damages in respect of unregistered agreements. This power has not been taken advantage of, possibly because the benefit to individuals in relation to cost may make it unattractive. Here surely there is a case for providing for a class action. The law should be amended so that a body representing consumers generally could claim damages on their behalf.

The problem in respect of mergers can be simply stated. Since they were brought under control in 1965 views about them have altered and the structural situation in industry has changed. As we noted in Chapter 4, at the time of the passing of the 1965 Act, and indeed for several years after, the attitude of ministers was that mergers were beneficial except in a minority of cases. Today many economists are sceptical about the benefits they confer,[8] and added to that is the fact that in industry generally, and in specific industries, output has come to be concentrated in fewer hands.[9] Further concentration could be dangerous – economically and politically. In short, the approach adopted in 1965 is out of date. That approach has been said not to be neutral but to be favourable to mergers. The idea that the law has not been neutral is founded on two points. First, mergers have been allowed to proceed unless they have been found to be contrary to the public interest. There has been no question of their being allowed to proceed only if they were positively to benefit the public interest. Second, and perhaps crucially in the light of the ministerial monopoly of reference, ministers have as we have seen been favourably disposed towards them.

Some of the dissatisfaction with the present approach has been focused on the way in which the law has been implemented. Quite simply, far too few of the mergers surveyed by the Mergers Panel have been referred to the Monopolies and Mergers Commission.[10]

There have been many proposals for a change in policy; for the most part they have emphasized the need for a tightening up.[11] Some have looked favourably on the idea of reversing the onus of proof – e.g., mergers should show net benefit to the public if they are to be allowed to proceed. Consideration has also been given to the idea of banning mergers involving the very biggest firms. Other proposals have suggested that some kinds of merger should automatically be referred to the Monopolies and Mergers Commission. In November 1977 the UK government announced that it intended to carry out a review of the law and institutions of competition policy. A consultative document, *A Review of Monopolies and Mergers Policy*,[12] was published in 1978 containing the fruits of the review group's thinking. It too suggested that a change was needed and it opted for what it called a neutral, as opposed to the existing favourable, policy. The group suggested that the government should warn firms of the new shift in policy with its greater emphasis on competition. In looking at mergers the Monopolies and Mergers Commission should be required to report first whether a merger was expected to prevent, restrict or distort competition significantly, or to have other adverse effects. If it did then the Commission should assess any likely benefits. Finally, it should balance detriments and benefits and recommend the action to be taken. It will be apparent that the review group fought shy of adopting some of the more radical suggestions discussed above. Clearly not everyone will be happy with such a limited change.

A number of other changes in merger policy are needed. Follow-up studies would be useful. In other words, do mergers that have been approved produce the benefits promised? The ministerial monopoly of merger references has attracted a lot of criticism. There have been cases where the Director-General recommended a reference but the Secretary of State decided against for political reasons. The Director-General should be allowed to refer mergers – this would not preclude the Secretary of State from doing so also.

A number of suggestions have been made on the monopoly front. Perhaps the most important is the proposal that in the light of the Commission's long-standing opposition to certain forms of monopoly firm practice – e.g. exclusionary devices – these should now be banned.[13]

Prices and Incomes Policy

In Chapters 1 and 5 we saw that an incomes policy was potentially a form of consumer protection, at least for some. We say 'potentially' because it all depends on the cause of inflation. If inflation is of the wage-push variety then incomes policy is an appropriate response. Such wage-pushfulness may represent an attempt to increase the real income of workers. It may however be defensive in character; unions may press for wage increases merely in order to preserve the purchasing power of wages in conditions where prices are rising because of the state of the world market. There is no doubt that in 1973 and 1974 the main inflationary impetus did come from rising import prices. This had a direct effect on prices as well as indirect effects through (a) rising raw material and fuel costs and (b) rises in wages designed to protect the purchasing power of workers' incomes. We also envisaged that, where expectations about future prices are an important factor in determining wage-pushfulness, an incomes, and for that matter a prices, policy may have a calming effect.

It is difficult to resist the conclusion that recently pressure for pay increases – well in excess of productivity increases – has been a major factor in the causation of inflation. If this condition continues, and it is arguable that in varying degrees this is likely, then there is a case for the institution of a permanent mechanism for controlling the increase of incomes. The sceptic may wonder whether incomes policies are likely to work. What does past experience prove? This is a matter of some controversy, but it does seem to be the case that when policy has been 'full-on' wage increases have been lower than might have been predicted. The problem is that in the subsequent 'half-on' or 'policy-off' periods there has been a flood of wage increases in which the ground lost has been made up. This suggests that if incomes policy is to have any significant effect it must be continuous. It must cease to be a political football. Within the parties and between the parties there should be agreement that control must be applied and must not be turned on and off for electoral advantage. It is ultimately necessary that the electorate be well persuaded of the need for such a permanent policy, although in the interim governments should recognize that they are there to govern.

No one should underestimate the difficulties inherent in seeking to operate an incomes policy. No doubt in the light of events in 1978–79 no one is likely to do so! Past experience indicates that voluntary policies do not work or do not work for very long. It has been suggested that voluntary policies may last for a couple of years – after that they begin to crumble. Reluctantly we are driven to the conclusion that incomes policy must have a statutory base. Even then we should not expect too much. It would require a veritable army of civil servants to vet every wage bargain, and clearly this is not on. Moreover the ingenuity of man is such that ways can be found of getting round any system of control. Jobs can be spuriously redefined in order to justify more pay, etc. It should not however be impossible to devise a system that, even if it does not produce absolute price stability, at least brings inflation down well below recent intolerable levels.

One of the problems of incomes policy is how to exercise control in a flexible manner. For example, an absolutely rigid norm frustrates the operation of the price mechanism and gives rise to inefficiency in the allocation of resources.[14] Industry X may be experiencing an increase in demand for its products but may not be able to respond if it is unable to get the extra labour because the norm prevents it bidding up wage rates in order to get it. Then again, the promotion of increased efficiency may require ways of giving increases above the norm where genuine increases in productivity can be negotiated. In all such cases the exception must not be taken as being the new norm for everyone else.

Incomes policies are likely to develop increasing strains and eventually to break down if they ride roughshod over the need for differentials. Some of the difficulties of recent years are almost certainly due to flat-rate increases which have favoured the lower paid. In so far as comparisons tend to focus on the gross wage or salary, it may be that a less explosive approach is to help the lower paid through the mechanism of the taxation system. Ultimately it does however seem to us that the lower paid must expect to see some of their absolute improvement coming from increased efficiency – a reality that faces the community as a whole.

In Chapters 1 and 5 we noted that incomes policies do not have much chance of proving acceptable if they do not also encompass some surveillance of prices. (In this context we must also say that government policy *generally* must be conceived in a way that is supportive of pay, and indeed price, restraint.) From what has gone before it is obvious that we do not believe that the government can leave wages to the forces of free collective bargaining and rely for its control on a policy of sitting on prices. The balance of power in society appears to be such that this would depress economic performance further below the present miserable level. Profits would be eroded and the funds for investment would thus be depleted. Lower investment would reduce the rate of increase of productivity and this would tend to generate higher costs and thus price increases. On the other hand, we do not advocate the disappearance of price control. We believe that the kind of role discharged by the Price Commission following the Price Commission Act 1977 is important. Here we would emphasize the importance of supervising prices in situations where the force of competition is absent or attenuated.

One of the obvious weaknesses in government pay strategy in recent years has been the absence of any central body to whom claims for exceptional treatment can be put and which can adjudicate dispassionately on the relativities issue.[15] The disbanding of the old National Board for Prices and Incomes was a great mistake, and we desperately need to bring such a pay adjudicating body back into existence. The problem that arises is, should that body's decisions merely be advisory, or should they be mandatory in effect? We would suggest that the basis of incomes policy should be a general percentage norm increase. The policy should however include an element of flexibility. It should specify very clearly the various grounds for increases in excess of the norm and should prescribe the maximum excess above the norm in those special cases. It should be expected that the great majority of collective bargains would be concluded within the ambit of flexibility. In cases where the parties were unable to settle within that ambit the matter should be referred to the central body for adjudication. Its decision would be final. Equally, the new body should be able to challenge settlements that did not conform to the rules and its decision would again be final.

In our view some organizational and functional changes are needed. At the top of our new structure we envisage a quadrupartite body made up of representatives of the government, the CBI, the TUC and the consumer interest. The latter could be supplied from the membership of the National Consumer Council. The task of the new body would be to deliberate on the prices and incomes targets for the coming year. It would *advise* the government as to what was desirable and feasible on the prices front and what increases in incomes would be compatible therewith. From this would emerge the norm increases. This supreme body would also *advise* the government on the incomes flexibility criteria and margins and the price increase criteria. Beneath it there would be another institution, organized in two divisions, whose task would be to seek to achieve the objectives finally laid down. We have noted a convergence in the roles of the Monopolies and Mergers Commission and the Price Commission. These two bodies could be amalgamated. Given the essential unity of competition policy there would be a case for integrating within the new structure the activities of the Director-General in making references to the Restrictive Practices Court. The prime task of this division would be to seek to increase efficiency and to arrest inflation (the two of course go together) through the agency of competition. Price control should be reserved for situations where competition is limited or largely non-existent, e.g. nationalized industries and private industry where, because of oligopoly or dominance, the normal force of competition is muted. The amalgamated body should be more adventurous in suggesting structural changes than the Monopolies and Mergers Commission has been. Regulation of prices should include the cutting down of excessive promotional activity which can create barriers to entry and may involve a misuse of scarce resources. The government has indicated a desire to regulate this kind of behaviour. The other division would be concerned with pay on the lines discussed earlier.

Courts, Contracts and Product Liability

We considered briefly in Chapter 10 the court system through which a consumer is required to take action to enforce civil law rights. Despite the special provisions that have been made to alleviate the problems relating particularly to small claims[16] we can understand the dismay with which a consumer views the prospect of a court appearance. Procedure is still not designed to allow the ordinary, unrepresented litigant to put his own case with ease and we would expect the lot of the consumer to be bettered in one of two ways. Either the system must be made simpler with special courts solely for small claims, or the law and procedure that is applicable in the present system must be simplified so that the layman can be more confident in the presentation and outcome of his case.

As to the former, both the Conservative Party, when in power, and the Labour Party have expressed themselves to be opposed to the creation of a new court performing the same sort of function that was envisaged for the County Court on its creation in 1846. It is fair to point out that the special provisions introduced recently may need time to become established and to work properly, but we feel that this type of tinkering with the system is unlikely to provide a permanent answer.

As to the latter, there are signs that the civil rights of consumers are being strengthened to such a degree that an appearance in court may be unnecessary by virtue of the fact that the defendant may have little left in the way of defence. The Unfair Contract Terms Act 1977 ought to be significant in preventing reliance on unfair exclusion clauses which rob the consumer of his rights, and there are signs that the courts may be increasingly willing to take into account the relative strengths of the parties in deciding the merits of the case.[17]

However, the introduction of strict liability for injuries caused by products would have the most far-reaching effect on the balance of rights between consumer and producer. We have mentioned the complexities of procedure in the courts, but we should also draw attention to the enormous difficulties that lie in the path of the consumer trying to prove that his injuries were caused by the negligence of a particular manufacturer. The frustrations of the law of negligence and the unfair results that follow from a requirement that fault must be proved to establish the manufacturer's liability were both strong arguments behind the Law Commission's recommendation that a system of product liability be adopted.[18] The Pearson Commission[19] weighed in heavily in support of the Law Commission's view, and they had both been preceded by an EEC Draft Directive and a Convention adopted by the Council of Europe.[20] We are fully conscious of the additional cost of insurance that manufacturers and others would have to bear, and the cost of other precautions, most of which would no doubt be passed on to the consumer. However, the Thalidomide tragedy is still fresh in the minds of many people and we are confident that the introduction of strict liability for injury caused by products is only a matter of time.

If the law is to be reformed in the way outlined and the contractual rights of consumers are to be strengthened, some of the grievances about the court system would disappear. There is a considerable connection between the two problems.

Consumer Credit

The reforms of credit law conceived in the Consumer Credit Act 1974 are undergoing a lengthy gestation period. We expect that it will be some time yet before they are fully implemented, and until they are the law of hire-purchase will soldier on with some of the less complex changes introduced by the Act grafted on. In respect of the remarks that we made in the preceding section about the willingness of the courts to consider the relative strength of the parties in deciding the merits, we look forward with anticipation to decisions about extortionate credit bargains. That, as much as anything, will test the willingness of the judges to implement the spirit of the Act in their decisions.

The adoption of a licensing system for the credit business may act as a pointer to the effect of licensing in a controversial area, and judgments as to the success of the system may inform decisions about measures to be introduced in other areas of the protection field, e.g. advertising.

Import Controls

There is no doubt, and we emphasized the point in Chapter 1, that import controls can have a significantly adverse effect on the consumer. They can reduce his range of choice and, even if domestic productive capacity is adequate to fill the gap, they can raise prices. A full discussion of the pros and cons of import controls would require more space than we have available. However, the following points will serve to indicate the kind of problems we have in mind.

There are some superficially attractive arguments in favour of import controls but we do need to be careful. As for general import controls we would incline to the view that a devaluation is to be preferred as a means of maintaining domestic competitiveness. If there is a case for import controls it must be on a selective basis. But again we do need to be vigilant. There is, for example, the infant industry argument. A new industry may not be able to withstand foreign competition. If for a limited period it can be shielded it will be able to grow and will come to derive the economies of large-scale production, etc., and then be able to stand on its own two feet without protection. But will it? The absence of foreign competition may mean that it lacks the incentive to become viable and it may become a permanent object of assistance. There is also the senile industry argument. An old industry may be encountering difficulties, but if given a breathing space it may be able to re-equip and thus become viable. A good example would be the shoe industry. But quite apart from the questions as to whether it will be galvanized into action and will actually ever become *fully* competitive, there is a doubt as to whether we ought to be concentrating on lower technology. Should we concentrate on products such as shoes and low cost clothing which less developed countries are well placed to produce? Should we not be shifting our resources into the newer and more advanced technologies?

Nationalized Industries

We believe that the position of the consumer needs to be strengthened in relation to the provision of domestic goods and services by the nationalized industries. This has been the subject of at least two major inquiries[21] and in both cases the conclusion was that significant improvements were necessary. The position of the consultative councils seems very variable. Thus POUNC – the Post Office Users' National Council – seems to be relatively well placed to do its job but others fall well short of its standard. In some instances there has been a lack of the information that was necessary if the consultative bodies were to do their jobs properly. In some cases the range of questions that the bodies have been able to consider has been too narrow. A statutory duty to consult on the part of the industry has been by no means universal. We have already suggested that the chairmen of the consultative councils should sit on the industry boards. It is also tempting to suggest that the councils should be represented in the pay bargaining process.

Food

As we have discussed in Chapters 5 and 6, the sale of food has been subjected to rigorous standards. The Food and Drugs Act 1955 imposes strict liability in respect of the quality of food sold in shops, and we have adverted to the regulations on labelling, presentation and unit pricing.

There is currently some discussion about whether it is proper to continue to impose upon the sellers of food the entire risk of the food being injurious. It could be argued that the consumer ought to expect to run a degree of risk when he purchases food; that certain foods are inherently harmful and that the state of medical knowledge is always adding to the list; that the manufacturer and the shopkeeper cannot ever entirely eliminate the risk to health from certain foods. Arguments like these will be under consideration by the government in the review that it is undertaking of the Food and Drugs Act 1955.

The harmonization of laws within the EEC which we have referred to earlier in this chapter is likely to result in the introduction of regulations to make it compulsory to display a shelf life on perishable food. It is equally likely that more and more foods will be brought under the regulations that require unit pricing. It is in areas like this that the consumer is particularly weak through an inability to judge value for money.

Advertising

Since we have been obliged to deal with the subject of advertising in many of the chapters of this book it will come as no surprise to the reader that we have identified it as one of the areas in which there is certain to be some developments in the fairly near future. The report of the OFT on advertising which was published at the end of 1978 contained an assessment of the self-regulatory system under which the advertising industry operates.

Self-regulation has always been claimed to be the most effective form of guarantee against low standards but hitherto there has been a lack of convincing evidence about that effectiveness. It is argued that there are areas of advertising that would be wholly inappropriate for legal control, and one might point to the difficulties experienced by the law in the field of obscenity as an example of the problems of definition in matters of taste.

The absence of effective sanctions has been criticized but there has yet to be a convincing scheme presented for monitoring advertisements and assessing them. The problem of enforcement is only one aspect and it assumes that there are acceptable standards to be enforced. The criteria by which advertisements are to be judged can also be the subject of heated debate.

We feel unable to make an adequate judgment on the merits of the self-regulatory system, but that in itself might indicate that there is more research to be done in exposing the workings of the system and its efficacy. The government's response to the report of the OFT will be available before too long and we suspect that it might sound the death knell for the present system.

The Office of Fair Trading

Last but not least we ought at least to hazard a guess at the fortunes of the OFT in the coming years. We think that it has made an auspicious start in dealing with a number of undesirable trade practices, and it is clearly a highly effective agency for the co-ordination of efforts to protect the consumer from all manner of difficulties.

The contribution of the OFT to the education of the consumer cannot be underestimated. The consumer education movement has always argued that an informed and educated purchaser is far less likely to make mistakes and to encounter difficulties, whether before or after purchase, than an ill-informed one. The education of the consumer has been undertaken with a will by the OFT and it deserves great credit for the imagination and flair with which it has presented some of the material that has formed the basis of this book. It is not in any carping way that we sound one warning note.

Laudable though the presentation of as much information as possible to the consumer may be, the danger that it creates is that it will induce exactly that state of complete reliance that it is trying to dispel. The informed consumer is supposed to be alert to make choices, but the over-informed consumer may be misled into thinking that any action that is not specifically prohibited by instructions or information is thereby safe. There is a story, no doubt apocryphal, from the United States of a lady who dried out her pet poodle in a microwave oven on the basis that the instructions said nothing about ovens being harmful to pets put inside them. We would argue that the consumer must not be induced to believe that he will be told *everything* that he needs to know!

The OFT will, of course, continue the work that it has begun in consumer affairs and we do not regard it as a criticism in the antitrust field that it has failed to effect any significant improvement in the situation. The legislation is not unduly helpful.

The production of Codes of Practice ought, we think, to continue, not least because the codes have sometimes given the consumer rights that were in advance of those that he might have had at common law. One may assume that the OFT will go ahead with a code only when it is satisfied that something worthwhile has been achieved for the consumer and so they are always likely to be of some help.

FINALE

We conclude this chapter where we began it, with an expression of hope that, without any diminution of the level of protection afforded to the consumer, the coming years may be ones in which there is some opportunity to take stock of achievements and assess the efficacy of the law, the institutions, the codes, and the agencies that now exist. The upsurge in consumerism which led to much of the legislation of the 1970s is just beginning to level out and a number of those who got carried along on a wave of enthusiasm are presently wondering quite where that wave has left them and in what direction they should now strike out. A period of consolidation would not in our view do any harm at all, provided that some of the remaining issues are dealt with.

We include a short bibliography in the book because we hope that some who find interest in the issues that we have discussed will pursue them further into the specialist works. We have tried to raise issues, provide information, rehearse arguments and stimulate debate over a wide field and in a way that we hope the reader will have found helpful.

> Ah! don't say that you agree with me. When people agree with me I always feel that I must be wrong.
>
> *Oscar Wilde*

Addendum

The foregoing account of institutions and policy reflects the position at the end of February 1979. However in May 1979 a new government took office. Below we discuss some of the changes which have already taken place and some which *may* take place.

First, we record that the functions of the Department of Prices and Consumer Protection have been merged into the Department of Trade. Statutes assign various roles to 'the Secretary of State', and under the new institutional arrangement this will be the Secretary of State for Trade, as the Secretary of State for Prices and Consumer Protection no longer exists. The former has a seat in the cabinet just as the latter had. There is now a Minister of State for Consumer Affairs without a seat in the cabinet. The Minister of State will be responsible for both competition and consumer protection policy. Although, as we have seen, the DGFT and his Office enjoy a degree of independence, the departmental link will now be with the Department of Trade.

Some changes in policy are also apparent. One of the most important is the rejection of price control. The new government believes that the activities of the Price Commission had a negligible effect on inflation and that they destroyed jobs and investment. The Price Commission and its activities (including pre-notification, etc.) will therefore be abolished. In respect of price control the new government places more emphasis on the strengthening of competition. The reader will recollect that after 1977 the Price Commission tended to focus its control on areas where the force of competition was weak. The new government intends to deal with this kind of problem through the agency of the Monopolies and Mergers Commission. A Competition Bill was published in early July and the DGFT will be charged with the responsibility for uncovering anti-competitive practices. These are defined as a course of conduct that has or is intended or is likely to have the effect of restricting, distorting or preventing competition in the U.K. These can be referred to the Commission. The important element here is that he could refer the *practices* of a firm or firms *even if the statutory monopoly condition was not satisfied*. Two points should be noted. Firstly, such a limited reference could be dealt with relatively expeditiously. Secondly, the firm or firms could offer to give voluntary undertakings and thus avoid the need for the investigation. If, however, an investigation did take place and a report was produced, the Secretary of State could make orders in the normal way. It is also intended that the Secretary of State could ask the DGFT to investigate prices in areas of public concern. It is also proposed that the Secretary of State shall be given powers to refer to the Commission abuses of monopoly power by nationalized industries – the Fair Trading Act 1973 does, however, already contain provisions relevant to nationalized industries.

Earlier in the book we referred to the *Review of Monopolies and Mergers Policy* 1978. In March 1979 a *Review of Restrictive Trade Practices Policy* was also published. The latter suggests a number of possible changes including the introduction of fines for failure to register and also that collusive tendering should be prohibited. Criminal penalties should apply in cases of infringement of the prohibition. Both these reviews have yet to be digested by the new government, after which a recasting of the present battery of antitrust laws may ensue.

The Minister of State has announced that Government grants for the running of Consumer Advice Centres will be terminated at the end of the financial year. This represents another shift away from protection through public institutions and may be further evidence of an end to the consumer protection boom.

The new government has rejected an incomes policy based on the imposition of rigid norms, and has instead chosen the application of strict cash limits in the public sector and control of the growth of the money supply. The theory is that if trade unions insist on pay increases in excess of what is provided for in the cash limits, or in the expansion of the money supply, then labour will price itself out of the market – i.e. unemployment will result. It is anticipated that this unpleasant experience, or the prospect of it, will induce realistic pay bargaining. However the government is also hoping to work through persuasion. A new economic forum is foreshadowed which will seek to educate the public as to the level of pay settlements which the economy can afford. Past experience indicates that governments have been forced to change course and it is difficult at this early stage to predict how successful this new phase of anti-inflation policy will be, particularly in the light of the changes in the tax structure and the rate of VAT which were announced in the budget on 12 June 1979

There now seems less prospect of significant change taking place in the way in which advertising is regulated. The Conservative government can be expected to be more accommodating towards the industry. Also the emphasis on public expenditure cuts suggests that we may see less rather than more regulation.

18 July 1979

Notes

CHAPTER 1

1 We readily admit that such policies are not necessarily *exclusively* concerned with the interests of consumers. For example, competition policy will also be concerned with the supply of raw materials, equipment, etc., bought by businessmen, nationalized industries, etc. However, it seems reasonable to argue in reply that if because of competition policy businessmen or nationalized industries pay less for the things they buy, then they are in a position to reflect that fact in the prices they charge to consumers. We also readily admit that when specific competition laws are examined it is apparent that serving the consumer has only been one of a number of aims in the minds of legislators. We allude to these other aims in this chapter and in Chapters 3 and 4. However we believe that competition and price policies do protect the consumer interest, even if not exclusively, and we therefore feel justified in including them in the discussion.
2 They have their own consumer councils.
3 J. K. Galbraith, *American Capitalism*, Houghton Mifflin, Boston, 1952.
4 D. Swann, *Competition and Consumer Protection*, Penguin, Harmondsworth, 1979, Chapter 3; W. S. Howe, *Industrial Economics An Applied Approach*, Macmillan, London, 1974, Chapter 3.

CHAPTER 2

1 The EC Commission now administers the three treaties establishing the three separate Communities.
2 Discussed in Chapter 5.
3 The DPCP is also responsible for the Metrication Board, the Hearing Aid Council and the British Hallmarking Council, and it sponsors the British Standards Institution.
4 It is odd that the statute nowhere mentions the OFT but it is clear that the Director-General of Fair Trading must have both a staff and offices to carry out his functions.
5 Fair Trading Act 1973, S.2(1) (a).
6 Ibid., S.2(1) (b).
7 Ibid., S.34, S.35.
8 Ibid., S.124.
9 E.g. *The Consumer Credit Act – what every shopper should know, what every trader must know*, OFT, London, 1976.
10 S.3.
11 Fair Trading Act 1973, schedule 2 and S.3(5).
12 Ibid., S.14 (4).

13 Ibid., S.13.
14 Ibid., S.17 (2)
15 Ibid., S.21.
16 *Disguised Business Sales – A Report on the Practice of Seeking to Sell Goods Without Revealing that they are being Sold in the Course of a Business.* House of Commons Paper No. 355. This report was implemented by the Business Advertisements (Disclosure) Order 1977 (S.I 1977 No. 1918).
17 *Rights of Consumers – A Report on Practices Relating to the Purported Exclusion of Inalienable Rights of Consumers and Failure to Explain their Existence.* House of Commons Paper No.6. Implemented by the Consumer Transactions (Restriction on Statements) Order 1976 (S.I 1976 No.1813).
18 *Prepayment for Goods – A Report on Practices Relating to Prepayment in Mail Order Transactions and Shops.* House of Commons Paper No.285. Implemented by the Mail Order Transactions (Information) Order 1976 (S.I 1976 No.1812).
19 Fair Trading Act 1973, S.50.
20 Ibid., S.51.
21 Ibid., S.44, S.45, S.46.
22 Ibid., S.56.
23 Ibid., S.88.
24 Ibid., S.64.
25 Ibid., S.88.
26 Ibid., S.86.
27 The number stood at 110 at the end of 1976. The financial help made available to the councils increased from £100,000 in 1975–76 to £1,289,000 in 1976–77 and £3,000,000 in 1977–78. It was the decrease in grant for the period beginning April 1978 that led a number of councils to think again.
28 Cmnd 5726.
29 Its reports have been concerned with consumers and the nationalized industries and with paying for fuel, and discussion papers have ranged over rent arrears, tenancy agreements, means-tested benefits and local advice services.
30 See the Consumer Council response in their Press notice, 'The Axing of the Consumer Council', 29 October 1970.
31 Reference may be made particularly to the discussion paper on local advice services where the Foreword says, 'From the beginning of its life the NCC has regarded the consumer as embracing the user of the social services. People can be just as done down in their dealings with government bureaucracy, sometimes more so, as by shopkeepers and manufacturers.'
32 In a magazine called *Consumer Reports.*
33 *The Good Food Guide, How to Sue in the County Court* and *The Which Guide to Contraception*, respectively.
34 *Final Report of the Committee on Consumer Protection*, Cmnd 1781, HMSO, London, 1962.
35 Ibid., Recommendation 108, referring to paras. 481, 491–3.
36 The Grant for the last period 1974–79 was in the region of £2.5 million.
37 *Annual Report 1977–8*, NACAB, London, 1978. Consumer matters are the second most popular category.
38 See, for example, The Unfair Advertising Act 1970–72 (South Australia).
39 *The British Code of Advertising Practice*, Preamble to 5th edition.
40 Ibid., para 3.1.
41 Ibid., Introduction to the 5th edition.
42 It is perhaps fair to add that in a number of jurisdictions the control of advertising has been achieved under statutes that give a government body power to bring into question trade practices, for example the Federal Trade Commission in the United States. This may give an indication of the way in which our own Director-General

of Fair Trading may use the powers under the Fair Trading Act to control advertising. See Fair Trading Act 1973 S.2(1), S.17 and the *First Report of the Director-General of Fair Trading*, HMSO, London, 1975, p.22.
43 The EEC is preparing a directive on misleading advertising; see R. G. Lawson, 'Advertising Controls in the EEC', *New Law Journal*, Vol.127, 1977, pp.563–6.
44 At the moment the sanctions are entirely dependent upon the advertising industry itself. If advertisers persistently infringe the code they may find their advertisements refused by newspapers and journals and trading privileges withdrawn. In addition the Authority may publish details of the outcome of complaints made against advertisements (*British Code of Advertising Practice*, Sanctions, p.11i). (For completeness we should also note that the Association of the British Pharmaceutical Industry has an advertising code of its own.)
45 See the Independent Broadcasting Authority Act 1973, S.1, S.2, S.4, S.8, S.10. The current IBA practice forbids advertisements in excess of six minutes per hour over the day, and seven minutes in any one clock hour.
46 E.g. the Electricity Consultative Councils, the Gas Consumers' Councils, the Domestic Coal Consumers' Council, the Post Office Users' National Council. For a view of their functions over the years see Consumer Council, *Consumer Consultative Machinery in the Nationalised Industries*, HMSO, London, 1968 and National Consumer Council, Report No.1, *Consumers and the Nationalised Industries*, HMSO, London, 1976.
47 See particularly, criticisms in Consumer Council, op.cit., and National Consumer Council, op.cit. There has also been criticism in the press – see 'Are watchdogs worth their £1m keep?', *Sunday Times*, 24 August 1975. We discuss the need for change in Chapter 11.

CHAPTER 3

1 *European Parliamentary Assembly Debates*, 19 October 1961 (official translation).
2 Other alleged implications are the sacrifice of potential competition and mutual forbearance and reciprocity effects. The reader who wishes to follow these ideas up should see C. D. Edwards, 'Conglomerate Bigness as a Source of Power', in NBER, *Business Concentration and Price Policy*, University of Princeton Press, 1955, pp. 331–59, and J. M. Blair, *Economic Concentration Structure Behaviour and Public Policy*, Harcourt Brace Jovanovich, New York, 1972, pp. 42–50.
3 *Official Journal of the European Communities*, (*OJ*), 21 December 1974.
4 Ibid., 5 August 1969.
5 *Common Market Law Reports* (*CMLR*), Vol.12, 1973, pp. 7–29.
6 Arrangement is the appropriate technical word for such a phenomenon in British antitrust law.
7 *OJ*, 7 August 1969.
8 *CMLR*, Vol.11, 1972, pp. 621–2.
9 Ibid., p. 622.
10 *OJ*, 13 March 1978.
11 Ibid., 7 August 1969.
12 *CMLR*, Vol.11, 1972, p. 629.
13 *OJ*, 13 March 1978.
14 Ibid., 17 January 1972.
15 Ibid., 31 December 1972.
16 See V. Korah, *Competition Law of Britain and the Common Market*, Elek, London, 1975, pp. 183–5.
17 *OJ*, 7 August 1969.

18 Ibid., 6 January 1966.
19 Ibid., 20 June 1971.
20 Ibid., 12 August 1968.
21 Ibid., 9 April 1964.
22 *CMLR*, Vol.8, 1969, pp. 273–83.
23 *OJ*, 2 June 1970.
24 Ibid., 29 December 1977.
25 Ibid., 18 June 1969.
26 Regulation 17 of 1962, *OJ*, 21 February 1962.
27 *OJ*, 23 December 1971.
28 For the status of old and new agreements see particularly *Portelange* case, *CMLR*, Vol.13, pp. 397–428 and *Brasserie de Haecht (No.2)* case, *CMLR*, Vol.12.
29 See, for example, the *Pittsburgh-Corning* case: *OJ*, 5 December 1972.
30 *CMLR*, Vol.22, 1978, p. 31.
31 European Communities Commission, *First Report on Competition Policy*, Brussels, 1972, p. 25.
32 H. W. De Jong, 'EEC Competition Policy Towards Restrictive Practices', in K. D. George and C. Joll (eds), *Competition Policy in the UK and EEC*, Cambridge University Press, 1975, pp. 33–60.
33 *OJ*, 17 June 1974.
34 *OJ*, 14 November 1968.
35 Ibid.
36 European Communities Commission, *Seventh Report on Competition Policy*, Brussels, 1978, pp. 94–5.
37 *OJ*, 17 January 1972.
38 European Communities Commission, *Eighth General Report on the Activities of the Communities*, 1965, p. 71 *Ninth General Report*, 1966, p. 71.
39 European Communities Commission, *Sixth Report on Competition Policy*, Brussels, 1977, pp. 69–70.
40 *OJ*, 26 January 1972.
41 *OJ*, 18 February 1978.
42 European Communities Commission, *Bulletin of the European Economic Community*, No.5, May 1964, Annexe II.
43 *CMLR*, Vol.17, 1978, pp. 509.
44 *OJ*, 13 January 1971.
45 European Communities Commission, *Third Report on Competition Policy*, Brussels, 1974, pp. 50–1.
46 European Communities Commission, *Sixth Report on Competition Policy*, Brussels, 1977, pp. 73–4.
47 *The Economist*, 29 July 1978.
48 *OJ*, 20 October 1964.
49 *CMLR*, Vol.5, 1966, pp. 418–81.
50 See *Diepenbrock and Riegers-Blondel* case, *OJ*, 17 July 1965 and *Hummel-Isbecque* case, *OJ*, 23 September 1965.
51 *OJ*, 22 February 1978.
52 *CMLR*, Vol.10, 1971, pp. 260–80.
53 *OJ*, 5 August 1969.
54 *OJ*, 7 August 1969.
55 *OJ*, 13 March 1978.
56 *OJ*, 20 June 1971; *CMLR*, Vol.11, 1972, pp. 694–8.
57 *OJ*, 8 January 1972; *CMLR*, Vol.12, 1973, pp. 199–239.
58 European Communities Commission, *Fourth Report on Competition Policy*, Brussels, 1975, pp. 35–6.

NOTES TO PAGES 63–82

59 *OJ*, 27 January 1978.
60 *OJ*, 9 April 1976; 'European Court: *The United Brands* Case', *Journal of World Trade Law*, Vol.12, 1978, pp. 248–9.
61 *OJ*, 16 August 1976.
62 European Communities Commission, *Sixth Report on Competition Policy*, Brussels, 1977, p. 88.
63 *OJ*, 31 December 1972: *CMLR*, Vol.13, 1974, pp. 309–46.
64 European Communities Commission, *Third Report on Competition Policy*, Brussels, 1974, pp. 60–1.

CHAPTER 4

1 This is a simplification of the legal position. For a more detailed account see R. Wilberforce, A. Campbell and N. Elles, *The Law of Restrictive Trade Practices*, Sweet and Maxwell, London, 1966, pp. 23–44, 47.
2 *Mogul S.S. Company v. McGregor, Gow* [1892] A.C.25; *Allen v. Flood* [1898] A.C.1; *Quinn v. Leathem* [1901] A.C.495.
3 [1925] A.C.700, 711–12.
4 *Nordenfelt v. Maxim Nordenfelt Guns and Ammunition Company* [1894] A.C.535, 565.
5 *Att-Gen. of the Commonwealth of Australia v. Adelaide S.S. Company* [1913] A.C.781, 796. The onus was made more difficult by virtue of rulings to the effect that evidence of the actual or likely consequences of an agreement by trade, technical or other expert witnesses was not admissible – see A. Hunter, *Competition and the Law*, Allen and Unwin, London, 1966, p. 71.
6 See R. B. Stevens and B. S. Yamey, *The Restrictive Practices Court*, Weidenfeld & Nicolson, London, 1965, p. 29. It is worth noting that judges showed little enthusiasm for competition and were reluctant to be drawn into public policy. The latter was likely if they opined as to what was and what was not in the public interest.
7 For a review see D. Swann, 'The Solus Site System in Law and Economics', *Northern Ireland Legal Quarterly*, Vol.18, No.1, 1967, pp. 1–32, 156–8.
8 These were subsequently published as Board of Trade, *Survey of International Cartels and Internal Cartels 1944–46*, Department of Industry, London, 1976. The seminal thinking was embodied in an internal memorandum 'The Control of Monopoly' written by the late Hugh Gaitskell and by Professor G. C. Allen.
9 *Employment Policy*, Cmnd 6257, HMSO, London, 1944.
10 A. Hunter, 'The Monopolies Commission and Price Fixing', *Economic Journal*, Vol.66, 1956, p.602.
11 Monopolies and Restrictive Practices Commission, *Collective Discrimination A Report on Exclusive Dealing, Collective Boycotts, Aggregated Rebates and other Discriminatory Trade Practices*, HMSO, London, 1955.
12 *In re Yarn Spinners' Agreement*, L.R.1 R.P., pp. 118–98.
13 *In re Water-Tube Boilermakers' Agreement*, L.R.1, R.P., pp. 285–346.
14 *In re National Sulphuric Acid Association's Agreement*, L.R.4 R.P., pp. 169–239.
15 *In re Chemists' Federation Agreement*, L.R.1 R.P., pp. 43–64.
16 *In re Tyre Trade Register Agreement*, L.R.3 R.P., pp. 404–62.
17 L.R.1 R.P., p. 189.
18 *In re Wholesale and Retail Bakers of Scotland Association's Agreements*, L.R.1 R.P. p. 377.
19 *In re Phenol Producer's Agreement*, L.R.2 R.P., pp. 1–50.

20 L.R.1 R.P., p. 188.
21 *In re British Bottle Association's Agreement*, L.R.2 R.P., pp. 345–91.
22 *In re Linoleum Manufacturers' Association's Agreement*, L.R.2 R.P., pp. 395–432.
23 *In re Federation of British Carpet Manufacturers' Agreement*, L.R.1 R.P., pp. 473–548.
24 *In re Associated Transformer Manufacturers' Agreement*, L.R.2 R.P., p. 339.
25 Ibid.
26 *In re Glazed and Floor Tile Home Trade Association's Agreement*, L.R.4 R.P., pp. 239–99.
27 *In re Permanent Magnet Association's Agreement*, L.R.1 R.P., pp. 119–77.
28 *In re Black Bolt and Nut Association's Agreement*, L.R.2 R.P., pp. 50–105.
29 *In re Cement Makers' Federation Agreement*, L.R.2 R.P., pp. 241–93.
30 D. Swann, D. P. O'Brien, W. P. J. Maunder and W. S. Howe, *Competition in British Industry Case Studies*, Department of Economics, Loughborough University of Technology, 1973.
31 *In re Galvanised Tank Manufacturers' Association's Agreement*, L.R.5 R.P., pp. 315–50; *In re Mileage Conference Group of the Tyre Manufacturers' Conference Ltd's Agreement*, L.R.6 R.P., pp. 49–114. For an account of how the word 'arrangement' was interpreted to deal with information agreements see D. P. O'Brien and D. Swann, *Information Agreements, Competition and Efficiency*, Macmillan, London, 1968, Chapters 4 and 5.
32 *In re Chocolate and Sugar Confectionery Reference*, L.R.6 R.P., p. 382. For an account of the rise and fall of rpm, with case studies, see W. S. Howe, *Resale Price Maintenance – History, Theory and Case Studies*, unpublished MSc thesis, Loughborough University of Technology, 1972.
33 Monopolies Commission, *A Report on the Supply of Flat Glass*, HMSO, London, 1968.
34 Monopolies Commission, *A Report on the Supply and Exports of Cigarette Filter Rods*, HMSO, London, 1969.
35 Monopolies Commission, *A Report on the Supply of Cigarettes and Tobacco and of Cigarette and Tobacco Machinery*, HMSO, London, 1967.
36 Monopolies Commission, *A Report on the Supply of Chlorodiazepoxide and Diazepam*, HMSO, London, 1973.
37 Monopolies Commission, *A Report on the Supply of Ready Cooked Breakfast Cereal Foods*, HMSO, London, 1973.
38 Monopolies Commission, *A Report on the Supply of Household Detergents*, HMSO, London, 1966.
39 Price Commission, *Southalls (Birmingham) Ltd. Sanitary Protection and Other Hygenic Products*, HMSO, 1978. This is essentially a duopolistic industry.
40 Monopolies and Restrictive Practices Commission, *A Report on the Supply of Certain Industrial and Medical Gases*, HMSO, London, 1956.
41 Monopolies Commission, *A Report on the Supply of Electrical Equipment for Mechanically Propelled Land Vehicles*, HMSO, London, 1963.
42 Monopolies Commission, *A Report on the Supply of Wallpaper*, HMSO, London, 1964.
43 Monopolies and Restrictive Practices Commission, *A Report on the Supply of Certain Industrial and Medical Gases*, HMSO, London, 1956.
44 Monopolies Commission, *A Report on the Supply of Petrol to Retailers in the United Kingdom*, HMSO, London, 1967.
45 Monopolies Commission, *A Report on the Supply of Asbestos and Certain Asbestos Products*, HMSO, London, 1973.
46 Monopolies and Mergers Commission, *A Report on the Supply of Indirect Electrostatic Reprographic Equipment*, HMSO, London, 1976.

47 See, for example, Monopolies Commission, *British Sidac Ltd. and Transparent Paper Ltd., A Report on the Proposed Merger*, HMSO, London, 1970.
48 See for example, Monopolies and Mergers Commission, *Charter Consolidated Investments Ltd. and Sadia Ltd., A Report on the Proposed Merger*, HMSO, London, 1974; Monopolies Commission, *Thorn Electrical Industries Ltd. and Radio Rentals Ltd., A Report on the Proposed Merger*, HMSO, London, 1968.
49 Monopolies and Mergers Commission, *Babcock and Wilcox Ltd., and Herbert Morris Ltd., A Report on the Existing and Proposed Mergers*, HMSO, London, 1977; Monopolies Commission, *The Rank Organisation Ltd. and The De La Rue Company Ltd., A Report on the Proposed Acquisition of the De La Rue Company*, HMSO, London, 1969.
50 Monopolies and Mergers Commission, *H. Weidmann, A. G. and B. S. and W. Whiteley Ltd., A Report on the Proposed Merger*, HMSO, London, 1975.
51 See, for example, Monopolies Commission, *British Sidac Ltd.*, and Monopolies Commission, *United Drapery Stores Ltd. and Montague Burton Ltd., A Report on the Proposed Merger*, HMSO, London, 1967.
52 See Monopolies Commission, *British Insulated Callendar's Cables Ltd., and Pyrotenax Ltd., A Report on the Merger*, HMSO, London, 1967. This was not very satisfactory affair in which the fact that the merger had taken place may have put the Commission at a disadvantage. The two firms controlled 90 per cent of the market but the Commission accepted assurances on the part of the acquiring company. This seems to have reduced the costs below what were the benefits of slim cost savings and alleged improvements in export prospects.

CHAPTER 5

1 The obvious other-things-being-equal factor is that there is no compensating fall in the price of imported raw materials and fuels.
2 This point was well illustrated towards the end of the life of the 1973–77 Price Code. Because of the depressed state of the market competition prevented businessmen from securing increases allowed under the Code. It was competition rather than the Code that was helping to limit the rate of inflation.
3 The Phillips curve embodies the idea that annual percentage wage increases may vary inversely with the annual percentage rate of unemployment. Low unemployment is associated with high wage increases, and high unemployment is associated with low or even negative wage increases.
4 In some degree this is true of the government, the real burden of whose debt falls as prices rise. This is bad for the holders of the debt but good for those who pay the taxes that service and repay it. They may of course be the same people.
5 See F. A. Filby, *A History of Food Adulteration and Analysis*, Allen & Unwin, London, 1934.
6 The use of nitrites and nitrates to prevent botulism illustrates the difficulties that arise in this field. Although nitrites and nitrates are effective they also tend under certain circumstances to combine with the amines in the meat to produce nitrosomine, which is known to produce cancer in animals. The UK approach in such circumstances is flexible: a ban does not automatically follow, although regulations can be made that will limit the quantity of the additive that can be used.
7 See A. G. Cameron, *Food – Facts and Fallacies*, Faber & Faber, London, 1971, pp. 114–21.
8 H. Yellowlees, 'Food Safety: A Century of Progress' in Ministry of Agriculture,

Fisheries and Food, *Food Quality and Safety: a Century of Progress*, HMSO, London, p. 72.
9 Ibid.
10 *Final Report of the Committee on Consumer Protection*, Cmnd 1781, HMSO, London, 1962.
11 *Interim Report of the Committee on Consumer Protection*, Cmnd 1011, HMSO, London, 1960.
12 Council on Productivity, Prices and Incomes, *Fourth Report*, HMSO, London, 1961, p. 24.
13 W. Fellner, *The Problem of Rising Prices*, OEEC, Paris, 1961.
14 Bank of International Settlements, *Thirty-First Annual Report, 1st April 1960 – 31st March 1961*, Basle, 1961, p. 26.
15 On the theory of incomes policy see A. R. Prest and D. J. Coppock (eds), *The UK Economy – A Manual of Applied Economics*, Weidenfeld & Nicolson, London, 1976, pp. 288–9; and F. Blackaby, 'Incomes Policies and Inflation', *National Institute Economic Review*, Vol.58, 1971, pp. 34–53.
16 If demand is not controlled and exceeds full capacity working, businessmen are under little or no pressure to compete for orders.
17 *Incomes Policy: the Next Step*, Cmnd 1622, HMSO, London, 1962.
18 A. Fels, *The British Prices and Incomes Board*, Cambridge University Press, 1972, p. 16.
19 *Prices and Incomes Policy*, Cmnd 2639, HMSO, London, 1965.
20 *Machinery of Prices and Incomes Policy*, Cmnd 2577, HMSO, London, 1965.
21 National Board for Prices and Incomes, *Report No.36 Productivity Agreements*, Cmnd 3311, HMSO, London, 1967; *Report No.65 Payment by Results Systems*, Cmnd 3627, HMSO, London, 1968; *Report No.83 Job Evaluation*, Cmnd 3772, HMSO, London, 1968; *Report No.123, Productivity Agreements*, Cmnd 4136, HMSO, London, 1969. The Board also investigated a number of productivity agreements in the context of specific wage and salary increase references.
22 *Prices and Incomes Policy: An "Early Warning" System*, Cmnd 2808, HMSO, London, 1965. The TUC in fact operated what was called a wage vetting system – see C. W. Jefferson, K. I. Sams and D. Swann, 'The Control of Incomes and Prices in the United Kingdom, 1964–1967: Policy and Experience', *Canadian Journal of Economics*, Vol.1, 1968, p. 286.
23 *Prices and Incomes Standstill*, Cmnd 3073, HMSO, London, 1966.
24 *Prices and Incomes Standstill: Period of Severe Restraint*, Cmnd 3150, HMSO, London, 1966.
25 *Prices and Incomes Policy after 30th July 1967*, Cmnd 3235, HMSO, London, 1967.
26 *Productivity, Prices and Incomes Policy in 1968 and 1969*, Cmnd 3590, HMSO, London, 1968.
27 There was also voluntary agreement to keep the increase of dividends to $3\frac{1}{2}$ per cent.
28 This included the dividend ceiling which was allowed to lapse.
29 A price freeze began in November 1972 prior to the operation of the Code, etc., in April 1973.
30 I. H. Lightman, 'Price Controls in the United Kingdom 1973–78: Natural Development or Radical Change?', *Journal of Agricultural Economics*, Vol.29, 1978, p. 312.
31 These Category I and II firms also had to make quarterly returns on their net profit margins.
32 See J. Sizer, 'Management Accounting and the Banker, Part 2 Financial Statements, Inflation and Company Liquidity', *Bankers' Magazine*, Vol.220, March 1976, pp. 33–8.

33 For a review of effects see R. Evely, 'The Effects of the Price Code', *National Institute Economic Review*, No.77, 1976, pp. 56–9.
34 However, originally quite generous rules were laid down which, provided they were satisfied, allowed firms under investigation to make interim price increases. Early in 1979 the government introduced the Price Commission (Amendment) Act which brought about significant changes in the interim price increase procedure. Some commentators see this as an alternative device for attacking excessive wage claims, the 1978–79 5 per cent norm policy having been severely undermined.
35 Price Commission, *Report for the Period 1 November 1977 to 31 January 1978*, HMSO, London, 1978, p. 9.
36 J. D. Gribbin, 'The United Kingdom 1977 Price Commission Act and Competition Policy', *Antitrust Bulletin*, Vol.23, 1978, p. 426.
37 Price Commission, *Report for the Period 1 November 1977 to 31 January 1978*, HMSO, London, 1978, p. 14.
38 Price Commission, *Margins of Coal Merchants in West Wales*, HMSO, London, 1978.
39 Price Commission, *Tea Prices*, HMSO, London, 1978.
40 Price Commission, *Fisons Ltd Agrochemical Division – Agrochemical and Horticultural Products*, HMSO, London, 1978.
41 See W. D. Reekie, *The Economics of the Pharmaceutical Industry*, Macmillan, London, 1975, Chapter 7; S. St P. Slatter, *Competition and Marketing Strategies in the Pharmaceutical Industry*, Croom Helm, London, 1977, Chapters 2 and 6.
42 See Rent Act 1977, which consolidates the Rent Act 1968, the Rent Act 1964 and the Housing Rents and Subsidies Act 1975.
43 See I. Paulus, *The Search for Pure Food: A Sociology of Legislation in Britain*, Martin Robertson, London, 1974.
44 See *Fitzpatrick* v. *Kelly*, (1873) L.R. 8 Q.B., p. 337; *Roberts* v. *Egerton*, (1874) L.R. 9 Q.B., p. 494.
45 We have omitted subsequent legislation. The 1879 amending Act, the subsequent Acts relating to specific products (e.g. Margarine Act 1887) and the subsequent Food and Drugs Acts are dealt with in Paulus, op.cit., and *Bell and O'Keefe's Sale of Food and Drugs*, 14th ed., Butterworths, London, 1968, pp. 1–11.
46 The Committee also advises on description, labelling and advertising of foods. For an account of the work of the FSC, including a list of reports up to 1975, see A. G. Ward, 'Advising on Food Standards in the United Kingdom 1. The Changing Role of the Food Standards Committee', in Ministry of Agriculture, Fisheries and Food, op.cit. (n.8 above), pp. 22–41.
47 Food Standards Committee, *Novel Proteins*, HMSO, London, 1975.
48 *(Interim) Date-Marking of Food*, HMSO, London, 1971; *Date-Marking of Food*, HMSO, London, 1972.
49 Mention should also be made of the European Pharmacopoeia. This is now coming into operation and products meeting its standards will carry the letters Ph.Eur.
50 Our source of information on this general topic, which we have drawn on closely, is the valuable study by T. Daintith and E. J. C. Carstairs, *Report on the Economic Law of the United Kingdom*, Competition – Approximation of Legislation Series No.20, Vol.5; Office for Official Publications of the European Communities, Luxembourg, 1974, pp. 83–4.
51 For more details on the English and Scottish Bars see Daintith and Carstairs, op.cit., p. 83.
52 *Licensing and Supervision of Deposit Taking Institutions*, Cmnd 6584, HMSO, London, 1976. For earlier experience under the Protection of Depositors Act see

also J. M. Holden, *The Law and Practice of Banking* 2nd ed., Pitman, London, 1974.
53 For example, under the Licensing Act 1964 liquor licences are required, but the concept of consumer protection does not arise other than to the extent that licencees have to be fit and proper persons. The position is similar in respect of betting, which is covered by the Betting, Gaming and Lotteries Act 1964. On all this see E. Anthony and J. D. Berryman, *A Guide to Licensing Law*, Butterworths, London, 1976.
54 The remit of the FHAC also extends to labelling – see below.
55 For an account of the work of the FACC see B. C. L. Weedon, 'Advising on Food Standards in the United Kingdom 2. Food Additives and Contaminants and the Role of the FACC', in Ministry of Agriculture, Fisheries and Food, op.cit. (n.8 above), pp. 42–61.
56 See Reekie, op.cit. (n.41 above), pp. 107–12; Price Commission, *Prices, Costs and Margins in the Production and Distribution of Proprietary Non-ethical Medicines*, HMSO, London, 1978, pp. 1–13.
57 On non-tariff barrier policy see D. Swann, *The Economics of the Common Market*, Penguin, Harmondsworth, 1978, Chapter 4; on food policy see M. Barthelemy, 'Harmonisation in the EEC of National Legislation on Foodstuffs', Ministry of Agriculture, Fisheries and Food, op.cit. (n.8 above), pp. 165–78.

CHAPTER 6

1 See Chapter 7.
2 E.g. The Trade Descriptions Act 1968.
3 The slogan, over a cartoon of a puzzled housewife with a heap of packaging, reads 'Don't be misled by deceptive packaging – it's not always as big as it looks!' The Office of Fair Trading have employed the device of the cartoon liberally in their own excellent information leaflets.
4 Above, pp. 118–129.
5 In 1976–77 the OFT received 11,224 complaints about the operation of the Act and 2,221 convictions were obtained under the statute. The majority of these were concerned with the provision of food not of the right quality (1,332) but there were 643 convictions under the Labelling Regulations. See *Annual Report of the Director-General of Fair Trading*, 1978.
6 Above, pp. 119–120.
7 Food and Drugs Act 1955, s.82.
8 The measure being used must be displayed on a notice in the public house.
9 See p. 136 below.
10 Price marking was extended to all food and drink sold in shops, market stalls, etc., by the Price Marking (Food) Order 1978, subject to certain exceptions for 'Counter service', delivery vans, etc.
11 S.8.
12 Draft Directive on the Labelling, Presentation and Advertising of Foodstuffs for sale to the consumer. See *Official Journal of the European Comunities*, 22 March 1976.
13 These tables are in fifteen parts and are a supplement to the Consumer Credit (Total Charge for Credit) Regulations 1977. The enabling provision in the statute is S.20.
14 More particularly to rules that require them to display a hazard symbol, but the poisons legislation applies to, for example, weedkiller and drycleaning fluid as far as labelling requirements are concerned.

15 There are other odd examples of particular disclosure requirements, for example the requirement that all new cars sold have information concerning their fuel consumption, which is government-approved.
16 For example, in Nottinghamshire studies were made of the efficiency and relative costs of both estate agents and solicitors. The comparisons between different members of the same profession was most interesting for the public, but was less warmly received by the professions.
17 Their arguments were supported by the very rapid growth in consumer inquiries handled by Citizens' Advice Bureaux in areas where consumer advice centres have been closed down.
18 *Consumerism*, NOP, London, 1976; National Consumer Council, *Consumers and the Nationalised Industries*, HMSO, London, 1976. See also F. Williams (ed.), *Why the Poor Pay More*, Macmillan, London, 1977.
19 Above, pp. 124–125.
20 Above, p. 120.
21 R. Cranston, *Consumers and the Law*, Weidenfeld & Nicolson, London, 1978, pp. 107–8.
22 Above, at pp. 33–34.
23 There are now quarterly magazines on, among other things, *Motoring* and *Do-it-yourself*; there are the regular publications of the *Good Food Guide*, and a whole host of other publications from cookery books to divorce and family planning.
24 Perhaps setting up in opposition to/co-operation with the National Consumer Council.
25 There are only limited safeguards against doorstep selling (see p. 187 below), but the government will soon have to respond to an EEC Draft Directive on the topic.
26 This was recognized by the government recently in an announcement that the Department of Prices and Consumer Protection are hoping to put through a series of amendments to the Fair Trading Act 1973 which will allow the Secretary of State to restrict advertising or promotional expenditure. It is alleged that heavy spending on advertising by monopoly holders results in the restriction of competition by the creation of barriers for new entrants to the market.
27 Discussed in R. G. Lawson, 'Advertising Controls in the EEC', *New Law Journal*, Vol.127, pp. 563–6.
28 Reported in *The Financial Times*, 27 September 1978.

CHAPTER 7

1 We are referring throughout this chapter, and in the remainder of the book, to the courts of England and Wales. The courts in Scotland and the law and remedies they apply are quite different. For the court structure see D. M. Walker, *The Scottish Legal System*, Green and Son, Edinburgh, 1976. In Northern Ireland the model system is similar to England but has important differences.
2 English law does not recognize the 'test case' or the 'class action'. It is up to each individual involved in a particular tort or breach of contract to bring his own action, although it is clear that the resolution of one case will have a direct bearing on others that are indistinguishable. To that extent the persons who have suffered similar damage may get together to put up one case and may even prevail upon the defendant to accept the result of that case as deciding the rest.
3 It is quite normal for a contract to provide for submission of any disputes under the contract to arbitration. This will not oust the jurisdiction of the court

ultimately but it will require the plaintiff to abide by the arbitration clause in the first instance.
4 As examples one can point to the increased activity in publicity and information (*How to Sue in the County Court*), and to the withdrawal of legal aid for undefended divorce with the consequence that most people will take action themselves.
5 The private prosecutions that are brought tend to be on notorious matters, e.g. obscenity, where a citizen feels especially strongly.
6 See n.2 above, and consider the case of the Thalidomide children who were grouped according to their particular disabilities so that they could eventually be compensated similarly.
7 The standard of proof in a criminal case is usually expressed as proof beyond reasonable doubt, whereas in a civil case the plaintiff is only required to prove his case on a balance of probabilities. Before the Civil Evidence Act 1968, a criminal conviction was no evidence in a civil court that the offence had in fact been committed.
8 The position has been ameliorated by the establishment of the Criminal Injuries Compensation Board with the object of compensating the victims of crimes of violence.
9 Theft Act 1968, S.15(1).
10 Ibid. S.15(4).
11 For further reading on the law of theft, see J. C. Smith and B. Hogan, *Criminal Law*, (4th ed.), Butterworths, London, 1978.
12 *Final Report of the Committee on Consumer Protection*, Cmnd 1781, HMSO, London, 1962.
13 Ibid., para. 575.
14 'Strict liability' is the term generally used to denote offences of which a person may be guilty without any knowledge or intention to break the law, or without even realizing that a risk of breaking the law exists.
15 In *Havering London Borough Council* v. *Stevenson* [1970] 1W.L.R.1375, the defendant operated a car-hire business and as a normal practice sold off those cars for which he no longer had any use. One such car had a false reading on the odometer and a charge was brought under S.1(1). The defendant's argument that he had not made the description in the course of trade or business was rejected – the selling of the cars was held to be an integral part of the business that the defendant operated.
16 *Fletcher* v. *Budgen* [1974] 2 All E.R.1243.
17 [1975] 2 All E.R.226.
18 TDA 1968, S.4(2). The Molony Committee thought that to include oral representations within the scope of the Act would be to put a very powerful weapon in the hands of the consumer and might lead to 'invidious conflicts' of evidence between consumer and trader (Report, paras. 658, 659).
19 *Cottee* v. *Douglas Seaton (Used Cars) Ltd.* [1972] 3 All E.R.750.
20 *Norman* v. *Bennett* [1974] 3 All E.R.351. Of course, the disclaimer would not be effective in a civil action.
21 OFT Review, see below. See also, G. J. Borrie, 'A Review of the Trade Descriptions Act 1968', *Criminal Law Review*, December 1975, pp. 662–70.
22 *Review of The Trade Descriptions Act 1968, a consultative document*, published by the OFT in October 1976.
23 Report, paras. 558, 636 and 813.
24 *John* v. *Matthews* [1970] 2 All E.R. 623.
25 [1971] 2 All E.R.296.
26 *Richards* v. *Westminster Motors Ltd* [1976] R.T.R. 88.

27 *Doble v. David Greig Ltd* [1972] 2 All E.R.195.
28 *Annual Report of the Director-General of Fair Trading*, HMSO, London, 1978, p. 15.
29 *VAT-Exclusive Prices*, House of Commons Paper, No.461, HMSO, London, 1977. The principle has been adopted by the government and a draft order has been made.
30 Although the effective difference may be small after the decision in *MFI Warehouses Ltd v. Nattrass*, considered below.
31 *R. v. Sunair Holidays Ltd* [1973] 2 All E.R.1233.
32 *R. v. Thomson Holidays Ltd* [1974] 1 All E.R. 823.
33 [1976] 1 All E.R.65.
34 [1973] 1 All E.R.762.
35 WMA 1963, S.24(2).
36 WMA 1963, S.24(3).
37 WMA 1963, S.24(4).
38 WMA 1963, S.24(7), e.g. in respect of the sale of coal, where a ticket is usually given to the customer with the weight of coal delivered.
39 WMA 1963, S.26(7).
40 WMA 1963, S.26(7): this allows the court a degree of flexibility, and the section also provides that in any event the court should have regard generally to all the circumstances of the case.
41 Council Directives 75/106/EEC and 76/211/EEC.
42 Food and Drugs Act 1955, S.6.
43 The Labelling of Food Regulations, above p. 135.
44 *Concentrated Foods Ltd v. Champ* [1944] KB 342.
45 Medicines Act 1968, Part VI.
46 Fabrics (Misdescription) Act 1913, as amended.
47 The remedy available will depend on the nature of the term which is broken. See further, Chapter 9.
48 The cases on this point are very difficult to reconcile, and the questions in the text illustrate a series of cases in which the particular factor has been regarded as important. The most contentious issue is the effect of the expertise of one of the parties, and reference might be made to three difficult cases that each concern statements made during the sale of a car: *Oscar Chess v. Williams* [1957] 1 WLR 370; *Dick Bentley Productions, Ltd v. Harold Smith (Motors) Ltd* [1965] 1 WLR 623; *Beale v. Taylor* [1967] 1 WLR 1193.
49 It was a further drawback that rescission, like all the equitable remedies, must be requested quickly by the petitioner or he risks a refusal. It is not unusual for the falsity of a statement to take some time to emerge.
50 Misrepresentation Act 1967, S.2(1). The subsection requires that a contact has been made and that the misrepresentation should have been made by a party to it. Not every false statement is a misrepresentation – sales talk, 'mere puffs', unverifiable statements of opinion will not give rise to an action. See further p. 166 below.
51 The nature of the action is not at all clear. It is not an action in contract for it rests on statements that are not, *ex hypothesi*, part of the contract, and some of the commentators have referred to it as a new statutory tort. See, for example, Smith and Thomas, *Casebook on Contract*, 6th edn, Sweet and Maxwell, p. 280.
52 Misrepresentation Act 1967, S.2(2).
53 [1964] A.C.465.
54 *Derry v. Peek* (1889) 14 App Cas 337.
55 See pp. 146–7 above.
56 For example, where a holiday brochure has made specific promises about the facilities at a resort.

57 *Inter alia*, the Indecent Advertisements Act 1889, Race Relations Act 1976, Sex Discrimination Act 1975. The control of credit advertising by the Consumer Credit Act 1974 is discussed at p. 187 below.
58 As the claim that money had been deposited with a bank made it clear that the advertisement of the Carbolic Smoke Ball was meant to be relied upon – *Carlill* v. *Carbolic Smoke Ball Co.* [1893] 1 Q.B.256.
59 Fair Trading Act 1973, S.2, S.13, S.14, S.17, S.22, S.23.
60 *Rights of Consumers – A Report on Practices Relating to the Purported Exclusion of Inalienable Rights of Consumers and Failure to Explain their Existence*, House of Commons Paper No.6, 1976. *Disguised Business Sales – A Report on the Practice of Seeking to Sell Goods without revealing that they are being Sold in the Course of a Business*, House of Commons Paper No.355, 1976.
61 The Consumer Transactions (Restriction on Statements) Order 1976, and the Business Advertisements (Disclosure) Order 1977 respectively.
62 The Secretary of State has recently announced that the government will be making an Order early in 1979 under price display legislation which will prohibit bogus bargain offers: *The Financial Times*, 19 October 1978. The government has further indicated that as soon as parliamentary time permits an order will be laid to require VAT to be shown on prices, or to be included in the price.

CHAPTER 8

1 Only an abbreviated discussion can be included since we consider that a full treatment of the economic aspects of credit control are beyond the scope of this book.
2 'Revolving' in the sense that, as the customer pays off the outstanding debt, the amount of the continuing credit available to him is increased by the amount of that payment.
3 For example, by the Hire Purchase Act 1964, the Supply of Goods (Implied Terms) Act 1973 and the Consumer Credit Act 1974. It is arguable that the Consumer Credit Act 1974 represents the first really careful control on the finance houses.
4 [1966] 2 Q.B.431.
5 The original slogan adopted by the banks operating the Access credit card was 'Access takes the waiting out of wanting'.
6 Consumer Credit Act (CCA), S.75.
7 The Committee on Consumer Credit began its work in the autumn of 1968 under the chairmanship of Lord Crowther. Its Report was published in March 1971 (Cmnd 4596, HMSO, London).
8 See below, pp. 184–6.
9 See the thorough discussion in R. Cranston, *Consumers and the Law*, Weidenfeld & Nicolson, London, 1978, pp. 206ff.
10 [1895] A.C.471.
11 Therefore incurring the liability of a supplier of goods.
12 This rate is fixed by the Bank of England in response to national and international pressures.
13 All the credit card companies employ very persuasive advertising of a general and a personal nature, particularly adjusted to seasonal requirements such as holidays and Christmas.
14 The current yield rate is 23.1 per cent for Barclaycard.
15 See n.7 above.
16 See the White Paper, *Reform of the Law of Consumer Credit*, Cmnd 5427, HMSO, London, 1972.

17 Report, paras. 4.2.2 et seq.
18 See p. 187 below.
19 See p. 192 below.
20 See the explanation of these forms of agreement at p. 175 above.
21 CCA, S.9(4), S.20(1) and S.189(1). This is different from the present position under the Hire-Purchase Act 1965 where the total purchase price is considered.
22 CCA, S.10 (3).
23 CCA, S.8(1).
24 CCA, S.16(6)(b).
25 A more elegant term than that coined by the draftsman.
26 CCA, S.75(1). Technically, the creditor is liable jointly and severally with the supplier and has a right of indemnity against the supplier.
27 See Chapter 2 above.
28 CCA, S.22(1).
29 See the parts of Chapters 2 and 6 dealing with advertising controls and the particular provisions of the Advertising (Hire-Purchase) Act 1967.
30 There are very few controls on doorstep selling generally. The consumer can tell the salesman to go away, but if he persists he may win orders. There is now an EEC Draft Directive on the topic which is being anxiously considered by the government.
31 CCA, S.65(1).
32 CCA, S.127.
33 Barclaycard and Access have issued statements to all cardholders saying that they have received advice that the section would not apply to any person who became a cardholder before 1 July 1977, but that they would assume liability voluntarily where it would otherwise have accrued under S.75.
34 This is a very interesting statutory provision which gives the court powers that have hitherto been eschewed by the judges. The court may set aside or amend the terms of the agreement in a way that runs counter to the previously accepted principles of freedom of contract. It will be interesting to observe the way in which the courts use their new powers.
35 See p. 192 above.
36 CCA, S.87.
37 CCA, S.88.
38 CCA, S.89.
39 CCA, S.90.
40 CCA, S.91.

CHAPTER 9

1 For a consideration of the contents of a contract, and an analysis of express and implied terms, see G. H. Treitel, *The Law of Contract*, 4th ed., Stevens, London, 1975, Chapter 6.
2 The judges have often talked about conditions as terms that 'go to the substance of the contract' or are 'essential to the very nature of the contract'; *Wallis, Son and Wells* v. *Pratt and Haynes* [1910] 2 K.B.1003. Warranties then become all terms that are not conditions, and are taken to be those terms that are subsidiary to the main purpose of the contract.
3 *Hong Kong Fir Shipping Co. Ltd* v. *Kawasaki Kisen Kaisha Ltd* [1962] 2 Q.B.26.
4 Although express agreement will not always be sufficient to categorize the terms

of the contract if it appears that the parties have not really addressed themselves to the consequences of the breach of a particular term; see *L. Schuler A.G.* v. *Wickman Machine Tool Sales Ltd* [1974] A.C.235, where the parties described a particular term as a condition in a written contract but the House of Lords decided it was really a warranty.

5 The Sale of Goods Act 1893, to be considered later, gave some protection even to nineteenth-century consumers, but allowed sellers to contract out of their liability under the Act by inserting exclusion clauses into their contracts.
6 The Supply of Goods (Implied Terms) Act 1973, and the Unfair Contract Terms Act 1977.
7 See, for example, *Lloyds Bank Ltd* v. *Bundy* [1974] 3 All E.R.757; *Clifford Davis Management Ltd* v. *W.E.A. Records Ltd* [1975] 1 All E.R. 237.
8 Similar terms are implied into hire-purchase agreements by virtue of Ss. 8–11, Supply of Goods (Implied Terms) Act 1973.
9 P. S. Atiyah, *The Sale of Goods*, 5th ed., Pitman, London, 1975; A. P. Dobson, *Sale of Goods and Consumer Credit*; Sweet and Maxwell, London, 1975; R. Lowe, *Commercial Law*, 5th ed., Sweet and Maxwell, London, 1976.
10 The warranty that the buyer will enjoy quiet possession of the goods is relatively little used.
11 As we shall see, the private seller is not permitted to exclude liability for breach of this particular condition – see below, p. 211.
12 *Grant* v. *Australian Knitting Mills Ltd* [1936] A.C.85.
13 *Beale* v. *Taylor* [1967] 1 W.L.R.1193.
14 [1972] A.C.441.
15 These are largely a codification of the factors that the courts had considered important in reaching their own definition of merchantable quality.
16 *Geddling* v. *Marsh* [1920] 1 K.B.668, where the court held that injuries caused by the bursting of a bottle in which mineral waters were contained could be compensated under the Act; *Wilson* v. *Rickett Cockerell and Co. Ltd* [1954] 1 Q.B.598, where an ingenious argument that the presence of explosive in Coalite did not render the Coalite itself unmerchantable was rejected.
17 On facts similar to the *Wilson* case in *Duke* v. *Jackson* [1921] S.C.362.
18 For the definition of credit-broker see the amended S.14(3) above, p. 200.
19 [1936] A.C.85.
20 The Family Practitioner Committee, operating under S.42 of the National Health Service Act 1946.
21 For an outline of the organization and obligations of the Law Society, see R. J. Walker, *The English Legal System*, 4th ed., Butterworths, London, 1976, Chapter 12.
22 This immunity was confirmed by the House of Lords in *Rondel* v. *Worsley* [1969] 1 A.C.191, but the restrictions were imposed by the same court in *Saif Ali* v. *Sydney Mitchell and Co. (a firm)* [1978] 3 All E.R.1033.
23 [1932] A.C.562.
24 *Donoghue's* case exploded the argument that the absence of an action in contract was fatal to an action in the tort of negligence. This old proposition was particularly unfair to the person to whom products were given, or who used them in his work.
25 See below, pp. 206–9. The proposals emanate from a number of quarters including the Law Commissions and the *EEC*.
26 See, for example, *Winfield and Jolowicz on Tort*, 10th ed., (ed. W. V. H. Rogers), Sweet and Maxwell, London, 1975; H. Street, *The Law of Torts*, 6th ed., Butterworths, London, 1976; R. F. V. Heuston, *Salmond on the Law of Torts*, 17th ed., Sweet and Maxwell, London, 1977.

27 [1932] A.C.562, at 599.
28 In this context manufacturer is given an extended meaning which will include almost anyone who can be shown to be at fault and is connected with the process from manufacture to delivery to the consumer.
29 As in *Donoghue's* case.
30 An employee may have a cause of action against his employer if he is injured at work while using defective equipment, but there are decisions that indicate an alternative action against the manufacturer of the equipment. See *Vacwell Engineering Co. Ltd* v. *B.D.H. Chemicals Ltd* [1971] 1 Q.B.88.
31 Even a tombstone! A young boy who was injured when a tombstone fell on him recovered damages; *Brown* v. *Cotterill* [1934] 51 T.L.R.21.
32 The maxim is known as *'res ipsa loquitur'* and the better view seems to be that, if the plaintiff can establish that the mere fact of the accident happening raises the inference of negligence, then the onus will be on the defendant to produce an explanation that is consistent with non-negligent conduct on his part.
33 For a consideration of the topic of breach of duty of care, see *Winfield and Jolowicz on Tort*, from p. 61.
34 The recovery of damages consequent upon a negligent statement that has caused loss is one example; *Hedley Byrne and Co. Ltd* v. *Heller and Partners* [1964] A.C.465.
35 *The Wagon Mound* [1961] A.C.388, and see pp. 229–30 below.
36 [1932] AC.562.
37 i.e. The Law Commission and the Scottish Law Commission.
38 The convention was adopted by the Committee of Ministers in September 1976 and has been open for signature since January 1977. The full title of the convention is the European Convention on Products Liability in regard to Personal Injury and Death.
39 The Report is entitled *Liability for Defective Products* and was published in June 1977 (Cmnd 6831) and followed the consultative Working Paper No.64 of the same name which had been published in 1975.
40 See para. 29.
41 Ibid., para. 38.
42 Presented by the Commission to the Council in September 1976; *Proposal for a Council Directive relating to the Approximation of the Laws, Regulations and Administrative Provisions of the Member States concerning Liability for Defective Products.*
43 *Liability for Defective Products*, para. 43.
44 Ibid., para. 132.
45 Ibid., para. 117 *et seq.*
46 Draft Directive, Article 7.
47 *Liability for Defective Products*, para. 135.
48 Ibid., para. 117 *et seq.*
49 Ibid., para. 137.
50 The Royal Commission on Civil Liability and Compensation for Personal Injuries, which reported in 1978. The Report is Cmnd 7054.
51 E.g. *Hollier* v. *Rambler Motors (A.M.C.) Ltd* [1972] 2 Q.B.71.
52 This generally referred to as the *contra proferentem* rule and is exemplified by *Wallis, Son and Wells* v. *Pratt and Haynes* [1911] A.C.394.
53 The 'ticket' cases are all concerned with the principle that adequate notice has been given of the terms of the contract and that they contain an exclusion clause; e.g. *Parker* v. *S.E.Railway* (1877) 2 C.P.D.416; *Thornton* v. *Shoe Lane Parking Ltd* [1971] 1 Q.B.163.
54 Beginning with the case of *Karsales (Harrow) Ltd* v. *Wallis* [1956] 1 W.L.R.936,

and continuing with varying fortunes through the years. For a very good monograph on the subject of exclusion clauses generally, see David Yates, *Exclusion Clauses in Contracts*, Sweet and Maxwell, London, 1978.
55 Nothing in the discussion later in the chapter about the effects of the Unfair Contract Terms Act 1977 should obscure the principle that the Act is applicable only where the clause in question is a part of the contract. Where a rule of law operates to exclude the terms from the contract for one reason or another there will be no need to rely on the Act. However, it might prove to be simpler to have the clause avoided under the Act than to prove that it should not be part of the contract in the first place.
56 Exclusion clauses are not always so unsubtle as simply to exclude liability. They can equally well operate by stipulating that one party does not have any obligation to do certain things that he has contracted to do.
57 Unfair Contract Terms Act 1977, S.11(2).
58 The same test is used to establish the validity of a clause purporting to exclude liability for misrepresentation – Unfair Contract Terms Act 1977, S.8.
59 So, for example, a professional man who bought goods or a car 'on the firm' would be outside the consumer provisions of the Act.
60 These types of transaction can never be consumer dealings; Unfair Contract Terms Act 1977, S.12(2).
61 Ibid., S.12(3).
62 A collateral contract operates to formalize the relationship whereby the purchaser of goods agrees to purchase goods made by a particular manufacturer in the knowledge that a guarantee of some sort is provided. Consideration is provided for the contract with the manufacturer by the making of the contract with the retailer. See, for example, *Shanklin Pier* v. *Detel Products Ltd* [1951] 2 K.B.854.
63 In this case the posting of the card by the purchaser is both the acceptance of an offer made to him by the manufacturer and the consideration for the contract.
64 See p. 22 above.
65 Fair Trading Act 1973, S.124(4).
66 See the *Annual Reports of the Director-General of Fair Trading* for details of all the codes of practice that have been agreed to date.
67 The Office of Fair Trading provide well illustrated informative leaflets about the various codes which is an indication to the consumer that the code in question has some 'official' sanction.

CHAPTER 10

1 We are confining our discussion to the court system in England and Wales. In Scotland the appropriate court would be the Sheriff Court, where there are special procedures for small claims – see D. M. Walker, *The Scottish Legal System*, Gray and Son, Edinburgh, 1976. In Northern Ireland an action would be started in County Court.
2 For example, there is a provision that permits the High Court to remit cases to the County Court for trial where they fall within the jurisdictional limits of the County Court, and also there are penalties in costs for the plaintiff who recovers only a small amount of damages in the High Court.
3 Even where the wrong alleged was wrongful exclusion from a beauty contest, the court was undeterred in putting a money figure on the damage suffered: *Chaplin* v. *Hicks* [1911] 2 K.B. 786.
4 See p. 233 below.

5 Administration of Justice Act 1969 and County Courts Jurisdiction Order 1977.
6 The whole procedure is described in the official booklet prepared by the Lord Chancellor's Office, *Small Claims in the County Court*, HMSO, London, 1978.
7 Of the 10,017 arbitrations heard in 1977, 9,879 were heard by the Registrar: *Judicial Statistics, Annual Report 1977*, HMSO, London, 1978.
8 At p. 140 above.
9 The figures contained in the report are now very old, since they refer to studies undertaken in 1967, but they indicated that of 1,238 cases considered by the study only 112 (9 per cent) were begun by an individual. 1104 (89.2 per cent) were begun by a firm or utility board.
10 By the County Court (New Procedure) Rules 1971, which took effect on 1 March 1972.
11 *Which?*, July 1975. See also N. E. Hickman, ' "Small Claims" and County Court Costs', *New Law Journal*, Vol.127, 1977, pp. 856–8.
12 See n.11 above.
13 The case has been argued in *Justice Out of Reach*, HMSO, London, 1970, and among others by T. G. Ison, 'Small Claims', *Modern Law Review*, Vol.35, 1972, pp. 18–37.
14 For a nice example of the application of this test see *Barnett v. Chelsea and Kensington Hospital Management Committee* [1969] 1 Q.B.428.
15 *Hadley v. Baxendale* (1854) 9 Exch. 341; *Victoria Laundry (Windsor) Ltd v. Newman Industries Ltd* [1949] 2 K.B.528; *Koufos v. Czarnikow Ltd* [1969] 1 A.C.350.
16 *Koufos v. Czarnikow Ltd*, n.15 above.
17 *The Wagon Mound* [1961] A.C.388.
18 [1973] 2 Q.B.27.
19 [1973] 2 Q.B.233.
20 Rare, but not impossible in certain circumstances, see *Beswick v. Beswick* [1968] A.C.58.
21 [1975] A.C.396.
22 There were 33,792 complaints concerning the Trade Descriptions Act 1968 in the year 1975–76, and 35,228 in 1976–77, but only 790 convinctions in 1976, and 946 in 1977. *Report of the Director-General of Fair Trading*, HMSO, London, 1978.
23 *R. v. Daly* [1974] 1 All E.R.290; *R. v. Kneeshaw* [1975] Q.B.57.
24 [1974] Q.B.592.

CHAPTER 11

1 *A Review of Monopolies and Mergers Policy. A Joint Response to the Consultative Document from the National Consumer Council, Consumer's Association and the National Federation of Consumer Groups*, November 1978.
2 The reader who wishes to know more about the CAP is referred to D. Swann, *The Economics of the Common Market*, 4th ed., Penguin, Harmondsworth, 1978.
3 See Swann op.cit., and J. S. Marsh, 'Europe's Agriculture: Reform of the CAP', *International Affairs*, Vol.53, No.4, 1977, pp. 604–14.
4 National Consumer Council, *Real Money Real Choice: Consumer Priorities in Economic Policy*, NCC, London, 1978, pp. 39–40.
5 National Consumer Council, *Submission by the National Consumer Council to the Review of Restrictive Trade Practices Legislation*, August 1978, p. 4.
6 L.R.6 R.P., pp. 532–68.

7   This was proposed by J. W. Rooker, MP, in the House of Commons in 1978 – see *Weekly Hansard*, No.1116, 18 July 1978, cols 284–90.
8   See A. Sutherland, 'The Management of Mergers Policy', in A. Cairncross (ed.), *The Managed Economy*, Blackwell, Oxford, 1970; G. D. Newbould, *Management and Merger Activity*, Guthstead, Liverpool, 1970, Chapter 4; A. Singh, *Takeovers*, Cambridge University Press, London, 1971; G. Meeks, *Disappointing Marriage: A Study of the Gains from Merger*, Cambridge University Press, London, 1977; J. Kitching, 'Why Acquisitions are Abortive', *Management Today*, November 1974, pp. 82–8.
9   S. J. Prais, *The Evolution of Giant Firms in Britain*, Cambridge University Press, London, 1976; L. Hannah and J. A. Kay; *Concentration in Modern Industry*, Macmillan, London, 1977.
10 Between 1965 and mid-1973 the Mergers Panel examined 800 mergers (excluding newspaper mergers). Out of this 20 (2.5 per cent) were referred. Allowing for those referred, which were also approved, Hannah and Kay, op.cit., doubt whether the public interest was promoted in rather less than 99 per cent of those surveyed by the panel.
11 See A. Sutherland, op.cit.; M. A. Utton, 'British Merger Policy' in K. D. George and C. Joll (eds), *Competition Policy in the UK and EEC*, Cambridge University Press, London, 1975, pp. 95–121; M. A. Crew and C. K. Rowley, 'Antitrust Policy: Economics versus Management Science', *Moorgate and Wall Street*, Autumn 1970, pp. 19–34; M. Howe, 'Antitrust Policy: Rules or Discretionary Intervention', *Moorgate and Wall Street*, Spring 1971, pp. 59–68; M. A. Crew and C. K. Rowley, 'Antitrust Policy: The Application of Rules', *Moorgate and Wall Street*, Autumn 1971, pp. 37–50; M. Howe, 'British Merger Policy Proposals and American Experience', *Scottish Journal of Political Economy*, Vol.19, 1972, pp. 37–61.
12 *A Review of Monopolies and Mergers Policy*, Cmnd 7198, HMSO, London, 1978.
13 For other desirable changes on the monopoly front see *A Review of Monopolies and Mergers*.
14 Some inefficiency may be tolerable in that the alternative to incomes policy may be deflation of demand and unemployment which also involves economic loss.
15 At the time of writing (February 1979) the government has announced its intention to create a pay board for the public sector in order to deal with problems of comparability – this goes some way to meet our criticism.
16 Arbitration in the County Court, the pre-trial review and the no-costs rule where the action is for less than £200, see pp. 223–26 above.
17 See, for example, the Unfair Contract Terms Act 1977, Schedule 2 (discussed at p. 213 above); the Consumer Credit Act 1974, S.138 and the observations of Lord Denning M.R. in *Lloyds Bank* v. *Bundy* [1974] 3 All E.R.757, and *Clifford Davis Management Ltd* v. *W.E.A. Records Ltd*, [1975] 1 All E.R.237.
18 See p. 207 above.
19 *The Royal Commission on Civil Liability and Compensation for Personal Injury Report*, Cmnd 7054, HMSO, London, 1978, paras. 1193–1278.
20 See pp. 206–8 above.
21 Consumer Council, *Consumer Consultative Machinery in the Nationalised Industries*, HMSO, London, 1978, and National Consumer Council, Report No.1, *Consumers and the Nationalised Industries*, HMSO, London, 1976.

Select Bibliography

ATIYAH, P. S., (1975) *The Sale of Goods* Pitman, London.

BENNION, F. A. R., (1978) *The Consumer Credit Act Manual* Oyez, London.
BLACKABY, F. (1971) 'Incomes Policy and Inflation' *National Institute Economic Review* Vol.58, pp. 34–53.
BORRIE, G. J. and DIAMOND, A. L. (1973) *The Consumer, Society and The Law* Penguin, Harmondsworth.
BRITTAN, S. and LILLEY, P. (1977) *The Delusion of Incomes Policy* Temple Smith, London.

COCKFIELD, SIR ARTHUR (1978) 'The Price Commission and the Price Control' *The Three Banks Review* March 1978, pp. 3–25.
CRANSTON, R. (1978) *Consumers and the Law* Weidenfeld & Nicolson, London.
CUNNINGHAM, J. P. (1974) *The Fair Trading Act 1973* Sweet and Maxwell, London.

DAINTITH, T. and CARSTAIRS, E. J. C. (1974) *Report on the Economic Law of the United Kingdom* Competition – Approximation of Legislation Series No.20, Vol.5, Office for Official Publications of the European Communities, Luxembourg.
DE JONG, H. W. (1975) 'EEC Competition Policy Towards Restrictive Practices' in K. D. GEORGE and C. JOLL (eds) *Competition Policy in the UK and EEC* Cambridge University Press, pp. 33–65.
DOBSON, A. P. (1979) *Sale of Goods and Consumer Credit* Sweet and Maxwell, London.

FELS, A. (1972) *The British Prices and Incomes Board* Cambridge University Press.

GEORGE, K. D. and JOLL, C. (1978) 'EEC Competition Policy' *The Three Banks Review* March 1978, pp. 55–80.
GILSTRA, D. J. (1976) *Leading Cases and Materials on the Competition Law of the EEC* Kluwer, Deventer.
GOODE, R. M. (1974) *Introduction to the Consumer Credit Act 1974* Butterworths, London.
GRIBBIN, J. D. (1974) 'The Operation of the Mergers Panel since 1965' *Trade and Industry* 17 January 1974, pp. 70–3.
GRIBBIN, J. D. (1978) 'The United Kingdom 1977 Price Commission Act and Competition Policy' *Antitrust Bulletin* Vol.23, pp. 405–39.

HARVEY, B. W. (1978) *The Law of Consumer Protection and Fair Trading* Butterworths, London.
HERMANN, A. H. and JONES, C. (1977) *Fair Trading in Europe* Kluwer-Harrap, London.
HOWE, M. (1972) 'British Merger Policy Proposals and American Experience' *Scottish Journal of Political Economy* Vol.19, pp. 37–61.

SELECT BIBLIOGRAPHY

HOWE, M. (1975) 'Policies Towards Market Power and Price Discrimination in the EEC and the UK' in K. D. GEORGE and C. JOLL (eds) *Competition Policy in the UK and EEC* Cambridge University Press, pp. 151–78.

KORAH, V. (1975) *Competition Law of Britain and the Common Market* Elek, London.

LAIDLER, D. (1975) 'Inflation and Its Control: A Monetarist Analysis' in R. M. GRANT and G. K. SHAW (eds) *Current Issues in Economic Policy* Philip Allan, Deddington, pp. 218–33.
LAWSON, F. H. (1972) *Remedies of English Law* Penguin, Harmondsworth.
LIGHTMAN, A. (1978) 'Price Controls in the United Kingdom: Natural Development or Radical Change?' *Journal of Agricultural Economics* Vol.29, pp. 311–20.
LOWE, R. (1976) *Commercial Law* Sweet and Maxwell, London.

MILLER, C. J. and LOVELL, P. A. (1977) *Product Liability* Butterworths, London.
MITCHELL, J. (1978) *Price Determination and Prices Policy* Allen & Unwin, London.
MORRIS, D. (ed.) (1977) *The Economic System in the UK* Oxford University Press.

O'KEEFE, J. A. (1971) *The Law Relating to Trade Descriptions* Butterworths, London.
O'KEEFE, J. A. (1977) *The Law of Weights and Measures* Butterworths, London.

PICKERING, J. F. (1966) *Resale Price Maintenance in Practice* Allen & Unwin, London.
PICKERING, J. F. (1974) 'The Abolition of Resale Price Maintenance in Great Britain' *Oxford Economic Papers* Vol.26, pp. 120–46.
PREST, A. R. and COPPOCK, D. J. (eds.) (1976) *The UK Economy A Manual of Applied Economics* Weidenfeld & Nicolson, London.

REEKIE, W. D. (1974) *Advertising* Macmillan, London.
ROWLEY, C. K. (1966) *The British Monopolies Commission* Allen & Unwin, London.

SIZER, J. (1977) 'Management Accounting and the Lending Banker Part 22: Pricing Decisions IV: Pricing in Inflation' *Banker's Magazine* Vol.22, pp. 25–32.
SUTHERLAND, A. (1970) *The Monopolies Commission in Action* Cambridge University Press.
SUTHERLAND, A. (1970) 'The Management of Mergers Policy' in A. CAIRNCROSS (ed.) *The Managed Economy* Blackwell, Oxford, Chapter 7.
SWANN, D. (1979) *Competition and Consumer Protection* Penguin, Harmondsworth.
SWANN, D., O'BRIEN, D. P., MAUNDER, W. P. J. and HOWE, W. S. (1973) *Competition in British Industry: Case Studies* Department of Economics, Loughborough University of Technology.
SWANN, D., O'BRIEN, D. P., MAUNDER, W. P. J., and HOWE, W. S. (1974) *Competition in British Industry* Allen & Unwin, London.

THOMPSON, P. K. (1978) *The Unfair Contract Terms Act 1977* Butterworths, London.
TREITEL, G. H. (1975) *The Law of Contract* Stevens, London.

UTTON, M. A. (197x) 'British Merger Policy' in K. D. GEORGE and C. JOLL (eds.) *Competition Policy in the UK and EEC* Cambridge University Press, pp. 95–121.

WALKER, D. M. (1976) *The Scottish Legal System* Gray and Son, Edinburgh.

WALKER, R. J. and WALKER, M. G. (1976) *The English Legal System* Butterworths, London.

Index

Additives, 2, 9, 102, 119, 125-6
Adulteration, food and drink, 101, 119
Advertising –
  general issues –
    deceptive, 17
    effect on competition, 17, 265 n26
    excessive expenditure on, 17
    and health, 17-18
    indecent, 145, 268 n57
    informational role, 16-17, 144-5
    persuasive role, 17, 144-5
    self versus state regulation, 37-8, 165-7, 249
  legal regulation –
    Advertising (Hire-Purchase) Act 1967, 146
    Consumer Credit Act 1974, 187-8
    Consumer Protection Advisory Committee, 23-6, 146, 167
    EEC draft directives, 137, 146-7, 264 n12
    Food and Drugs Act 1955, 160-2
    Medicines Act 1968, 162
    Misrepresentation Act 1967, 146, 163-4
    Monopolies and Mergers Commission, 93
    Office of Fair Trading Report, 146, 249
    Price Commission, 93
    Trade Descriptions Acts 1968, 1972, 146, 153-60, 165-6
    Weights and Measures Act 1963, 161
  voluntary regulation –
    Advertising Association, 36, 146
    Advertising Standards Authority, 36-8, 147-8
    Association of the British Pharmaceutical Industry, 257 n44
    British Code of Advertising Practice, 36-8, 147-8
    Code of Advertising Practice, 36
    other codes of practice, 215

Independent Broadcasting Authority, 38
Independent Broadcasting Authority Act 1973, 38
Advertising Association, 36, 146
Advertising Standards Authority, 36-8, 147-8
Advisory Committee on Foodstuffs (EEC), 131
Advisory Committee on Pesticides and other Toxic Chemicals, 126
Advisory Committee on Restrictive Practices and Monopolies (EEC), 54
Antitrust –
  and consumer protection, 9-12, 73-4, 78-9, 80-4, 86-8
  in mixed economy, 10
  phenomena, 41-5
  policy in EEC –
    Article 85, 40-1, 46-52, 70, 71, 240
    Article 86, 40-1, 62, 70, 236, 240
    enforcement, 52-4
    dominant firm cases, 62-6
    merger cases, 63, 67
    restrictive practice cases, 54-62
  policy in ECSC –
    Article 65, 67
    Article 66, 67-8
  policy in UK –
    Director General of Fair Trading, 22-3, 26-8, 76, 85, 90, 95, 239-41, 245
    Fair Trading Act 1973, 21, 23-5, 26, 27, 31, 39, 85-6, 89, 90, 91, 94, 146, 161
    information agreement cases, 84-5
    merger law and cases, 94-6, 240, 241
    Office of Fair Trading, 22-3, 76, 90
    Monopolies and Mergers Act 1965, 85, 89, 94, 240
    Monopolies and Restrictive Practices (Inquiry and Control) Act 1948, 27, 71, 73-6, 85, 89
    monopoly law and cases, 89-93, 241

280 INDEX

Resale Prices Act 1964, 27, 87-8
Resale Prices Act 1976, 21, 27
resale price maintenance law and cases, 86-8
restrictive practices law and cases, 76-8, 79-84, 238-40
Restrictive Practices Court Act 1976, 27
Restrictive Trade Practices Act 1956, 10, 27, 76-84, 85, 86, 88, 89
Restrictive Trade Practices Act 1968, 27, 84-5, 239
Restrictive Trade Practices Act 1976, 21, 39, 76-84, 239
service agreements, 85-6
Arbitration in County Courts, 223-4
Architects, registration of, 121
Association of British Travel Agents, 124
Automobile Association, 234

Bank for International Settlements Report, 105
Banking, regulation of –
  Banking Act 1979, 123
  Protection of Depositors Act 1963, 123
Bargain offers, bogus, 158, 167, 268 n62
Bar, General Council of, 122, 203
Barristers, professional standards of, 203
Betting, gaming, etc, regulation of –
  Betting, Gaming and Lotteries Act 1963, 264 n53
Board of Trade, 74, 90
Borrie, G. J., 22
British Code of Advertising Practice, 36-8
British Electrotechnical Approvals Board, 141
British Hallmarking Council, 255 n3
British Pharmaceutical Codex, 121
British Pharmacopoeia, 121
British Pharmacopoeia Commission, 141, 254 n3
British Standards Institution, 141, 255 n3
Brougham, Henry, 220

Caveat Emptor, 8-9, 103 202
Citizen's Advice Bureaux Service, 21, 31, 34-6, 176, 185

Civil and criminal proceedings *see* Courts, civil and criminal proceedings
Civil Aviation Authority, 124
Class actions, 240
Code of Advertising Practice Committee, 36
Codes –
  voluntary –
    advertising, 36-8, 146-8, 215
    hygiene, 125
    trade practices, 215, 250
Committee for the Review of Medicines, 127
Committee on Safety of Drugs, 127
Committee on Safety of Medicines, 127
Committee on Trusts, 71
Common Agricultural Policy, 117, 130, 236-7
Confederation of British Industry, 107, 109, 244
Consumer –
  adequacy of protection of, 235-6, 250-1
  and advertising, 17-18, 37-8, 144-5, 165-7
  and competition, 9-12, 73-4, 78-9, 80-4, 86-8
  and free enterprise system, 5-6, 8-9
  and inflation, 13-15, 97-100
  meaning of, 18
  in mixed economy, 4-17
  sovereignty of, 5, 8, 16-17
Consumer Advice Centres, 31, 138-40
Consumers' Association, 33-4, 139-40, 142-3, 146, 226, 235
Consumer Consultative Committees (Nationalized Industries), 38, 248
Consumer Council, 32, 224, 256 n47
Consumer credit *see* Hire-Purchase
Consumer Groups, 39
Consumer Protection Advisory Committee, 22, 23-5, 146, 148, 167, 184
Consumer Protection Officers, 30-1, 120, 152, 154, 155, 233
Contaminants, 102, 125-6
Contract *see* Sales of goods (and services)
Council of Europe, 206-8, 246
Council of Law Society in Scotland, 121
Council on Productivity, Prices and Incomes, 104

INDEX 281

County Councils, 30
County Courts *see* Redress and enforcement of rights
Courts, civil and criminal proceedings, 150-2, 217
Credit *see* Hire-Purchase
Credit cards, 170, 174-5, 182
Criminal and civil proceedings *see* Courts, civil and criminal proceedings
Crowther Committee on Consumer Credit, 171, 176, 177, 178, 180, 182, 183-4
Countervailing power, 13

Damages, 150-2, 164, 204-13, 218, 228-31
Date marking, 2, 120, 137
Datsun, 2
Deceptive practices –
 CPAC, 23-5, 167
Deceptive statements –
 advertising, voluntary controls, 36-8, 146-8
 criminal offences –
  Fabrics (Misdescription) Act 1913, 162
  Food and Drugs Act 1955, 160-1
  Medicines Act 1968, 162
  Theft Acts 1968, 1978, 146, 153
  Trade Descriptions Acts 1968, 1972, 146, 154-60
  Weights and Measures Acts 1963, 1979, 161
 civil rights –
  fraudulent misrepresentation, 165
  innocent misrepresentation, 163-4
  negligent misrepresentation, 164-5
  Misrepresentation Act 1967, 146, 165
  representations as terms of a contract, 162-3
Dennison, S. R., 79
Dentists, registration of, 121
Department of Commerce (Northern Ireland), 30
Department of Economic Affairs, 105
Department of Health and Social Security, 29, 125, 126
Department of Industry, 30, 122
Department of Prices and Consumer Protection, 20-1, 35, 39, 135, 192

Department of Trade, 21
Department of Trade and Industry, 32, 84
Deposit Protection Board, 123
Design Centre, 141
Dillon Round, 2
Director General of Fair Trading, 22-8, 76, 78, 88, 90, 95, 122, 146, 154, 158, 162, 166, 167, 171, 179, 184-6, 191, 192, 215, 216, 239, 241, 245
Disguised business sales, 25, 167
District Councils, 30, 120
Doctors, registration of, 121
Doorstep selling, 144, 188, 265 n25
Drugs –
 advertising controls –
  Medicines Act 1968, 162
 labelling –
  Medicines Act 1968, 135-6
 misuse of –
  Misuse of Drugs Act 1971, 128
 pricing *see* Pharmaceutical Price Regulation Scheme
 standards –
  Medicines Act 1968, 121, 126-7

Economic Development Committees, 105
Employment Policy White Paper 1944, 73
Environmental and Consumer Protection Service (European Community), 20
Environmental Health Officers, 30-1, 120
Estate agents, regulation of, 123
European Atomic Energy Community, 19
European Coal and Steel Community –
 antitrust policy, 67-8
 pricing rules, 68-9
European Community Commission, 19-20, 46-69
European Community Council of Ministers, 20
European Community Court of Justice, 20
European Council, 19-20
European Economic Community –
 and advertising, 146-7
 antitrust policy, 46-62, 236
 Common Agricultural Policy, 117, 130, 236-7
 consumer protection policy, 129-31, 137-8

INDEX

and date marking, 137
and doorstep selling, 265 n25
harmonization of standards, 129-31, 137-8, 237-8
and product liability, 208-9, 246
and tariff barriers, 3, 40-1
Exclusion clauses *see* Sale of goods (and services)
Exclusion of consumers' inalienable rights, 25, 167

Fabrics, misdescription of, 128
Financial dealers, regulation of, 122
Fireworks, control of sale, 129
Fitness for purpose, 201-2
Food (and drink) –
  additives in, 2, 9, 102, 119, 125-6
  adulteration of, 101, 119
  advertising of, 160-2
  Common Agricultural Policy and, 236-7
  composition of, 135
  date marking, 2, 120, 137, 264 n12
  EEC labelling draft, 137, 264 n12
  Food Additives and Contaminants Committee, 124-6
  Food and Drugs Act 1955, 30, 39, 101, 119-20, 124-6, 134-5, 136, 161, 249
  Food and Drugs Act (Scotland) 1956, 39, 118
  Food and Drugs Act (Northern Ireland) 1958, 39, 118
  Food and Drugs (Control of Food Premises) Act 1976, 125
  Food Hygiene Advisory Council, 124
  Food Standards Committee, 120, 135
  labelling, 134-5, 137, 264 n12
  meat inspection, 125
  price display, 136
  standards, harmonization of in EEC, 129-31
  standards, guarantee of in UK, 118-20
  sale in prescribed quantities, 135
  Scientific Committee on Food (EEC), 131
  Slaughterhouses Act 1974, 125
  strict liability, 118-19, 249
  subsidization of, 15, 99, 113-14
  unit pricing, 136
Food Additives and Contaminants Committee, 125-6
Food Hygiene Advisory Council, 124

Food Standards Committee, 120, 135

Galbraith, J. K., 13
Goldman, P., 34
Gribbin, J. D., 116
Gun barrels, guarantee of standards, 128
Guarantees *see* Sale of goods (and services)

Hallmarking –
  British Hallmarking Council, 254 n3
  Hallmarking Act 1973, 140-1
Heath, E., 109
Hire Purchase –
  Advertising (Hire-Purchase) Act 1967, 146, 268 n5
  Consumer credit – development and sources, 169-70, 172-6
  Crowther Committee Report on Consumer Credit, 171, 176-8, 180-4
  Consumer Credit Act 1974 –
    advertising, 187-8
    agreements covered, 179-82
    classification of agreements, 182-4
    'cooling off' period, 190
    credit enquiries and references, 191
    defaulter, protection of, 171-2, 193-4
    DGFT and, 184-6, 191-2
    doorstep selling, 188
    ending agreements, 190-1
    fair trading, 192
    incidents during agreements, 189-90
    judicial control, 192-3, 247
    licensing, 184-6, 247
    making agreements, 188-9
    seeking business, 187-8
    total charge for credit, 180, 263 n13
    true interest rates, 137, 187
  Hire-Purchase Act 1938, 169
  Hire-Purchase Act 1964, 267 n3
  Hire-Purchase Act 1965, 173, 178, 268 n21
Home Office, 30
Housing –
  building standards, 121
  rent control, 118
Howe, Sir Geoffrey, 21, 225
Hunter, Alex, 75-6

Import controls, 2, 247

INDEX

Incomes policy –
  emergence of, 103-6
  1965–70, 106-9
  1970–74, 109-12
  1974–78, 109-12
    Social Contract, 111-12
    Phases I to IV, 111-12
  future of, 242-5
  National Incomes Commission, 106
  National Board for Prices and Incomes, 107-9, 244
  Pay Board, 111-12
  rationale of, 15-16, 97-100, 105
Independent Broadcasting Authority, 38
Independent Broadcasting Authority Act 1973, 38
Industrial Reorganisation Corporation, 94
Inertia selling, 216
Inflation –
  causes of, 14-15, 97-9
  and demand control, 14-15, 98-100
  effects of, 97-100
  and expectations, 16, 98-9
  and incomes policy, 15-16, 97-9, 103-11
  and price control, 15, 99, 104, 106-18
  and protection of consumers, 13-15, 99-100
  and subsidies, 16, 99, 113-14
Injury, prevention of –
  UK policy –
    Advisory Committee on Pesticides and other Toxic Chemicals, 126
    British Pharmacopoeia Commission, 121
    child resistant containers, 128-9
    Committee for the Review of Medicines, 127
    Committee on Safety of Drugs, 121
    Committee on Safety of Medicines, 127
    consumer durables, 3, 103
    Consumer Protection Acts 1961, 1971, 127
    Consumer Safety Act 1978, 127-8
    crash helmets, etc, 128
    dangerous drugs, 3, 103, 126-7
    Explosives (Age of Purchase, etc) Act 1976, 129

  fabric inflammability, 128
  Fabrics (Misrepresentation) Act 1913, 128
  fireworks, 129
  food additives and contaminants, 2, 9, 102, 119, 125-6
  Food Additives and Contaminants Committee, 125-6
  Food and Drugs Act 1955, 30, 39, 101, 119-20, 124-6, 134-5, 136, 161, 249
  Food and Drugs (Control of Food Premises) Act 1976, 125
  Food and Drugs (Scotland) Act 1956, 39, 119
  Food and Drugs (Northern Ireland) Act 1958, 39, 119
  food hygiene, 102, 124-5
  Food Hygiene Advisory Council, 124
  gun barrels, 128
  Gun Barrel Proof Acts 1868, 1950, 128
  meat inspection, 125
  medicines (drugs), 3, 103, 126-7
  Medicines Act 1968, 29, 39, 119, 121, 126-7, 129, 136
  Medicines Commission, 126-7
  Misuse of Drugs Act 1971, 128
  pesticides, 126
  Pharmacy and Poisons Act 1933, 129
  poisons, 129
  Poisons Act 1972, 129
  Poisons Board, 129
  road vehicles, 128
  Road Traffic Acts 1960, 1972, 128
  Slaughterhouses Act 1974, 125
  Veterinary medicines, 126
  Veterinary Products Committee, 126
  EEC policy –
    Advisory Committee on Foodstuffs, 131
    harmonization, 129-31, 237-8
    Scientific Committee for Food, 131
Inns of Court, Senate of, 203
Insurance, regulation of –
  Companies Act 1967, 122
  Insurance Brokers (Registration) Act 1977, 121
  Insurance Companies Act 1974, 122
  Policyholders Protection Act 1975, 123

Inter-Departmental Mergers Panel, 27, 95, 241
Interest rates, true, 137

Kennedy Round, 2
Keynesian economic policy, 7

Labelling –
  care, 9
  cautionary –
    chemicals, 137
    cigarettes, 137
    Medicines Act 1968, 135-6
    asbestos products, 137-8
  composition –
    Food and Drugs Act 1955, 135
  date-marking –
    advisory, 120
    compulsory – EEC draft, 137
  quantity –
    Weights and Measures Act 1963, 135
  quality –
    Hallmarking Act 1973, 140-1
    BSI kitemark, 141
    BEAB, 141
    Design Centre, 141
  unit pricing and price display –
    Prices Act 1974, 136
Laissez-Faire, 9-10
Lancet, The, 118
Law Commissions (strict liability), 206-8, 246
Law Society, 203
London boroughs, 30

Margarine standards, 263 n45
Meat inspection, 125
Medicines, control of *see* Drugs
Medicines Commission, 126-7
Merchandise marks, 154
Merchantable quality, 200-1
Mergers, control of, *see* Antitrust
Methven, Sir John, 22
Metrication Board, 255 n3
Metropolitan County Councils, 30
Minister for Trade and Consumer Affairs, 21
Ministry of Agriculture, Fisheries, and Food, 120, 124, 126
Mixed economy, rationale of –
  advertising and, 16-18
  caveat emptor, limitations of, and, 8-9
  competition, restrictions of, and, 9-12
  general, 6-7
  inflation, control of, and, 13-16
Molony Committee on Consumer Protection, 35, 103, 154, 156, 157, 266 n18
Monopolies Commission, 26-7, 74-6, 89-96, 241, 245
Monopoly, control of *see* Antitrust
Motor vehicle, control of *see* Vehicles

National Association of Citizens' Advice Bureaux, 35, 185
National Board for Prices and Incomes, 107-9, 244
National Consumer Council, 21, 33, 116, 140, 235-6, 237, 243, 244, 257 n47
National Economic Development Council, 105
National Federation of Consumer Groups, 39, 235
National Health Service, professional conduct in, 203, 270 n20
National Incomes Commission, 106
Nationalized Industry Consumer Councils, 38, 248
Negligence *see* Supply of goods (and services)
Nixon (Tokyo) Round, 2
Nuffield Foundation, 226

Office of Fair Trading, 22, 35, 39, 76, 90, 133, 134, 148, 158, 159-60, 179, 192, 215, 233
Opticians, registration of, 121
Organization for European Economic Cooperation, 105

Paris Treaty, 3, 19, 41
Pay Board, 110-12
Pearson Commission Report (personal injury), 209
Pharmaceutical Price Regulation Scheme, 118
Pharmaceutical Society, 128
Poisons, control of –
  Pharmacy and Poisons Act 1933, 129
  Poisons Act 1972, 129
  Poisons Board, 129
  Poisons List, 129
  Poison Rules, 129
Post Office Users' National Council, 248

Prepayment for goods, 26
President of the Board of Trade, 24, 94
Price Commission, 15, 17, 21, 109-18, 234-5
Prices and prices policy –
  Counter-inflation Act 1973, 110
  false statements as to price, 157-8
  National Board for Prices and Incomes, 107-9
  Prices Act 1974, 113-15, 136
  Price Code 1973–77, 109-14
  Price Code 1977, 114-18
  Price Code exceptions, 117-18
  Price Commission –
    constitution, 29
    future of, 242-5
    and Monopolies and Mergers Commission, 116, 245
    Price Commission Act 1977, 39, 88, 114, 244
    Price Commission (Amendment) Act 1979, 263 n34
    Price Commission reports, 113, 116-19, 249
  price control 1967–70, 106-9
  price display, 136, 158
  subsidies, 15, 99, 113-14
  Trade Descriptions Acts 1968, 1972, 157-8
  unit pricing, 136
Product liability *see* Sale of goods (and services)
Product performance –
  comparative data and testing, 32-4, 142-3
    Consumers' Association, 31, 138-40
    Consumer Advice Centres, 39
    Consumer Groups, 39
  other sources of information –
    manufacturers, 143
    specialist publications, 143
Public Health Officers, 30-1, 120
Pyramid selling, 216

Rag, flock and fillings, standards, 121
Regional and Island Councils (Scotland), 30
Redress and enforcement of rights –
  civil and criminal actions, 150-2, 217
  compensation in criminal cases, 233
  County Courts –
    action in, 221-3
    arbitration in, 223-4

    innovations outside, 226
    jurisdiction of, 217-21
    reform of, 225-6
    small claims in, 224-5
  remedies –
    damages, 151, 228-31
    specific performance and the injunction, 151, 231-2
    self-help and extra-legal remedies, 233-4
    small claims court proposal, 227
Registrar of Restrictive Trading Agreements, 76, 78
Rents –
  control of, 118
  Rent Officers, 118
  Rent Tribunals, 118
Resale price maintenance, control of, *see* Antitrust
Restrictive Practices Court, 27-8, 78-88, 238-40
Restrictive practices, control of, *see* Antitrust
Review of Monopolies and Mergers Policy 1976, 241
Rights of Consumers (EEC), 130
Road vehicles, regulation of *see* Vehicles
Rome Treaty 1957 (Euratom), 20, 67-9, 70
Rome Treaty 1957 (European Economic Community), 3, 19, 40-1, 46-67, 70, 130-1, 236-8

Safety *see* Injury, prevention of
Sale of goods (and services) –
  codes of practice, 215
  contractual rights –
    conditions, 196-7, 198
    warranties, 196-7, 198
  exclusion clauses –
    Sale of Goods Act 1893, 209-10
    Unfair Contract Terms Act 1977, 210-12
  fitness for purpose, 201-2
  guarantees –
    Unfair Contract Terms Act 1977, 214
  implied terms, 197-202
  merchantable quality, 200-1
  negligence and products liability –
    Council of Europe, 206, 246
    EEC draft, 208-9, 246

Law Commission recommendations, 206-8, 246
negligence, 203-6
strict liability, move to, 206-9, 246
sale by description, 198-200
supply of services, 202-3
Scientific Committee for Food (EEC), 131
Secretary of State for Industry, 128-9
Secretary of State for Prices and Consumer Protection, 21, 25, 26, 29, 31, 95, 113, 116, 117, 123, 158, 167, 180, 186, 187, 241
Secretary of State for Northern Ireland, 120
Secretary of State for Scotland, 120, 125
Secretary of State for Social Services, 120, 125
Secretary of State for Trade, 122
Seeds, standards of, 121
Select Commission on Adulteration of Food 1855, 118
Sinclair, Upton, 102
Slaughterhouses, hygiene in, 125
Small claims courts *see* Redress and enforcement of rights
Smith, Adam, 13
Solicitors (England and Wales), registration of, 121
Solicitors, professional conduct of, 203
Solicitors (Scotland), registration of, 121
Standards, guaranteeing –
  general, 8-9, 101-2
  EEC policy –
    Advisory Committee on Foodstuffs, 131
    harmonization policy, 130-31, 237-8
    Scientific Committee for Food, 131
  UK policy –
    banking –
      Banking Act 1979, 123
      Protection of Depositors Act 1963, 123

building –
  Public Health Act 1936, 121
dealing in securities –
  Prevention of Fraud (Investments) Act 1958, 122
drugs –
  British Pharmacopoeia Commission, 121
estate agency –
  Estate Agents Act 1979, 123
food and drink –
  Food Standards Committee, 120
insurance –
  Companies Act 1967, 122
  Insurance Brokers (Registration) Act 1977, 121
  Insurance Companies Act 1974, 122-3
  Policyholders Protection Act 1975, 123
liberal professions, 121-2, 203
rag, flock and fillings, 121
seeds, 121
travel agents, 123-4
Strict Liability *see* Sale of goods (and services) *and* Food *and* Deceptive Statements

Trading Standards Officers, 30-1, 120, 152, 154, 155, 184
TUC, 106, 107, 109-12, 244

VAT – exclusive prices, 158, 167, 267 n29, 268 n62
Vehicles, regulation of, 128
Veterinary Products Committee, 126

Weights and measures –
  EEC directives, 161
  quantity regulations, 161
Wilde, Oscar, 251